INTERPRETING
FOR INTERNATIONAL ORGANIZATIONS:
A PRACTICAL TRAINING GUIDE

国际组织
口译人才培养实用教程

赵 睿 马菁雪 编著

中山大学出版社
SUN YAT-SEN UNIVERSITY PRESS
·广州·

图书在版编目（CIP）数据

国际组织口译人才培养实用教程/赵睿，马菁雪编著 . —广州：中山大学出版社，2023.10

ISBN 978 – 7 – 306 – 07917 – 6

Ⅰ.①国…　Ⅱ.①赵…②马…　Ⅲ.①国际组织—口译—人才培养—教材　Ⅳ.①H059

中国国家版本馆 CIP 数据核字（2023）第 189157 号

GUOJIZUZHI KOUYI RENCAI PEIYANG SHIYONG JIAOCHENG

出　版　人：王天琪

策划编辑：陈　霞

责任编辑：陈　霞

封面设计：曾　斌

责任校对：邱紫妍

责任技编：靳晓虹

出版发行：中山大学出版社

电　　话：编辑部 020 – 84110283，84113349，84111997，84110779，84110776
　　　　　发行部 020 – 84111998，84111981，84111160

地　　址：广州市新港西路 135 号

邮　　编：510275　传　真：020 – 84036565

网　　址：http://www.zsup.com.cn　E-mail：zdcbs@ mail.sysu.edu.cn

印　刷　者：广东虎彩云印刷有限公司

规　　格：787mm × 1092mm　1/16　15.5 印张　246 千字

版次印次：2023 年 10 月第 1 版　2023 年 10 月第 1 次印刷

定　　价：48.00 元

前　言

党的二十大报告指出："中国积极参与全球治理体系改革和建设，践行共商共建共享的全球治理观，坚持真正的多边主义，推进国际关系民主化，推动全球治理朝着更加公正合理的方向发展。"① 国际组织是参与全球治理的重要平台，国际组织职员作为主权国家在国际事务中施展影响力、参与全球事务的代表，作用日益凸显。国际组织的超国家、次国家或非政府组织在运行和履行职责时需要大量的专业翻译人才。在国际组织中，我国任职的主要力量也是翻译人才。然而，我国在国际组织中任职人数少、职位低、影响力小，与中国的国际地位和国际影响力不相匹配。在全球治理背景下，加大力度培养参与国际组织运行的翻译人才，提高我国在国际组织中的地位和影响力，已成为一项紧迫工作。

目前，市面上的口译教材主要围绕"口译技能"或者"口译专题"进行编写，鲜有满足国际组织口译人才培养需求的教材。本教材以国际组织为编写主线，详细阐述了国际组织的历史、现状以及运行规则，并选取国际组织重要活动的演讲作为学习材料，在提升口译学习者语言水平、培养其口译技能的同时，开阔其国际视野，为培养国际组织翻译人才提供教材支撑。

教材特点：

1. 知识技能协同发展

本教材不仅注重口译技能训练，也重视背景知识积累，通过广泛的背景阅读，口译学习者将了解关于国际组织的基本知识、积累相关的专业术语，建立口译背景知识的图式结构，为提升口译技能打下基础，实现知识积累与技能发展相结合。

2. 密切契合市场需求

本教材深谙市场需求，精心挑选了联合国下属 18 个专门机构中的 8 个最

---

① 见中华人民共和国中央政府网（https://www.gov.cn/guowuyuan/2022 – 11/08/content＿5725232.htm?eqid＝ed082df70007bb5500000002648a740c），引用日期 2023 年 9 月 1 日。

为常见和关键的机构，内容覆盖了口译领域中关注热度最高的八大核心话题（经济、金融、健康、环保、教育文化、旅游、农业以及工业），这些话题也是国际社会当前和未来的重要议题。这些深层次的领域知识不仅有助于口译学习者在口译中更准确地传达信息，还有助于其更好地进行各种专业领域的口译工作。

3. 口译材料真实适用

教材中的演讲材料均源自真实的会议演讲，以为口译学习者提供真实的口译场景，让口译学习者深入了解口译任务的挑战和责任。此外，编者在教材建设中，根据英语专业及翻译专业本科生的语言和知识水平，对选取的演讲材料进行了适度的精简和修改，确保内容与口译学习者的水平更加契合。

4. 课程思政润物无声

本教材通过介绍国际组织的历史、结构，帮助学生深入了解国际法规，开阔国际视野，了解国际事务，从而帮助学生形成正确的国家观、民族观和历史观；另一方面，教材挑选了中国国家领导人参加国际组织高层次活动时的演讲，如习近平主席在世界卫生大会上的致辞，以及国际组织中的中国籍高层领导人（如国际货币基金组织副总裁张涛、联合国世界旅游组织执行主任祝善忠）的演讲，有助于口译学习者了解中国在国际舞台上的立场和影响力，强化口译学习者的政治、思想和情感的认同，激发口译学习者树立"四个自信"。

教材构成、安排及学习建议：

本教材包含 8 个章节，涵盖了 8 个联合国专门机构，分别对应不同的口译话题。每个章节的具体模块分为：一、背景阅读，包括国际组织的汉英介绍，汉语介绍选自外交部网站，英语介绍来自国际组织的官网。本部分作为课前预习材料，建议口译学习者提前阅读，掌握背景知识，积累词汇，为口译学习打下基础。二、口译实践，包括英译汉和汉译英篇章，每个篇章配有"实践解析"和"长难句点拨"。"口译实践"是本教材的核心部分，口译篇章均选自真实的会议发言，供课堂使用。在练习之前，口译学习者可阅读解析部分，了解讲话者的背景、会议主题和专业术语解释，启动长期记忆中的知识储备，为课堂练习做准备。"长难句点拨"小节聚焦演讲中的难点，分析口译中存在的困难并提供相应的口译策略。三、口译练习，包括英译汉和汉译英篇章，每个篇章配有"词汇准备"和"长难句点拨"，可作为课后作业让口译学习者加强练习。其中"词汇准备"是口译篇章中的生词，口译学习者既可以在自主练习前进行学习，也可以在课后进行拓展学习。"长难句点拨"与"口译实践"

节的设置一致。四、参考译文，包括"口译实践"和"口译练习"中各个篇章对应的译文，主要是来自官方提供的译文版本，供口译学习者在学习后参考使用。

编写人员介绍：

本教材的两位主编来自中山大学国际翻译学院，从事口译相关研究，是学院口译教学团队的核心教师，拥有丰富的口译实践与教学经验。

赵睿，中山大学国际翻译学院讲师，中山大学外国语学院口译研究方向博士生，美国迈阿密大学访问学者，从事口译教学十五年以上，在各类重大外事活动和国际会议中承担交替传译和同声传译任务，担任"中译杯"2018 年全国口译大赛（英语）交替传译总决赛一等奖、"中译杯"2019 年全国口译大赛（英语）交替传译总决赛二等奖、2023 年"CATTI 杯"全国翻译大赛决赛特等奖、第十二届全国口译大赛二等奖选手的指导老师，拥有丰富的口译教学经验。

马菁雪，中山大学国际翻译学院教师，中山大学国际翻译学院英语文学方向博士生，从事口译教学近十年，在各类重大外事活动和国际会议中承担交替传译和同声传译任务，担任"中译杯"2019 年全国口译大赛（英语）交替传译总决赛二等奖选手的指导老师，拥有丰富的口译教学经验。

特别鸣谢：

本教材内容涉及话题广泛，其中部分材料编选自外交部网站、甘肃省文化博览局网站、英文巴士网、中国日报网以及世界银行、国际货币基金组织、世界卫生组织、世界气象组织、世界旅游组织、联合国教科文组织、联合国粮农组织、联合国工业发展组织等国际组织的官网，在此特别感谢。

本教材在编写过程中得到了来自各方面的大力支持和帮助：受到中山大学2022 年本科教学质量工程项目的资助，得到中山大学国际翻译学院各位领导、同事特别是常晨光院长、郑华书记、周慧副院长、黄爱成副书记、赖军院长助理的关心和支持，得到校内外热心的同学如吴逸熙、陈歆怡、王晶晶、王楚凝、莫晓莹、赵胤祺等的协助（资料收集、听写整理和校对工作）；同时，中山大学出版社的领导和编辑，尤其是陈霞编辑，为本书的编辑出版做了大量的工作，我们在此一并表示衷心感谢。由于编写水平和经验有限，书中疏漏、错误在所难免，欢迎专家、同行和读者批评指正。

赵　睿

2023 年 6 月 17 日

目　录

第一章 世界银行集团

➡ 一、背景阅读

⬤ （一）汉语简介

世界银行集团（简称"世界银行"）是联合国系统下的多边开发机构，包括五个机构：国际复兴开发银行、国际开发协会、国际金融公司、多边投资担保机构和国际投资争端解决中心，其中前三个机构是世界银行集团的主体。

国际复兴开发银行（International Bank of Reconstruction and Development，IBRD）

【成　立】于 1944 年 7 月 1 日成立，1946 年开始运作，1947 年 11 月 15 日起成为联合国专门机构。是世界银行集团下属五个机构之一。

【负责人】彭安杰（Ajay Banga，美国籍），2023 年 6 月上任，任期 5 年。2016 年 1 月，世界银行任命时任中国财政部国际财金合作司司长杨少林担任世界银行常务副行长兼首席行政官。

【总　部】美国华盛顿

国际开发协会（International Development Association，IDA）

【成　立】于 1960 年成立，是世界银行集团下属五个机构之一。

【宗　旨】通过向世界上最贫困国家提供无息贷款和赠款，促进其经济发展，减少不平等现象，提高人民生活水平。

【成　员】目前包括 173 个成员国。

【负责人】彭安杰（Ajay Banga，美国籍），2023 年 6 月上任，任期 5 年。

【总　部】美国华盛顿。

国际金融公司（International Finance Corporation，IFC）

【成　立】于 1956 年成立，是世界银行集团下属五个机构之一。

【宗　旨】帮助和促进发展中国家私营部门发展。

【成　员】目前包括 184 个成员国。

【负责人】彭安杰（Ajay Banga，美国籍），2023 年 6 月上任，任期 5 年。

【总　部】美国华盛顿

［资料来源：见中国外交部网站（https://www.mfa.gov.cn/web/gjhdq_676201/gjhdqzz_681964/lhg_681966/jbqk_681968/201103/t20110329_9380021.shtml），引用日期：2023 年 8 月 17 日。］

（二）World Bank 英语介绍

1. What is World Bank?

The World Bank Group (also known as World Bank) is one of the world´s largest sources of funding and knowledge for developing countries. It has two missions. One is to end extreme poverty by reducing the share of the global population that lives in extreme poverty to 3 percent. The other is to promote shared prosperity by increasing the incomes of the poorest 40 percent of people in every country.

The World Bank is like a cooperative, made up of 189 member countries. These member countries, or shareholders, are represented by a Board of Governors. Generally, the governors are member countries' ministers of finance or ministers of development. They meet once a year at the Annual Meetings of the Boards of Governors of the World Bank Group and the International Monetary Fund.

2. History

In July 1944—one year before the end of World War Ⅱ—delegates from 44 countries met for the United Nations Monetary and Financial Conference held in Bretton Woods, New Hampshire. The conference aimed to create the framework for post-war international economic cooperation and reconstruction. The conference resulted in the formation of two institutions: the International Monetary Fund (IMF) and the International Bank for Reconstruction and Development (World Bank).

3. Institutions

With 189 member countries, staff from more than 170 countries, and offices in over 130 locations, the World Bank Group is a unique global partnership: five institutions working for sustainable solutions that reduce poverty and build shared prosperity in developing countries.

The International Bank for Reconstruction and Development (IBRD) lends to governments of middle-income and creditworthy low-income countries. The International Development Association (IDA) provides interest-free loans—called credits—and grants to governments of the poorest countries. Together, IBRD and IDA make up the World Bank.

The International Finance Corporation (IFC) is the largest global development institution focused exclusively on the private sector. We help developing countries achieve sustainable growth by financing investment, mobilizing capital in international financial markets, and providing advisory services to businesses and governments.

The Multilateral Investment Guarantee Agency (MIGA) was created in 1988 to promote foreign direct investment into developing countries to support economic growth, reduce poverty, and improve people's lives. MIGA fulfills this mandate by offering political risk insurance (guarantees) to investors and lenders.

The International Centre for Settlement of Investment Disputes (ICSID) provides international facilities for conciliation and arbitration of investment disputes.

4. What does World Bank do?

The World Bank provides low-interest loans, zero to low-interest credits, and grants to developing countries. These support a wide array of investments in such areas as education, health, public administration, infrastructure, financial and private sector development, agriculture, and environmental and natural resource management. Some of our projects are co-financed with governments, other multilateral institutions, commercial banks, export credit agencies, and private sector investors.

［资料来源：见世界银行网站（https://www.worldbank.org/en/about），引用日期：2023年8月17日。］

5. 词汇表 Vocabulary List

the Bretton Woods Conference　　　　　　　　　　　布雷顿森林会议

UN specialized agencies	联合国专门机构
minister of finance	财政部部长
member country	成员国
Board of Governors	理事会
shared prosperity	共享繁荣
delegate	代表
policymaker	决策人
International Bank for Reconstruction and Development（IBRD）	国际复兴开发银行
International Development Association（IDA）	国际开发协会
International Finance Corporation（IFC）	国际金融公司
Multilateral Investment Guarantee Agency（MIGA）	多边投资担保机构
International Centre for Settlement of Investment Disputes（ICSID）	国际投资争端解决中心

➡ 二、口译实践

● （一）英译汉

Rich and Poor：
Opportunities and Challenges in an Age of Disruption（Excerpt）
Jim Yong Kim，World Bank Group President
（April 10，2018）

（1）Before 1800, just about everybody was poor. You had royalty, you had these huge landowners, but they were a tiny, tiny minority and just about everyone lived in poverty. And everyone lived very much wedded to their land. This was the entire history of humanity. There were some huge changes, of course：agriculture. What happened was that mostly people were hunters and gatherers before agriculture. And then, when agriculture started, food production was then brought to people rather than vice versa. People didn't go out looking for food. There were places where they knew that a steady supply of food would be created.

But wealth was tied to land, and those who controlled land, controlled much of the world's wealth. And the difficulty was in shipping or moving anything: things, ideas, people. It was very difficult to move anything, so there wasn't very much trade. And so, the cost of moving things really mattered and shaped the way societies were formed.

In the 17th century, only 3000 European ships sailed to Asia. In the 18th century, for the next hundred years, about 6000 ships sailed. It was very difficult to move anything.

Now, around 1800-1820, some very important things happened. And the two most important ones that most historians will look at are the Industrial Revolution and steam power. So, around 1820, steam power allowed the movement of goods, and the movement of goods fueled industrialization, trade, and economic growth.

(2) But at that time, also was the start of—one of the great economists, Deirdre McCloskey, talked about right around that time, with the advent of the Industrial Revolution and steam, you had the beginning of what she called the great divergence, meaning that certain areas, especially Europe and the United States, grew rich very, very quickly.

(3) She talks about the founding—the formation of the so-called bourgeoisie. And the bourgeoisie were former peasants who were close enough to royalty that they wanted to live like that. And so, she sees the development of the bourgeoisie as a very important development because they were the precursors of the middle class.

Now, in the two centuries from 1820 until now, what happened was that the availability of goods, of services just exploded. It wasn't a little bit of change, it was just huge amounts of change, because before 1820, people were born and they died in pretty much the same world. The world, from the time they were born to the time they died did not change very much. But starting in 1820, the world started changing very, very quickly.

Two centuries ago, four out of five U. S. adults worked to grow food for their families. Now, one farmer feeds 300 people.

(4) So, the reason I talk about this is because we have to put these things in perspective. We have to put the evolution of sort of human advancement—which is what we work on at the World Bank, development—we have to put it in the

perspective of what happened.

……

This is what I see everywhere I go: Everywhere I go I see young people who may not own a smart phone, but who have access to smart phones. By 2025, many analysts are saying that the entire world will have access to broadband.

Now, when you get access to broadband, when you can see things on the Internet, a couple of things happen. First of all, people are much more satisfied with their lives when they have Internet access. When they have Internet access, they can see how the world works. They can watch movies, television shows. The satisfaction with life goes up.

(5) But the other thing that happens is their reference income goes up, and this is something that we actually study at the World Bank Group. The income to which they compare their own goes up. And when that happens, your income also has to go up or you're not very satisfied.

And so, there is so much aspiration, there is so much desire to have access to education, to make sure that your children are not underfed. There is so much aspiration out there, and once people get access to the Internet, the aspiration will continue to go up. How do we possibly respond to this situation?

Well, it gets right to the core of what we are as an institution. The World Bank Group—at the time, it was just one part of the World Bank Group—was founded in 1944 out of the ashes of World War Ⅱ. In a, I think, just brilliant—what's the right word? In a brilliant move, … we have to build institutions that, on the one hand can bring stability—because before World War Ⅱ and during World War Ⅱ, currency wars were happening. Countries would devalue their currency, would try to do everything they could to gain an advantage, and the status of global currencies was in a mess. So, they needed to bring some stability to the global system.

……

When I first walked into the World Bank, I saw this sign: "Our dream is a world free of poverty." And I asked, why is this a dream? Why don't we turn this into a real target and a goal, and we did.

After three to four months of arguing—and that's what we do at the World Bank, we argue. We argue with data, we argue with politics and ideologies—we argue with many different kinds of tools. We came to a conclusion: We wanted to end extreme poverty, that is, people living under ＄1. 90 a day, by 2030. And we also were committed to boosting shared prosperity, reducing inequality. And we decided that there would be three ways for us to get there.

The first, traditionally, we've always focused on economic growth but, in this case, we're focusing on inclusive, meaning everyone benefits; sustainable, meaning that it doesn't destroy the planet—inclusive, sustainable economic growth.

（6）The second, because there are so many crises that are affecting the world every day, pandemics, climate change, refugees, fragility, conflict, violence, we wanted to focus on fostering resilience to those kinds of problems in the world that affect more and more people.

And finally, the third pillar was to invest more and more effectively in people. So, inclusive, sustainable economic growth; resilience to the various shocks that are happening in the world today; and investing more and more effectively in people.

Now, we have had to change because the world has changed, and the world has changed pretty dramatically.

［资料来源：见世界银行网站（https://www.worldbank.org/en/news/speech/2018/04/10/rich-and-poor-opportunities-and-challenges-in-an-age-of-disruption），引用日期：2023 年 8 月 17 日。］

1. 实践解析

本演讲选自 2018 年 4 月时任世界银行行长 Jin Yong Kin（金墉）于 2018 年世界银行－国际货币基金组织春季会议前在美利坚大学的演讲。本演讲主要围绕经济话题开展，演讲涉及的时间跨度较大，既有对工业革命前世界经济发展的总结，也谈到了近 200 年世界的变迁。金墉在阐述观点时旁征博引，出现了一些相对陌生的名字如 Deirdre McCloskey（迪尔德丽·麦克洛斯基），还有不少结构复杂的长难句，对于口译学习者来说有一定挑战性。

2. 长难句点拨

（1）演讲者首先提到了人类社会发展的不同阶段，使用了 hunters 和 gatherers 等词，如果直接将其译为"狩猎者"和"采集者"，则稍显生硬，可以考虑进行词性转换，译为"从事狩猎和采摘"，让译文更加流畅。在翻译"And then, when agriculture started, … rather than vice versa."这一句时，有必要把 vice versa 的具体含义补充清楚，帮助听众更好地理解原文。

（2）该段提到了 Deirdre McCloskey，她是世界著名经济学家和经济史学家，认为世界变得富裕的主要原因，是一种对中产阶级及其平等自由主义的崇拜，而非物质原因。① 在进行口译的过程中，如果遇到人名，首先要确保把身份（即经济学家）准确翻译，人名可以采取音译或者直接按照英语发音朗读的方式译出。本演讲由于是即兴发言，多次出现了演讲者自我纠正的情况，例如 the start of 后面的信息未讲完就跳跃到下一个信息 one of the great economists, Deirdre McCloskey。因此，口译学习者在听力理解过程中要把握该段中 the start of 后面的内容实际就是此演讲后半段中的 the great divergence。在口译场景中，口译学习者可以适度整合译文。

（3）该段开头也出现了即兴演讲中的自我纠正，演讲者实际上想说的是 the formation of the so-called bourgeoisie，因此在口译过程中可以省略 the founding。"And the bourgeoisie were former peasants … like that."一句的结构略显复杂，peasants 作为引导词，引导了一个定语从句，而定语从句中又有 enough … that … 结构，因此在听辨过程中要注意分析逻辑层次。precursor 一词既有"先锋"的意思，也有"前身"的意思，结合上下文可以知道该段主要论述资产阶级的形成，因此译为"前身"更合适。

（4）该段中 perspective 出现了两次，但是意思却有差别，put sth. in perspective 就是"客观看待"的意思，这里的 perspective 的英语解释是"the capacity to view things in their true relations or relative importance"。而段末的 perspective 则意为"a mental view or prospect"②，可以译为"角度，思考方法"。在进行口译的过程中应注意把握不同语境下同一个的词的不同含义。第二句中插入了一个由 which 引导的从句，由于汉语中也有类似的插入结构，因而在口译中可以保留原文顺序，以补充说明成分的形式译出。但是这样难免有翻译腔的嫌疑，口译学习者也可以尝试整合句子信息，调整句序，让译文更加流畅。

（5）该句中的 reference income 实际上就是后句的 the income to which they compare their own，因此，将 reference income 译为"收入参考标准"更佳。在英译汉的过程中，由于语言结构的特点，有些词汇的具体含义会在句子或者文章的后半部分出现，如果在听辨过程中遇到了不熟悉的词语，不妨适当等待，结合上下文的内容来更好地理解词语意义。

---

① 参见［美］迪尔德丽·南森·麦克洛斯基《理想的经济学》，赵晓曦译，中译出版社 2023 年版，封底。

② 见韦氏词典网站（https://www.merriam-webster.com/dictionary/perspective），引用日期：2023年8月17日。

（6）该段中出现了多个列举，给口译学习者进行短时记忆和做笔记带来一定的挑战，但是列举的这些话题（流行病、气候变化、暴力、难民等）都是国际政治议题中的常见话题，因此，口译学习者应该熟练掌握这些话题的表达方法。英译汉的长句翻译常用技巧是切分，将一个长句切分成若干个小句，再根据句子逻辑适当调整句序，让译文更加流畅。该句中 resilience 后面以介词短语作为修饰语，补充说明是什么样的 resilience，由于定语过长，翻译时可以在介词 to 的位置断句，再利用词性转换，将介词 to 灵活处理为动词，再重复阐述 resilience，从而让译文更加清晰。

（二）汉译英

世行看中国 2022 年：具挑战性的再平衡之路（节选）

继 2021 年的强劲反弹之后，世界经济进入充满挑战的 2022 年。在大规模刺激政策和疫苗接种快速推进的作用下，发达经济体迅速复苏，但许多发展中国家仍在苦苦挣扎。

（1）世界银行在美东时间 1 月 11 日发布的《全球经济展望》报告强调指出，在疫苗接种率差异巨大的情况下，包括新冠病毒变异株蔓延、食品和商品价格上涨、资产市场动荡、美国和其他发达经济体的政策可能收紧，以及地缘政治紧张局势持续等这些因素，均使得发展中国家面临具有挑战性的经济环境。

全球环境也将影响 2022 年的中国经济前景。

中国的出口表现可能受到抑制，而出口是 2021 年中国经济增长的主要动力。（2）世界银行预测，继 2021 年呈现 8% 的强劲周期性反弹后，2022 年中国经济增速将放缓至 5.1%，更接近于潜在增长率——即满负荷生产状态下的可持续增长率。

由于 2021 年下半年的增速低于这一水平，我们在预测中假设政策将适度放松。尽管我们预计增长势头有望回升，但中国经济前景仍然面临全球和国内经济下行风险。

…………

面对这些不利因素，中国的政策制定者应沉着应对。

（3）世界银行的最新一期《中国经济简报》认为，随着中国公共基础设施存量接近饱和，通过以投资为主导的刺激措施来提振内需的传统策略只会加剧房地产行业的风险，投资回报也会越来越低。相反，要实现经济持续增长，中国需要从三个方面坚持走具有挑战性的经济再平衡之路：第一，经济增长从外需拉动转向内需拉动，从投资和工业主导转向更多依靠消费和服务业；第二，让市场和私营部门在创新推动和资本、人才配置方面发挥更大作用；第三，从高碳经济转向低碳经济。

这些再平衡举措并非易事。《中国经济简报》指出，结构性改革有助于中国减少向高质量增长新路径转型所面临的权衡取舍。

首先，可以通过财政改革建立更具累进性的税收制度，同时增加社会安全网和教育卫生支出。这将有助于降低预防性家庭储蓄，促进国内消费，减少家庭之间的收入不平等。

其次，继收紧针对数字平台的反垄断约束以及针对线上消费服务的一系列限制措施之后，中国政府可考虑将注意力转向更广泛的市场竞争壁垒，以刺激创新和生产率增长。……

（4）第三，通过扩大碳排放交易范围和强化碳排放交易制度来扩大碳定价的使用，同时推动电力部门改革，以促进可再生能源的市场渗透和全国范围内的交易与调度。这不仅会产生环境效益，也有助于推动中国经济向以创新为基础的更可持续的增长模式转型。

此外，（5）强化企业和银行处置框架将有助于减少道德风险，从而缓和货币政策宽松与金融风险管理之间的权衡取舍关系。私营企业和国有企业之间长期存在的利差体现了信贷获取的扭曲。消除这种扭曲，有助于推动中国经济向更多依靠创新驱动、私营部门引领的增长转型。

在过去40余年的改革开放过程中，中国的生产率增长一直由私营部门主导。通过在较小的私营企业中推广现代技术与实践，未来生产率提升的空间仍然很大。实现这些收益需要为国有企业和私营企业营造公平的竞争环境。

[资料来源：乔伊布、叶卡捷琳娜·瓦沙克马泽、李雨纱：《世行看中国2022年：具挑战性的再平衡之路》，见世界银行网站中文版（https://www.shihang.org/zh/news/opinion/2022/01/12/rebalancing-act-china-s-2022-outlook.），引用日期：2023年8月17日。]

1. 实践解析

本材料是世界银行中国局高级经济学家乔伊布（Ibrahim Chowdhurg）、世界银行预测局高级经济学家叶卡捷琳娜·瓦沙克马泽（Ekaterine T. Vashakmadze）和世界银行经济学家李雨纱于2022年1月发表的关于2022年中国经济走势的评论。评论认为，中国面临着经济再平衡的挑战，世界银行预测中国经济因受到疫情、房地产行业低迷等因素的影响，增速将放缓至5.1%。中国需要从三个方面进行经济再平衡：转向内需拉动、加强市场和私营部门的作用、实现从高碳经济到低碳经济的转变。为此，作者提出了一系列建议。这则材料隶属评论，文风严谨，里面出现了不少结构复杂的长难句，且涉及大量金融经济和相关领域背景知识，难度较大。

潜在增长率即潜在经济增长率，一般被定义为"一个经济体潜在产出的增长率"。潜在产出（Potential Output）是宏观经济理论中的一个重要概念，Nelson Barbosa Filho 在前人讨论基础上，综合不同的视角，提出"潜在产出是在高的资源利用水平下的生产能力，而在宏观经济学中，潜在产出也对应于在一个稳定的通货膨胀率水平下的国内生产总值（GDP）水平"[1]。

累进性的税收制度即 progressive tax system，累进税率。这是一种随课税对象数额的增大而相应提高计征比例的税率制度，即根据课税对象数额的大小，划分为若干等级，分别规定不同的税率。课税对象数额越大，则税率越高。[2]

碳定价即 carbon pricing，是一种降低温室气体排放的工具，将碳排放的外部成本内化为碳价，也就是对温室气体排放以每吨二氧化碳为单位给予明确定价的机制，主要包括碳税（carbon tax）、碳排放交易体系（Emission Trading Scheme）、碳信用机制（carbon crediting mechanism）、基于结果的气候金融（results-based climate finance）、内部碳定价（internal carbon pricing）五种形式。[3]

2. 长难句点拨

（1）首先，该句的信息密度很大，整体结构是主句＋宾语从句。而在宾语从句中，作者列举了多个影响经济环境的因素，对于口译学习者的听力理解和笔记产生了较大压力。其次，每个列举项都是主谓结构。如果保留原文结构，则译文会显得松散，口译学习者需要灵活采取策略。建议放弃原文的主句＋从句结构，将列举项转化为形容词＋名词的偏正短语，并将其作为并列主语。在一些政治、经济类演讲中，主谓结构的并列短语并不少见，将主谓结构转化为

① 见知网百科（https://xuewen.cnki.net/read-R2017030020000007.html），引用日期：2023 年 8 月 17 日。
② 见知网百科（https://xuewen.cnki.net/read-R2006110530011583.html），引用日期：2023 年 8 月 17 日。
③ 韩枫、彭华福、唐肖彬等：《全球碳定价机制发展趋势，现状及对我国的启示》，载《环境保护》2021 年第 24 期，第 66 页。

偏正结构的名词短语是一个常用策略，这样可以避免直接翻译造成小句过多、译文啰唆的问题，主谓结构转换为名词短语后，可选择的句型也会更多。

（2）该句结构并不复杂，但是"周期性反弹""潜在增长率""满负荷生产状态下的可持续增长率"等专业术语的翻译可能会对不少口译学习者造成困扰。在积累专业词汇时不仅要记住英语译文，还要理解术语的真正含义。以该句为例，在阅读句子的时候，读者可以看到破折号，从而理解"满负荷生产状态下的可持续增长率"是对"潜在增长率"的解释说明。但是在听力理解过程中没有标点符号的提示，需要口译学习者根据上下文来理解两者之间的关系。

（3）该句结构看似复杂，但句子主干可以简化为"《中国经济简报》认为，随着基础设施存量接近饱和，传统策略只会加剧风险，投资回报也会越来越低"。如果口译学习者能在听辨、做笔记和口译过程中抓住句子的核心主干，那么进行口译时就会事半功倍。其他部分主要是修饰语，英语的修饰语位置更加灵活，可以根据句意和语言特点，以动名词短语和介词短语的形式进行后置。除了句子结构外，"基础设施存量""饱和"这些表达也可能有难度，口译学习者应注意词汇积累。许多学习者听到"传统策略"一词时，下意识就会将其翻译成"traditional/conventional strategies"，参考译文使用的是"old playbook"，英语单词 playbook 的释义是"any plan or set of strategies, as for outlining a campaign in business or politics"①，非常符合本文语境。显得译文更加地道。

（4）该段句子较为冗长，是典型的多动词、无主语的句子。如果在译成英语的过程中，将每个动词短语都独立成句，则译文显得冗余、啰唆。因此，在口译过程中应充分考虑到汉英两种语言的差异。该句的核心是"采取一系列措施（扩大碳排放交易范围、强化碳排放交易制度、推动电力部门改革）从而实现目标（扩大碳定价的使用、促进可再生能源的市场渗透和全国范围内的交易与调度）"。而目标最终产生的效果则是该段的第二句"这不仅会产生环境效益，也有助于推动中国经济向以创新为基础的更可持续的增长模式转型"。在厘清这两个句子的逻辑关系后，口译学习者可以采取整合策略，利用词性转换技巧，将第一句以并列主语方式译出，与第二个句子的谓语部分整合，从而化繁为简。

（5）该段的第一句与难点（4）类似，也具有多动词、无主语的特点，因

---

① 见柯林斯英语字典网站（https://www.collinsdictionary.com/zh/dictionary/english/playbook），引用日期：2023 年 8 月 17 日。

此，口译时应采用的技巧也是一致的，即通过词性转换的方式来补充句子主语，一般是动词转名词，或者动词转形容词。该句采取的是将"强化企业和银行框架"这一动宾短语处理为形容词＋名词的偏正结构。值得注意的是，在翻译"消除扭曲"时，应避免直译为"eliminating distortion"，这是因为：首先，这样的搭配在英语中不常见，让人觉得译文生硬、晦涩；其次，如果探究发言的真正含义，"消除扭曲"实际指的是"私营企业和国有企业之间长期存在的利差"这个问题，因此用"address distortion"更加符合讲话者的意图。

三、口译练习

（一）英译汉

International Finance Forum (IFF) 2021 Spring Meetings:
Global Governance and International Co-operation in the Post-pandemic Era (Excerpt)
Session on the Global Sustainable Finance: Green and
Low-carbon Circular Development
Victoria Kwakwa, Vice President East Asia and Pacific International
[May 29, 2021 (DC time)]

Good afternoon. It is a great pleasure to join today's forum. I would like to thank the International Finance Forum for inviting me back to the IFF Spring Meetings to discuss the World Bank's approach to green and low carbon development in the post pandemic recovery.

When we met last November, most parts of the world were under lockdown, struggling to cope with the COVID-19 pandemic. Now six months later, some countries have begun to turn the corner thanks to the vaccine rollout, while others are experiencing a painful resurgence of the virus, particularly in South Asia. Clearly, the global pandemic is far from over. (1) Moreover, there is a growing divergence between developed and developing countries in terms of accessing vaccines and jump-starting economic recovery which is of grave concern.

Looking beyond the immediate task of fighting the COVID-19 pandemic, we need to make sure we seize the crisis to work towards a green, inclusive and resilient development path. The pandemic has starkly exposed the interdependence between people, the planet and the economy. It therefore highly welcomes that climate change is increasingly recognized as the defining development challenge of our time.

(2) The science on this is unequivocal: the consequences of climate change and pandemics are severe and irreversible, and it is the developing countries that continue to bear the brunt. The global pandemic has already pushed over 100 million people into extreme poverty in 2020 and worsened inequality. Climate change risks aggravating this bleak picture: we estimate an additional 130 million people could be pushed into extreme poverty by 2030 as a result of the effects of a warming climate.

Action is therefore urgent. We are lagging behind the *Paris Agreement* target to limit global warming to well below 2 degrees Celsius compared to pre-industrial levels. With COP26 in Glasgow on the horizon, we have a unique opportunity as well as a duty to intensify our efforts.

I am therefore pleased to note that the World Bank Group recently adopted a new *Climate Action Plan* (*CAP*) 2021-2025. (3) The new Action Plan aims to increase the WBG's impact on Green House Gas (GHG) emissions and adaptation outcomes by increasing climate finance, and expanding diagnostics to prioritize climate-related actions, including direct support to clients Nationally Determined Contributions (NDC).

We emphasize that climate action and development are intrinsically linked. (4) Indeed, we need a whole of economy approach to deliver growth and climate goals and embed climate priorities in country macroeconomic frameworks and financial sector regulation.

We will need transformational actions in key systems like energy, agriculture and food, cities, transport, and manufacturing, which drive the economy, account for around 90 percent of global greenhouse gas emissions and are the primary consumers and polluters of other scarce resources such as land and water.

We will also need to accelerate the move away from coal but to achieve this transition will require a range of social and labor market policies that addresses adverse impacts and safeguard the vulnerable. Without attention to a just transition, the energy transition cannot be sustained.

Significant reforms of fiscal systems will also be needed to mobilize domestic resources in a way that promotes inclusiveness. The financing needed for investment at scale far exceeds the possibilities of the public sector, requiring strong private sector involvement. Public-private partnerships, key upstream policy reforms and innovative financing can help spur private investment.

Fortunately, we have some good examples of these integrated whole of economy approaches already, including from our own work in the World Bank Group. Let me highlight a few:

In Greater Cairo in Egypt, the World Bank is supporting reducing air and climate emissions from critical sectors and increasing resilience to air pollution. The 200 million project focuses on reducing vehicle emissions, improving the management of solid waste, and developing and implementing a strong, economically feasible climate impact mitigation program.

(5) In coastal city of Beira in Mozambique, the World Bank financed a city-wide storm water drainage system, and flood control systems to build urban resilience to floods, the Project also showcased the effectiveness of nature-based solution for climate change adaptation, while leveraging additional resources for climate finance. The project investments improved the lives of more than 284000 people.

......

Turning to China, our partnership today is increasingly focusing on greening of China's economy and providing global public goods. China's recent pledge to achieve carbon neutrality by 2060 provides an important opportunity for us to further strengthen our partnership in the climate change and green development agenda.

(6) We are starting to work with the Development Research Center (DRC) of the State Council on a *Green China* Flagship study to identify evidence-based policy options to accelerate China's transition to a sustainable, carbon neutral and more resource-efficient economy.

And we are directly supporting China's decarbonization efforts. In Shanxi, one of China's top coal exporting provinces, we have ongoing support for policy reforms to pioneer an accelerated and just transition away from coal. A new Green and Low Carbon Investment Fund we have put together with the Ministry of Finance will catalyze private capital into private green businesses and projects, anchored on the application of international green and ESG standards. Our program in the Yellow

River Basin will support eco-system restoration and nature-based solution to climate change mitigation. Our cities programs will promote low carbon mobility, planning and financing solution. Finally, our green agriculture and rural revitalization program will target GHG emission reduction in the agriculture sector and support climate smart agriculture practices.

To conclude, countries face a historic opportunity to establish a better way forward. The damage wrought by the pandemic and worsening climate change, the exceptional crisis response offers a unique opportunity for a reset that addresses past policy deficiencies and chronic investment gaps. China could lead by example in decarbonizing its economy and expanding green development. And we stand ready to contribute in any way that we can to the success of green and low carbon development.

Thank you.

[资料来源:见世界银行网站（https://www.worldbank.org/en/news/speech/2021/05/29/remarks-by-victoria-kwakwa-vice-president-east-asia-and-pacific-at-the-international-finance-forum-iff-2021-spring-meeti），引用日期:2023 年 8 月 17 日。]

1. 词汇准备

Green and Low-carbon Circular Development	绿色低碳循环发展
Nationally Determined Contributions (NDC)	国家自主贡献目标
Development Research Center (DRC)	国务院发展研究中心
Green China Flagship study	《绿色中国》旗舰研究
Green and Low Carbon Investment Fund	绿色低碳投资基金

2. 长难句点拨

（1）口译学习者对该句中 jump-starting economic recovery 这一表达可能比较陌生，翻译时可以根据英语合成词的特点猜测词义，start 表示开始，jump 是跳，可以猜测这个词是"快速开始"或者"快速启动"的意思。在句子听辨过程中，如果能准确判断 which 引导的定语从句修饰的对象实际是 growing divergence …… 整个短语，而不是 economic recovery，可以减少理解偏误。在口译过程中，应根据汉语语言特点适当调整语序，将后半句 in terms of 引导的状语提前，再翻译句子前半段。

（2）该句的难点不在于字词层面，而是在翻译的时候如何流畅自然地承上启下，"The science on this"中的"this"明显是指代上一段句末的"climate change is increasingly recognized as the defining development challenge of our time."，"science"一般而言指"科学"，此处直接译成"科学"不容易理解。结合语境理解，此处意为气候变化是我们这个时代发展的决定性挑战方面的科学证据。

（3）虽然该句句子主干结构简单，但是谓语的动词不定式短语及方式状语较长，可能会引起理解困难。因此，准确切分意群有助于准确理解原文。该句意群切分如下："The new Action Plan // aims to // increase the WBG's impact on … // by increasing climate finance，and expanding diagnostics … //，including direct support to …"。由于汉语的状语一般是在谓语之前，因此在翻译成汉语时要进行较大的语序调整，先翻译 by 引导的方式状语，再翻译 increase the WBG'S impact on 这个短语。因此，该句参考译文为：新的行动计划旨在通过增加气候融资，扩大诊断以期优先考虑气候相关行动，包括直接支持客户国的国家自主贡献，从而扩大世界银行集团对温室气体减排和适应两方面的影响力。

（4）对该句应灵活处理 a whole of economy approach 这个短语。approach 的释义是"the way you deal with or think about a task/ problem/situation"①，即（思考问题的）方式方法，但是在该句的语境下，如果直译为"全经济方法"，则会显得译文生硬、拗口，不妨根据上下文翻译为"全经济模式"。deliver growth and climate goals 表示"实现增长与气候目标"，embed sth. in sth. 表示"把××嵌入/插入××中"，这两个表达非常地道，口译学习者应该熟记这两个短语，在汉译英任务中灵活使用。

（5）对于大部分学习者来说，该句中的 Mozambique（莫桑比克）这个国家并不陌生，但是 Beira（贝拉）这个城市可能比较陌生了。如果不知道这个城市的具体译法，可以采取两种方法：一是模糊化处理，即翻译为"在莫桑比克的一个沿海城市，世界银行资助建设了全市范围的雨水排水系统和防洪系统"；另一种则是音译，即在口译笔记上记下发音，口译时直接朗读发音。该句后半段中 showcase 短语和 leveraging 短语都是在阐述贝拉这个项目的成果，虽然语法结构上未体现并列关系，但是根据实际意思应该处理成并列关系。短语 the effectiveness of nature-based solution for climate change adaptation 包含了多个抽象名词（effectiveness，solution，adaptation），可能会对理解原文造成一定

---

① 见柯林斯英语字典网站（https://www.collinsdictionary. com/zh/dictionary/english/approach），引用日期，2023 年 8 月 17 日。

困难，要能够借助介词理解这些词之间的逻辑关系，可译为"基于自然的解决方案对适应气候变化的有效性"。

（6）该句是典型的英语长句，最常用的技巧就是切分，先要按照意群切分句子，再根据汉语习惯调整表达："We are starting to //work with … // on a Green China Flagship study // to identify … // to accelerate China's transition // to … economy"。

● （二）汉译英

借鉴国际经验，助力中国建设韧性基础设施

过去 40 年来，中国的快速城市化发展增大了其城市暴露于自然灾害之下的风险，环境退化和气候变化更加剧这一趋势。（1）2021 年 7 月，郑州市受强台风"烟花"输送的大量水汽的影响，发生了历史罕见的洪灾。此次洪灾不仅使得大量的基础设施损毁，还对整个系统构成了显著的威胁。（2）此次暴雨的降雨量超过 100 毫米每小时，打破了全中国 2418 个气象台站的一小时降雨记录。郑州部分地铁站被淹，数百人被困其中。这次灾情也显示出该市地铁系统应急处置存在不足。

郑州地铁站被淹事件的发生让改进中国地下交通基础设施设计和加强此类设施保护显得尤为紧迫。（3）郑州暴雨事件之后，极端天气事件下交通基础设施的韧性成了"灾害风险管理与韧性基础设施"深度技术研讨会的一项关键议题。此次深度技术研讨会由世界银行东京发展学习中心与世界银行东京灾害风险管理中心合作主办。

通过一周的知识分享和培训，来自阿塞拜疆、中国、约旦、马尔代夫、尼日利亚、卢旺达、突尼斯七国的政府官员和研究人员分享了各自在应对基础设施规划、投资和管理风险方面面临的挑战。此次研讨会上分享的国际经验为中方与会人员就未来如何预防并应对极端天气事件提供了启示。（4）中方与会人员就减轻中国城市轨道交通系统被淹风险这一问题特别介绍了解决方案。

在此次研讨会中，神户市在阪神大地震后修订了其灾害风险管理规划的经验给中国也带来了启发。正如世界银行报告所强调的，随着气候变化加剧和城市范围迅速扩大，政府部门必须定期重新考虑以前对灾害风险所作假设并重新设计极端情形下的响应措施。（5）就地下轨道交通系统的防洪措施来说，若想确保地铁在洪灾期间能持续运营，相关研究人员要定期对最极端淹没情形的应

对措施进行更新。

就加固城市轨道交通设施而言，福冈市的《彩虹规划》和《（东京）涩谷站改建计划》是暴雨管理方面的两个相关实例……此外，很多城市会利用雨水花园和透水路面来过滤并吸收暴雨，以防地面有过多积水。比如，日本多个城市已采用便于雨水渗入地下的绿色解决方案，以环境友好方式降低地铁站被淹风险。除了上述两个经验分享以外，此次研讨会给中国和其他国家就如何加强灾前预防的准备工作的主题提供了以下几点启示：

一是应急管理专业人士在协调有效响应行动方面起着不可或缺的作用。城市需要招聘专业人员并确保在职官员和相关部门人员得到全面的应灾培训。

二是公众的防灾意识很重要。地方政府部门在这方面可以发挥重要作用。宣传和定期开展应急演练能够助力提升人们在紧急情况下自救和互救的技能。

三是（6）信息透明是很关键的。灾害袭来时，相关部门和组织能够迅速、及时分享准确疏散线路和救灾信息对挽救生命和预防人员和财产损失起到至关重要的作用。

随着中国在应对环境退化和气候风险的挑战增大的同时继续推进城市化，政策制定者和城市居民都将更加重视韧性基础设施和韧性社区的建设。世界银行的项目所积累的全球知识以及日本从其灾害预防和灾后响应行动中所得出的重要经验不仅有助于中国和其他国家去更好地应对愈加频繁的自然灾害，还能帮助他们更高效地预防未来的重大灾害风险。

［资料来源：汪伟平、倪晓勇、Francis Ghesquiere、肖媛、张子晴：《借鉴国际经验，助力中国建设韧性基础设施》；见世界银行博客（https://blogs.worldbank.org/zh-hans/eastasiapacific/leveraging-international-experience-resilient-infrastructure-china，引用日期：2023 年 8 月 17 日。］

1. 词汇准备

台风"烟花"	Typhoon In-fa
"灾害风险管理与韧性基础设施"	
	Disaster Risk Management and Resilient Infrastructure
深度技术研讨会	Technical Deep Dive（TDD）
神户	Kobe
阪神大地震	Hanshin-Awaji Earthquake
福冈市	Fukuoka
《彩虹规划》	*Rainbow Plan*
《（东京）涩谷站改建计划》	*Shibuya Station（Tokyo）'s redevelopment plan*

2. 长难句点拨

（1）该句中含有一个专有名词台风"烟花"，此处切忌望文生义，按照拼音翻译为"Yanhua"。此处涉及台风命名的规则。按照世界气象组织要求，亚太地区的柬埔寨、中国、朝鲜、日本、韩国、泰国、美国以及越南等成员，每个国家或地区提供10个名字。这140个名字分成10组，每组14个名字，按每个成员国的英文名称的字母顺序依次排列，按顺序循环使用。因此，有些台风名字如"鸿雁"（Kirogi，由朝鲜提供）、"鹦鹉"（Nuri，由马来西亚提供）听起来像是汉语名字，但是其英文名具有典型的地方特色，应谨慎处理。①

（2）打破纪录（break the record）是一个常见表达。该句中的难点是在动词和宾语之间插入了较为复杂的修饰信息，如"全国2418个气象台站"和"一小时降雨"。因此，在听力理解和做笔记的过程中，口译学习者应首先抓住核心信息，完成句子主干的搭建，然后再结合英语修饰语的特点，灵活利用英语的一些构词法来进行翻译。在英语中，还有reach a record high/low（创历史新高/低）这一表达，汉译英中也经常会遇到，应重视积累。

（3）虽然原文包含两个句子，但实际都是围绕一个主题，即"极端天气事件下交通基础设施的韧性是深度技术研讨会的关键议题"。如果能妥善利用英语的各种语法手段，将两个句子进行整合，译文就非常符合英语"形合"的特点。这种方式对语言能力要求较高，口译学习者要能够根据意群之间的关系，利用合适的语言手段，利用介词、非谓语动词和名词词组。除此之外，该部分和前面一句话实际上暗含了因果关系，在口译过程中，也要把因果关系进行显化处理。

（4）城市轨道交通（urban rail transit）泛指在城市中沿特定铁轨运行的公共交通工具。根据我国出版的《城市轨道交通技术规范》，采用专用轨道导向运行的城市公共客运交通系统包括地铁（metro/underground railway）、轻轨（light rail transit，LRT）、单轨（monorail）、有轨电车（streetcar/tram）、磁悬浮列车（magnetic levitation vehicle，maglev）、市域快速轨道（rapid rail transit）等。口译学习者应对上述术语有所了解，并熟记汉语及英语表达。尽管文中多次提到城市轨道交通，由于文章主要集中讨论地铁，因此，参考译文基本都翻译为"underground railway"。

---

① 《台风是如何命名的?》，见中国气象局网站（https://www.cma.gov.cn/2011xzt/2012zhuant/20120420/2012042009/201204/t20120423_3095568.html），引用日期2023年8月17日。

（5）该句中的"对最极端淹没情形的应对措施进行更新"中"更新"一词不宜直译为"update"，因为 update 的意思是"to bring（information，esp. written material or material recorded in some other form）up to date"[①]，一般使用 update sb. on sth. 这一词组。然而该句中"更新"的实际意思是每隔一段时间，假设可能发生的极端天气情况，并相应调整应对最极端淹没的应对预案。因此，使用 reconsider 和 redesign 更符合句意。

（6）"信息透明是很关键的"很容易令人想到"It's critical/key to keep information transparent."这样翻译从语法上看并没有问题，但是联系上下文看，所谓的"信息透明"指的就是第二句中的"迅速、及时分享准确疏散线路和救灾信息"。考虑到上下文的连贯与衔接，还有更加简便的处理方法。第二句中"相关部门和组织"也不一定要翻译为"related department and organization"，该句的核心是"迅速、及时分享准确疏散线路和救灾信息对挽救生命和预防人员和财产损失起到至关重要的作用"，翻译时可以省略原文中的主语，直接翻译核心主干部分。

➡ 四、参考译文

● （一）口译实践

1. 英译汉

富与穷：颠覆时代的机遇与挑战（节选）

世界银行集团行长　金墉

（2018 年 4 月 10 日）

1800 年以前，几乎人人都很穷，虽然有皇室，有那些大地主，但他们只是极少数，几乎人人都生活在贫困中，人人都依靠土地为生。这就是整个人类历史。当然也有些巨大的变化，即，农业。这件事情的发生是，在农业出现之

[①] 见牛津英语字典网站（https://www.oed.com/search/dictionary/? scope = Entries&q = update），引用日期 2023 年 8 月 17 日。

前，大多数人都从事狩猎和采摘。农业出现之后，就有了粮食生产，人民不再需要出去寻觅食物，他们知道哪里可以生产源源不断的粮食。

但是，财富是和土地拴在一起的，控制了土地就控制了世界上大部分财富。困难在于输送东西，包括货物、思想、人。输送任何东西都很困难，所以没有多少贸易。因此，真正重要的是运输成本，它决定了社会形成的方式。

在 17 世纪，只有 3000 艘欧洲船舶驶往亚洲。在 18 世纪，在此后的 100 年里，约有 6000 艘船驶往亚洲，运输任何东西都很困难。

到了 1800—1820 年，发生了一些非常重要的事情。在大多数历史学家看来，两件最重要的事情是工业革命和蒸汽机的出现。所以，在 1820 年前后，蒸汽机使运输货物成为可能，而货物运输推动了工业化、贸易和经济增长。

但是，与此同时，也是另一个开始，是伟大的经济学家之一迪尔德丽·麦克洛斯基当时所谈到的，随着工业革命和蒸汽机的出现，开始出现了她所说的大分流，意思是某些地区，特别是欧洲和美国很快富起来。

她谈到创始，即所谓资产阶级的形成。而资产阶级过去是农民，他们足够接近皇室，希望像皇室那样生活。所以，她认为资产阶级的发展是非常重要的发展，因为资产阶级是中产阶级的前身。

现在，从 1820 年到现在的 200 年里，货物和服务的供应出现爆炸式增长。这不是微小的变化，这是巨大的变化，因为 1820 年之前，人们基本上是在同样的世界里出生和死去。这个世界从他们出生到他们死去没有多大变化。但是从 1820 年开始，世界开始快速变化。

两个世纪前，美国成年人中的五分之四从事粮食生产以养活家人；现在，一个农民可以养活 300 个人。

所以，我讲这些的原因是，我们必须客观地看待这些事情。我们必须把人类进步（这就是我们世界银行所从事的发展工作）的演变过程，从历史的角度来看。

…………

现在，我每到一处都能看到，年轻人不一定拥有智能手机，但有机会获得智能手机。到 2025 年，很多分析人士说，全世界都会有宽带接入。

现在，当你有了宽带，当你能够上网浏览，就会发生两件事。首先，当人们能上网，他们的生活满意度就会大大提高。当他们能上网，他们就能看到世界是如何运行的。他们能够看电影、电视节目，生活满意度上升。

但是发生的另一件事是，他们的收入参考标准也上升了，这实际上是我们世界银行集团研究的课题。他们用来比较自己收入的标准提高了。在这种情况下，收入也必须上升，否则就会引起不满。

…………

所以，有那么多愿望，有那么多希望有机会受教育的愿望，保证孩子们不饿肚子的愿望。世界上有那么多愿望，一旦人们能够上网，愿望会继续增加。我们怎么应对这种情况呢？

这就直接触及我们这个机构的核心。世界银行集团，当时只是世界银行集团的一个机构，成立于1944年，诞生于第二次世纪大战的灰烬之中。我认为，怎么表述好呢？作为一个明智之举，……我们必须建立制度，一方面能够带来稳定，因为在"二战"之前和"二战"期间发生了货币战争。国家为使货币贬值，使尽浑身解数以占优势，全球货币状况一团混乱。所以，他们需要给全球体系带来稳定。

…………

我第一次走进世界银行，我看到了这个标语："我们的梦想是一个没有贫困的世界。"我问道，为什么这是一个梦想？我们不能把它变成一个实际目标吗？我们也确实这样做了。

经过三四个月的争论，这是我们世界银行的做法，我们争论。我们用数据争论，我们用政治和意识形态争论，我们用多种不同类型的工具争论。我们得出一个结论：我们要在2030年终结极端贫困，即终结每天生活费不足1.9美元的人口的贫困。我们还承诺促进共享繁荣，减少不平等。我们觉得有三条路能让我们达到目的。

首先，按照传统，我们一向着眼于经济增长，但是，在这种情况下，我们着眼于包容，意思是人人受益，可持续，意思是不破坏地球，包容、可持续的经济增长。

其次，由于每天都有那么多危机影响着世界，流行病、气候变化、难民、脆弱性、冲突、暴力，我们要着眼于加强韧性，以应对世界上那些影响越来越多人的问题。

最后，第三个支柱是更多更有效地投资于人。这指的是包容、可持续的经济增长；抵御当今世界发生的各种冲击的韧性；更多更有效地投资于人。

现在，我们必须改变，因为世界改变了，世界发生了巨大的变化。

［资料来源：见世界银行网站中文版（https://www.shihang.org/zh/news/speech/2018/04/10/rich-and-poor-opportunities-and-challenges-in-an-age-of-disruption），引用日期2023年8月17日。］

2. 汉译英

China's 2022 Outlook：Rebalancing Act

After a strong rebound last year, the world economy is entering a challenging 2022. The advanced economies have recovered rapidly thanks to big stimulus packages and rapid progress with vaccination, but many developing countries continue to struggle.

The spread of new variants amid large inequalities in vaccination rates, elevated food and commodity prices, volatile asset markets, the prospect of policy tightening in the United States and other advanced economies, and continued geopolitical tensions provide a challenging backdrop for developing countries, as the World Banks *Global Economic Prospects* report published today highlights.

The global context will also weigh on China's outlook in 2022, by dampening export performance, a key growth driver last year. Following a strong 8 percent cyclical rebound in 2021, the World Bank expects growth in China to slow to 5.1 percent in 2022, closer to its potential—the sustainable growth rate of output at full capacity.

Indeed, growth in the second half of 2021 was below this level, and so our forecast assumes a modest amount of policy loosening. Although we expect momentum to pick up, our outlook is subject to domestic in addition to global downside risks. ...

In the face of these headwinds, China's policymakers should nonetheless keep a steady hand. Our latest *China Economic Update* argues that the old playbook of boosting domestic demand through investment-led stimulus will merely exacerbate risks in the real estate sector and reap increasingly lower returns as China's stock of public infrastructure approaches its saturation point.

Instead, to achieve sustained growth, China needs to stick to the challenging path of rebalancing its economy along three dimensions：first, the shift from external demand to domestic demand and from investment and industry-led growth to greater reliance on consumption and services；second, a greater role for markets and the private sector in driving innovation and the allocation of capital and talent；and third, the transition from a high to a low-carbon economy.

None of these rebalancing acts are easy. However, as the *China Economic Update points out, structural reforms could help reduce the trade-offs involved in transition to a new path of high-quality growth.*

First, fiscal reforms could aim to create a more progressive tax system while boosting social safety nets and spending on health and education. This would help lower precautionary household savings and thereby support the rebalancing toward domestic consumption, while also reducing income inequality among households.

Second, following tightening anti-monopoly provisions aimed at digital platforms, and a range of restrictions imposed on online consumer services, the authorities could consider shifting their attention to remaining barriers to market competition more broadly to spur innovation and productivity growth. ...

Third, the wider use of carbon pricing, for example, through an expansion of the scope and tightening of the emissions trading system rules, as well power sector reforms to encourage the penetration and nationwide trade and dispatch of renewables, would not only generate environmental benefits but also contribute to China's economic transformation to a more sustainable and innovation-based growth model.

In addition, a more robust corporate and bank resolution framework would contribute to mitigating moral hazards, thereby reducing the trade-offs between monetary policy easing and financial risk management. Addressing distortions in the access to credit—reflected in persistent spreads between private and State borrowers—could support the shift to more innovation-driven, private sector-led growth.

Productivity growth in China during the past four decades of reform and opening-up has been private-sector led. The scope for future productivity gains through the diffusion of modern technologies and practices among smaller private companies remains large. Realizing these gains will require a level playing field with State-owned enterprises.

[资料来源: Ibrahim Chowdhury, Ekaterine T. Vashakmadze and Li Yusha. *Rebalancing Act: China's 2022 Outlook*; 见世界银行网站 (https://www.worldbank.org/en/news/opinion/2022/01/12/rebalancing-act-china-s-2022-outlook), 引用日期2023年8月17日。]

● （二）口译练习

1. 英译汉

国际金融论坛 2021 年春季会议
后疫情时代：全球治理与国际合作（节选）
全球可持续金融：绿色低碳循环发展
世界银行东亚与太平洋地区副行长　维多利亚·克瓦
［2021 年 5 月 29 日（华盛顿时间）］

下午好。很高兴出席今天的论坛。感谢国际金融论坛邀请我出席春季会议，介绍世界银行关于疫后复苏的绿色低碳发展理念。

在去年 11 月国际金融论坛召开之际，世界大部分地区处于封闭状态，竭力应对新冠肺炎疫情。6 个月后的今天，由于疫苗推出一些国家形势开始好转，而另一些国家特别是南亚则经历着病毒卷土重来。显然，全球范围的疫情远未结束。此外，在获取疫苗和启动经济复苏方面，发达国家和发展中国家之间的差距不断扩大，令人严重关切。

除了抗击新冠疫情的当务之急外，我们需要确保以危机为契机，走向绿色、包容和韧性发展之路。这场疫情凸显出人、地球、经济三者之间的相互依存关系。因此，我们对气候变化日益被看成当今时代的决定性发展挑战深表欢迎。

这方面的科学明确无误：气候变化和流行病的后果是严重且不可逆转的，而发展中国家仍首当其冲。新冠疫情在 2020 年已使 1 亿多人陷入极端贫困，并加剧了不平等现象。气候变化有可能令这一暗淡局势更加雪上加霜：我们估计，由于气候变暖的影响，到 2030 年可能还会有 1.3 亿人陷入极端贫困。

因此，采取行动刻不容缓。我们在将全球升温幅度限制在相比工业化前水平低于 2 摄氏度的《巴黎协定》目标方面进展滞后。随着在格拉斯哥举行的第 26 届联合国气候变化大会的临近，我们有独特的契机也有义务加倍努力。

因此，我很高兴介绍，世界银行集团最近通过了新的《气候行动计划（2021—2025 年）》。新的行动计划旨在通过增加气候融资，扩大诊断范围以期优先考虑气候相关行动，包括直接支持客户国的国家自主贡献，从而扩大世界银行集团对温室气体减排和适应两方面的影响力。

我们强调气候行动与发展具有内在联系。确实，我们需要采取一种"全经济"的模式来实现增长与气候目标，并将气候优先事项纳入国家宏观经济框架和金融部门法规。

我们需要在能源、农业与食品、城市、交通和制造业等关键系统采取转型措施，这些系统推动经济增长，约占全球温室气体排放量的90%，也是土地和水等其他稀缺资源的消费大户和主要污染源。

我们还需要加快脱煤步伐，但要实现这一转型，需要一系列社会和劳动力市场政策，以应对不利影响和保护弱势群体。如果转型中忽视公平，能源转型就无法持续。

对财政制度也需要进行重大改革，从而以促进包容性的方式调动国内资源。大规模投资所需要的资金远远超出公共部门的能力，需要私营部门的大力参与。公私伙伴关系、关键性上游政策改革和创新性融资有助于刺激私人投资。

令人欣慰的是，我们已有一些采取这些综合性"全经济"模式的良好案例，包括我们世界银行集团自身工作中的案例。我介绍几个案例。

在埃及的大开罗，世界银行支持减少关键行业的空气污染和排放，增强对空气污染的抵御能力。这个2亿美元的项目着重于减少车辆尾气排放，改善垃圾管理，并制订和实施一项强有力的、经济上具有可行性的气候影响缓解计划。

在莫桑比克沿海城市贝拉，世界银行资助建立了全市范围的雨水排水系统和防洪系统，增强城市抗洪能力。该项目还示范了基于自然的解决方案对适应气候变化的可行性，同时也为气候融资撬动了更多资源。该投资项目改善了超过28.4万人的生活。

⋯⋯⋯⋯⋯

在中国，我们目前的合作日益侧重于中国经济的绿色发展和提供全球公共产品。中国最近承诺到2060年实现碳中和，这为我们进一步加强在气候变化和绿色发展议程中的合作提供了重要机遇。

我们开始与国务院发展研究中心合作开展《绿色中国》旗舰研究，明确基于实证的政策选择，以加快中国实现可持续发展、碳中和以及提高资源利用效率的经济转型。

我们也直接支持中国的脱碳努力。在作为中国煤炭输出大省的山西，我们一直在支持政策改革，率先加快脱煤公平过渡。我们与财政部共同策划的一个新的绿色低碳投资基金，将以运用国际绿色和ESG标准为基础，促进私人资本投入私营绿色企业和项目。我们的黄河流域项目将支持生态系统恢复和基于自然的缓解气候变化解决方案。我们的城市项目将促进低碳出行、规划和融资解决方案。最后，我们的绿色农业和乡村振兴项目将以减少农业温室气体排放为目标，并支持气候智慧型农业实践。

总而言之，各国面临着确立更好的前进方向的历史机遇。尽管新冠疫情和气候变化加剧造成了破坏，但非同寻常的危机应对为"重设"提供了独特机遇，可以弥补过去的政策不足之处和长期投资缺口。中国可以在经济脱碳化和扩大绿色发展方面以身作则。我们随时准备为绿色低碳发展取得成功作出贡献。

谢谢各位。

[资料来源：见世界银行网站（https://www.shihang.org/zh/news/speech/2021/05/29/remarks-by-victoria-kwakwa-vice-president-east-asia-and-pacific-at-the-international-finance-forum-iff-2021-spring-meeti），引用日期2023年8月17日。]

2. 汉译英

Leveraging International Experience for Resilient Infrastructure in China

China's rapid urban growth over the last 40 years has increased its cities exposure to natural hazards, a trend exacerbated by environmental degradation and climate change. The risk to infrastructure systems became obvious in July 2021, when extreme rainstorms, formed by Typhoon In-fa, caused flood and widespread destruction in the city of Zhengzhou. The storm broke the single-hour rainfall record of 2418 national meteorological stations in mainland China. Subway stations in Zhengzhou were flooded and paralyzed, trapping dozens of people inside. The prevention measures in place to protect the city's subway operations proved inadequate.

The flooding in Zhengzhou's subway stations highlights the urgency of improving the design and enhancing the protection of underground transportation in China. Consequently, resilience of transportation infrastructure under extreme weather events was a key topic discussed at a recent one-week online Technical Deep Dive (TDD) on Disaster Risk Management and Resilient Infrastructure organized by the World Banks Tokyo Development Learning Center (TDLC) in collaboration with the

World Bank Tokyo Disaster Risk Management (DRM) Hub.

Through a week of knowledge sharing and training, government officials and researchers from seven countries Azerbaijan, China, Jordan, Maldives, Nigeria, Rwanda, and Tunisia shared the challenges they were facing in addressing risks in infrastructure planning, investment and management. The international experience shared at the TDD provided inspirations to participants from China on how to prepare and handle unexpected extreme weather events in the future. They especially reflected on potential solutions to mitigating flood risk to underground railway transportation systems in Chinese cities.

An important step, as highlighted in World Bank reports, is for researchers to carry out a systemic update of maximum inundation scenarios. The Chinese participants also learned from Kobe's experience in handling the aftermath of Hanshin-Awaji Earthquake, which led Kobe City to revise its disaster risk management plan. With accelerating climate change and rapidly expanding city footprints, authorities must regularly reconsider previous assumptions on disaster risks and redesign responses in extreme scenarios.

On strengthening underground rail transportation, Fukuoka City's *Rainbow Plan and Shibuya Station (Tokyo)'s redevelopment plan* for storm-water management are relevant examples. ... Further, various Japanese cities have utilized green solutions to facilitate rainwater infiltration to alleviate flooding in an environmentally friendly way. In many cases, rain gardens and permeable pavements can be utilized to filter and absorb storm water. The TDD offered additional takeaways on how to strengthen disaster preparedness for China and other countries.

First, emergency professionals are essential to coordinate an effective response. Cities need to recruit specialized staff and ensure existing officials are appropriately trained.

Second, public awareness is important. This is an area where local authorities can play an important role. Information campaigns and regular emergency drills can help improve people's skills in rescuing themselves and helping one another in an emergency.

Last but not least, information is key. When disasters hit, promptly sharing accurate information on evacuation routes and disaster relief is critical in saving lives and preventing losses.

As China continues to urbanize with the challenges of environmental degradation and increasing climate risks, policy makers and residents alike will pay greater attention to resilient infrastructure and communities. The global knowledge accumulated through World Bank operations, as well as the lessons from Japan's disaster prevention and post-disaster responses, provide important experiences that could help China and other countries better cope with increasing natural hazards and prevent major disasters in the future.

［资料来源：Wang weiping, Ni Xiaoyong, Francis Ghesquiere, Xiao Yuan and Zhang Ziqing. *Leveraging international experience for resilient infrastructure in China*；见世界银行博客（https://blogs. worldbank. org/eastasiapacific/leveraging-international-experience-resilient-infrastructure-china），引用日期2023 年8 月17 日。］

第二章 国际货币基金组织

➡️ 一、背景阅读

🔵 (一) 汉语简介

【成　立】于1944年7月成立，1947年3月1日开始运作，1947年11月成为联合国专门机构。

【宗　旨】稳定国际汇兑，消除妨碍世界贸易的外汇管制，在货币问题上促进国际合作，并通过提供短期贷款，解决成员国国际收支不平衡时产生的外汇资金需求。

【成　员】目前共190个成员国。

【负责人】现任总裁是克里斯塔利娜·格奥尔基耶娃（Kristalina Georgieva，保加利亚籍），2019年10月1日就任基金组织总裁，任期5年。

【总　部】美国华盛顿。

【组织结构】理事会是最高权力机构，执行董事会负责处理日常业务。

【主要活动】与世界银行每年联合举办一次春季会议和一次年会。春季会议和年会期间举行货币与金融委员会会议。

【股本和资金来源】主要来源于各成员国认缴的份额。各成员国的份额由其国内生产总值、开放度、经济波动性、国际储备等经济指标确定。

　　[资料来源：见中国外交部网站（https://www.mfa.gov.cn/web/gjhdq_676201/gjhdqzz_681964/lhg_681966/jbqk_681968/200802/t20080229_9380009.shtml），引用日期：2023年8月17日。]

（二） IMF 英语介绍

1. What is International Monetary Fund（IMF）？

The International Monetary Fund（IMF）is an international organization that promotes global economic growth and financial stability, encourages international trade, and reduces poverty. Quotas of member countries are a key determinant of the voting power in IMF decision. Votes comprise one vote per 100000 special drawing rights（SDR）of quota plus basic votes. SDRs are an international type of monetary reserve currency created by the IMF as a supplement to the existing money reserves of member countries.

2. History

The IMF was conceived in July 1944 in the aftermath of the Great Depression of the 1930s at the United Nations Bretton Woods Conference in New Hampshire, United States. The 44 countries in attendance sought to build a framework for international economic cooperation and avoid repeating the competitive currency devaluations that contributed to the Great Depression of the 1930s. The IMF's primary mission is to ensure the stability of the international monetary system—the system of exchange rates and international payments that enables countries and their citizens to transact with each other.

3. Institution

The IMF is accountable to its member country governments. At the top of its organizational structure is the Board of Governors, consisting of one governor and one alternate governor from each member country, usually the top officials from the central bank or finance ministry. The Board of Governors meets once a year at the IMF-World Bank Annual Meetings. 24 of the governors serve on the International Monetary and Financial Committee, or IMFC, which advises the IMF's Executive Board on the supervision and management of the international monetary and financial system. The day-to-day work of the IMF is overseen by its 24-member Executive Board, which represents the entire membership and supported by IMF staff. The

Managing Director is the head of the IMF staff and Chair of the Executive Board and is assisted by four Deputy Managing Directors.

4. Three Major Systems

（1）Surveillance

In order to maintain stability and prevent crises in the international monetary system, the IMF monitors member country policies as well as national, regional, and global economic and financial developments through a formal system known as surveillance. The IMF provides advice to member countries and promotes policies designed to foster economic stability, reduce vulnerability to economic and financial crises, and raise living standards. It also provides periodic assessments of global prospects in its *World Economic Outlook*, in addition to a series of regional economic outlooks.

（2）Financial assistance

The IMF provides loans—including emergency loans—to member countries experiencing actual or potential balance of payments problems. The aim is to help them rebuild their international reserves, stabilize their currencies, continue paying for imports, and restore conditions for strong economic growth, while correcting underlying problems.

（3）Capacity development

The IMF provides technical assistance and training to help member countries build better economic institutions and strengthen related human capacities. This is a core mandate of the IMF and accounts for nearly a third of its budget. The IMF's capacity development efforts are also focused on helping member countries tackle development priorities—such as income inequality, corruption, climate change and gender inequality—helping them make progress toward the Sustainable Development Goals（SDGs）.

5. Central Terms

（1）Reserve position

Reserve position in the IMF is the sum of（a）the "reserve tranche", that is, the foreign currency（including Special Drawing Rights）amounts that a member country may draw from the IMF at short notice; and（b）any indebtedness of the IMF （under a loan agreement）in the General Resources Account that is readily available to the member country, including the reporting country's lending to the IMF under the General Arrangement to Borrow（GAB）and the New Arrangement to Borrow（NAB）.

（2）Special Drawing Right

The Special Drawing Right（SDR）is an interest-bearing international reserve asset created by the IMF in 1969 to supplement other reserve assets of member countries.

The SDR is based on a basket of international currencies comprising the U. S. dollar, Japanese yen, euro, pound sterling and Chinese Renminbi. It is not a currency, nor a claim on the IMF, but is potentially a claim on freely usable currencies of IMF members. The value of the SDR is set daily by the IMF on the basis of fixed currency amounts of the currencies included in the SDR basket and the daily market exchange rates between the currencies included in the SDR basket.

［资料来源：见国际货币基金组织网站（https://www. imf. org/en/About/Factsheets/IMF-at-a-Glance），引用日期：2023 年 8 月 17 日。］

6. 词汇表 Vocabulary List

International Monetary Fund	国际货币基金组织
international monetary system	国际货币体系（汇率体系）
system of international payments	国际支付体系
International Monetary and Financial Committee	国际货币与金融委员会
IMF-World Bank Annual Meetings	基金组织/世界银行年会
Special Drawing Right	特别提款权
quota	份额
surveillance	监督系统
financial assistance	资金援助
capacity development	能力建设

➡ 二、口译实践

● （一）英译汉

Opening Remarks at Peer-Learning Series on Digital Money/Technology: Central Bank Digital Currency and the Case of China

Krishna Srinivasan, Asia and Pacific Department Director, IMF

(July 7, 2022)

Good morning, everyone, and good evening if you're in the Western Hemisphere. Thank you for joining in today's event on Central Bank Digital Currency and the Case of China. As Alfred indicated, this is the second event in our new series of events on digital money and technology in the Asia-Pacific region.

Digital money and technologies can significantly change the landscape for financial systems and bring important benefits to the public at large. Among other things, they could foster financial inclusion, create new value-added in the economy, and reduce transaction costs, including across borders. The digital money/technology series covers a broad range of topics, and so allow me to make a few general points.

As with any innovation, the challenge is to find the right balance between fostering innovation and maintaining stability and protection for consumers and investors. (1) We will hear about CBDCs in greater detail today, but let me also highlight the critical point we find ourselves in for crypto assets. For example, the recent crypto market crash— triggered by the de-pegging of a large algorithmic stablecoin and exacerbated by the collapse of overleveraged financial institutions in digital asset banking and trading—highlights the risks created by regulatory shortcomings. As the size of digital assets grow, without proper regulation, the systemic risks that the sector poses will increase.

(2) The stakes are particularly high for Asia and the Pacific, where many people see digital finance as an opportunity to build and exploit new drivers of growth

and innovation. Several countries in the region are at the cutting edge of new developments stemming from the rise of private and public digital assets. (3) New crypto assets and associated products and services proliferated in the region with transaction volumes of crypto assets in many countries among the highest in the world.

Policy makers are keen to monitor the risks emanating from the digital finance sector, with many activities still unregulated but expected to have broader impact. We can and should learn from each other's experiences. (4) This peer-learning series thus highlights the experiences of countries in the region in regulatory guidance for the development of digital finance. Today's event focuses on China's experience with central bank digital currency, the e-CNY.

The IMF has set out an ambitious agenda for understanding the implications of fintech and digital assets for the global economy. For the Asia and Pacific Department, our goal will be to monitor and advise on these rapidly evolving areas for our member countries, and establish much closer interaction with member countries and key stakeholders. In particular, we'll strive to provide timely advice and capacity development assistance to small states, low-income countries, and emerging markets and developing countries in coordination with the IMF's Monetary and Capital Market Department.

As such, a lot of analytical work is underway on a broad set of issues. (5) As it related to CBDCs, I want to highlight a survey of 36 Asian economies we conducted earlier this year to help us understand the steps countries have taken in their consideration of CBDCs and how crypto falls into this landscape. The note summarizing the survey will be released later this year, but for now let me share four key findings with you:

First, we find that the Asia and Pacific region is at the forefront of the CBDC exploration, and interest in CBDCs continues to rise. Even though no Asian country has formally launched a CBDC yet, China and India—the world's most populous countries—are frontrunners for doing so in the near future. Other economies, such as Singapore are relatively advanced in their work on CBDC, while some countries including Japan, Korea, and Australia have done extensive research.

Second, several factors drive CBDC interest: The higher income countries seek to enhance the efficiency and safety of the payment system, while emerging market economies are looking to promote financial inclusion and financial stability. Some countries simply do not want to fall behind the curve, either because of regional peers or the private sector.

Third, the decision to adopt or explore CBDCs is closely linked with the rapid increase in the use of crypto assets in the economy, as well as attempts at regulation. (6) For example, in Indonesia, the Philippines, and Vietnam, the uptick in crypto usage for remittances and investment among individuals has policymakers considering the tangible benefits of technological innovation, including lower cost and improvements in payment systems.

Finally, while there is a significant interest in CBDCs, very few countries are actually likely to issue them in the near to medium terms. Most countries in the region have shown interest, with work ranging from preliminary research and development to launching live pilots.

Let me also use this forum to highlight that in addition to our work on CBDCs, we have done several studies on private digital assets, including empirical analyses on the drivers of crypto asset adoption across countries and the impact of policy action.

Regarding the effect of policy on adoption, we find that crypto bans reduce crypto activities in the short term. However, because bans are difficult to enforce, the effect diminishes over the long term, even when regulations are strict. Also interesting, announcing a plan to issue a CBDC, likewise, dampens crypto activities.

(7) Our research also shows that the crypto market can increase dollarization, as U. S. dollar stablecoins crowd out local currencies in crypto markets. This effect is stronger in countries with higher inflation and currency instability. The study points to regulated, local currency-backed stable coins issued by the private sector as an alternative to retail CBDCs.

We find that the rate of crypto adoption is greater in countries with higher digital penetration and remittances as well as weaker macroeconomic fundamentals—such as high inflation. Informality, corruption and the degree of capital controls are also positively associated with higher crypto adoption. These highlight the importance of implementing proper tracking of crypto activities and improving regulation.

Looking forward, we have several analytical projects at various stages of execution.

We're also planning a series of more technical CBDC research to our support our capacity development efforts. This includes CBDC infrastructure and design options for emerging markets and developing economies. It also includes a framework for deciding if and how to adopt a CBDC, and the implications for monetary policy and cross-border transmission of shocks.

(8) For the Pacific Island countries, we are undertaking analytical work to examine the prospects for digital currencies (including CBDCs) and to set up a framework to help the countries assess the costs and benefits of digital currency adoption as well as potential policy implication.

Given the importance of these topics for our membership and the IMF, digitalization is now regularly discussed with the authorities during our annual Article IV dialogues and covered in corresponding IMF staff reports. In particular, the Article IV consultations will focus on digital money issues for countries at the forefront of these issues (such as some Pacific Island countries and we will continue to closely cover developments in China) and countries with the potential to adopt CBDCs and/or encounter other digital finance issues soon.

I am very pleased that today we can bring together colleagues and friends from the People's Bank of China and the Hong Kong Monetary Authority, as a well as international experts on these issues. China's experience and pilots with the e-CNY could hold useful lessons for other countries as they search for ways to navigate the fast-changing digital finance landscape.

I am sure that this series of events in general and today's event on CBDC and the case of China in particular will be very useful for us all. Thank you.

[资料来源：见国际货币基金组织网站（https://www.imf.org/en/News/Articles/2022/07/07/sp070722-central-bank-digital-currency-and-the-case-of-china），引用日期：2023 年 8 月 17 日。]

1. 实践解析

本口译实践选自 2022 年 7 月 8 日，国际货币基金组织亚太部主任 Krishna Srinivasan（克里希纳·斯里尼瓦桑）在"央行数字货币及中国的案例"活动上的致辞。在致辞中，斯里尼瓦桑表明 IMF 已经制定了一项议程以了解金融科技和数字资产对全球经济的影响，此外，还介绍了 IMF 亚太部的发展目标，并公布了针对 36 个亚洲经济体在央行数字货币方面调查的四项主要发现，以及对私人数字资产研究的发现。

本演讲的口译难点是原文涉及许多数字资产术语，只有了解了相关术语含义，才能准确翻译相关内容。

Crypto asset 即加密资产，是利用加密、分布式记账技术存在的一种数字化资源，是替代现有货币的一种技术凭证、通过密码学和分布式账簿等技术来实现的私人资产，具有交易支付等功能。常见的加密资产有比特币（Bitcoin）、代币（Token）等基于区块链等加密技术形成的一种虚拟货币。①

Stable coin 即稳定币，与目标价值（如美元）保持价格稳定的一种可以全球流通的加密数字货币，稳定币不依赖任何国家的中央银行。鉴于其价值稳定，稳定币成为了传统金融市场和加密数字货币生态系统之间的桥梁。②

Algorithmic stable coin 即算法稳定币，它与一般的稳定币不同，不需要依靠其他抵押资产，而是通过调节市场的供需关系来维持价格稳定。③

2. 长难句点拨

（1）该部分有两个难点：首先，文中出现了数字资产相关的专业术语，如 crypto asset（加密资产），stablecoin（稳定币），digital asset（数字资产），如果缺乏相应的背景知识，可能无法理解原文的具体含义。其次，第二句的句子结构稍显复杂，主语和谓语之间插入了一个由两个并列的过去分词短语组成的长定语，口译学习者在听辨过程中应快速理解 crypto market crash，由 triggered by 引导的短语和由 exacerbated by 引导的短语之间的修饰关系和逻辑先后关系，即算法稳定币与支持资产脱钩引发了加密资产市场脱钩，而杠杆过高的金融机构倒闭进一步加剧了机密资产市场的恶劣形势，这些事件凸显了监管不力的风险。

（2）Stake 的英语解释是"an interest or share in an undertaking or enterprise"④，根据上下文语境这里可以译为"这对亚太地区而言尤其具有重大的意义"。该句中 Asia and the Pacific 后面接了一个非限制性定语从句，由于

---

① 参见张洋《加密资产的金融风险识别与监管问题研究》，载《财会通讯》2020 年第 22 期，第 140 页。

② 参见赵炳昊《应对加密数字货币监管挑战的域外经验与中国方案——以稳定币为切入点》，载《政法论坛》2020 年第 2 期，第 177 – 178 页。

③ 参见岳品瑜、廖蒙《加密货币大跌 算法稳定币还靠谱吗》，载《北京商报》2022 年 5 月 12 日第 8 版。

④ 见韦氏词典网站（https://www.merriam-webster.com/dictionary/stake），引用日期：2023 年 8 月 17 日。

句子较长，为让译文更加流畅，翻译时可以将定语从句拆成两个短句，通过增补技巧，将 opportunity 后面的动词不定式短语译为独立的短句，即"这对亚太地区而言尤其具有重大的意义——在亚太地区，很多人将数字金融视为一个机遇，认为其能为经济增长与创新带来新的动力"。

（3）Proliferate 的英语解释是"to increase in number very quickly"①，这里结合语境可以译为"快速发展"，其名词形式为 proliferation，如 nuclear proliferation（核扩散），*Treaty on the Non Proliferation of Nuclear Weapons*（《不扩散核武器条约》）；在医学口译场景下 proliferation 一般译为"增生"。

（4）Peer-learning 是教育学中的词语，一般译为"同伴学习"，但是在本文语境下，直接借用这个译法是欠妥的，该文是国际货币基金组织亚太部主任 Krishna Srinivasan 在"央行数字货币与中国实践"研讨会上的开幕词，旨在推动各国之间的经验交流，译为"同行学习"更加贴切。central bank digital currency（缩写为 CBDC）即"央行数字货币"，是"央行数字货币是数字化的具有支付功能或者存储价值的央行负债"，"能激发支付市场的竞争活力、降低支付成本、提高国内支付以及跨境支付效率等，因此具有替代和补充现有支付工具的潜能"②。中国的央行数字货币被称为"数字人民币"（e-CNY）。

（5）该句句式稍显复杂，句子的主干是"I want to highlight a survey … to help us understand …"，survey 后面有定语从句，understand 有两个并列宾语：steps 和 how crypto falls into this landscape，"steps"后面也有定语从句。这对口译学习者的听辨能力有较高的要求。口译学习者要厘清意群之间的逻辑关系，在语言转换过程中，可以采用顺句驱动的技巧，将长句进行拆分，即"I want to highlight // a survey of 36 Asian economies we conducted earlier this year// to help us understand the steps countries have taken in their consideration of CBDCs // and how crypto falls into this landscape."除此之外，该句中有两个抽象名词"consideration"和"landscape"，大部分口译学习者对这两个词都不陌生，但是口译过程中如果只翻译字面意思"认真思考"或者"风景、景色"，译文就会稍显生硬，应结合语境将这两个词的具体含义解释清楚，使译文更加清晰明了。

（6）Remittance 的汉语意思是汇款金额，如 outward remittance（汇出汇

---

① 见柯林斯英语字典网站（https：//www. collinsdictionary. com/zh/dictionary/english/proliferate），引用日期：2023 年 8 月 17 日。

② 王博、赵真真：《央行数字货币对支付体系的影响研究》，载《广东财经大学学报》2023 年第 1 期，第 63 页。

款），inward remittance（汇入汇款）；tangible 一词的解释是"that is clear enough or definite enough to be easily seen, felt, or noticed"①，反义词为 intangible，如 tangible asset（有形资产），tangible cultural heritage（物质文化遗产），intangible asset（无形资产），intangible cultural heritage（非物质文化遗产）。该句的结构并不复杂，但是主语过长，且句子中包含多个抽象名词（uptick，usage，improvement）可能会造成理解困难，因此，在口译过程中首先要厘清抽象名词之间的逻辑关系，再利用拆分的技巧，将主语独立翻译成一个短句，在处理句子其他成分时灵活进行词性转换，以便更加符合汉语表述习惯。

（7）Dollarization（美元化）是指一国居民在其资产中持有相当大一部分外币资产（主要是美元），美元大量进入流通领域，具备货币的全部或部分职能，并呈现逐步取代本国货币，成为该国经济活动的主要媒介的趋势，因而美元化实质上是一种狭义或程度较深的货币替代现象。Crowd out 的英语解释是"to push，move，or force（sth. or sb.）out of a place or situation by filling its space"②。

（8）这是一个典型的英语长句，句子主干是"we are undertaking analytical work to examine … and to set up a framework to …"，framework 后面有一个较长的动词不定式短语做后置定语。鉴于句子的意群较多，可以采用顺句驱动技巧。虽然顺句驱动技巧多应用在同声传译中，但是英文长句翻译是交替传译中的常见难点，如果能在听力理解过程把握意群之间的关系，把一个长句切分成若干个小短句，不仅可以减轻听力理解的负担，也可以让译文更加流畅，如"For the Pacific Island countries, // we are undertaking analytical work //to examine the prospects for digital currencies（including CBDCs）//and to set up a framework //to help the countries assess the costs and benefits of digital currency adoption as well as potential policy implication."

---

① 见柯林斯英语字典网站（https://www.collinsdictionary.com/zh/dictionary/english/tangible），引用日期：2023 年 8 月 17 日。

② 见韦氏词典网站（https://www.merriam-webster.com/dictionary/crowd% 20out），引用日期：2023 年 8 月 17 日。

（二）汉译英

为亚洲经济的持续成功提供政策保障（节选）（上）

国际货币基金组织副总裁　张涛

（亚洲货币政策论坛 2018 年 5 月 25 日）

女士们、先生们，

早上好，我很高兴来到新加坡，参加第五届亚洲货币政策论坛。

…………

在此，我想谈谈加强政策储备的一个关键问题，这就是要对通胀持续保持警惕。今天在座的各位央行人士都很清楚，尽管近年来通胀低迷，但我们没理由放松警惕。一些特殊的因素正在发挥作用，需要我们给予额外的特别关注。

让我们仔细看看最近的情况。

我们在最新一期《亚太地区经济展望》中分析了通胀趋势。（1）我们看到，2012 年至 2015 年之间，很多国家的物价水平急剧下跌。在这一时期，各种通胀指标都显示各类产品、服务的通胀水平出现普遍下降。截至 2017 年，通胀预测都保持不变或有所下调。

（2）但现在我们看到，澳大利亚、日本、韩国和部分东盟五国经济体的整体通胀率都在上升。这与其他发达经济体和新兴市场的情况一致，部分反映了近期大宗商品价格的上涨。

我们的研究有三个主要结论：

一是低通胀主要源于临时性因素，包括输入性通胀。（3）我们的测算显示，亚洲发达国家的通胀低于目标水平，有一半是由包括大宗商品在内的进口价格走低造成的；而在亚洲新兴国家，大部分则是由上述原因造成的。

二是通胀变化更多受到了前期因素的影响。各国的通胀预期普遍十分稳定，这在亚洲发达国家和采用通胀目标制的经济体尤其如此。不过，近年来通胀预期的重要性有所下降，而前期的通胀状况起到了更大的作用。

三是通胀水平对劳动力市场缺口变动的敏感度下降。我们在亚洲之外的其他新兴市场国家也发现了类似的现象。菲利普斯曲线似乎已变得平坦化，这与各国融入全球价值链和制造自动化水平上升有关。这些因素削弱了劳动者的谈判能力。

（4）展望未来，我们的研究结果显示：随着大宗商品价格上涨以及发达经济体货币政策正常化下低通胀的逆转，亚洲的通胀率可能会上升。而本地区汇率走弱，也可能成为另一个推动因素。与此同时，技术变革会对价格产生何种长期影响，目前还看不清楚。

（5）因此，央行应该对输入型通胀保持警惕，而灵活的汇率制度可以提供有用的防护墙。改善货币政策框架和加强央行政策沟通十分重要，这能让预期在驱动通胀中发挥出更大的作用，并将这些预期锚定在目标水平。

［资料来源：见国际货币基金组织网站（https://www.imf.org/zh/News/Articles/2018/05/24/sp052518-policies-to-ensure-asia-s-sustained-economic-success），引用日期：2023 年 8 月 17 日。］

1. 实践解析

本口译实践文章选自国际货币基金组织副总裁张涛在 2018 年第五届亚洲货币政策论坛上的发言。亚洲货币政策论坛成立于 2014 年，旨在讨论亚洲政策制定者在货币政策中面临的挑战。在本演讲中，张涛副总裁代表国际货币基金组织就亚洲所面临的重要经济问题谈了相关看法。本部分选取了发言中关于"亚洲通胀"话题的相关内容，翻译难点在于通货膨胀的相关术语。

输入性通胀（imported inflation）是"是由国外出现的通胀通过国际贸易的形式传导进入国内，因外部经济因素传导而引起的物价总水平上涨"。输入性通胀传导的三个路径分别是：国外商品的价格、货币供给和成本。[1]

菲利普斯曲线（Phillips Curve）是"表示失业率和通货膨胀率之间替换关系的曲线"[2]，最早由新西兰经济学家威廉·菲利普斯在《1861—1957 年英国失业和货币工资变动率之间的关系》一文中提出。

2. 长难句点拨

（1）在对经济话题进行口译的过程中经常会涉及关于经济发展趋势的表达，如"下降""猛降""稍降"等，口译学习者应有意识积累这一类词汇，以便在口译中快速、准确翻译。英语中表示"下降"的词汇有：decrease，decline，drop，fall，go down，reduce 等；表示"猛降"的词汇有 plunge，tumble，plummet，drop dramatically，be slashed；表示"稍降"的词汇有 dip，slip，be trimmed。口译学习者应重视词汇积累，让译文表达更加准确。该句后

---

① 沈怡林：《输入性通胀与汇率波动》载《经济研究导刊》2011 年第 28 期，第 90 - 91 页。

② 见知网百科（https://xuewen.cnki.net/read-R2006061250001149.html），引用日期：2023 年 8 月 17 日。

的"在这一时期"指的就是 2012 年至 2015 年期间，可以利用定语从句将重合的时间段进行整合，让译文更加精简。该句可以译为："We saw sharp price declines between 2012 and 2015，when disinflation was broad-based by various inflation measures. Inflation forecasts through 2017 stayed constant or were revised down."

（2）英语中表示"上升"的词汇有：increase，grow，rise，go up，等；表示"猛升"的词汇有 skyrocket，soar，jump up，surge，hike up，zoom up；表示"缓慢增长"的词汇有 pick up。该句含有三个小句，参考译文中将第三个小句处理为结果状语，很好地体现了前后的逻辑关系，也使得译文更加简洁。

（3）发达国家译为 developed countries，与发展中国家相对，但是该句中"亚洲发达国家"的对比项是"亚洲新兴国家"，是相对来说经济发展更前沿的国家，鉴于新兴国家用 emerging economies，亚洲发达国家可以考虑译为"advanced economies"。汉语是具有"动态"特点的语言，一个句子中常有多个动词，在汉译英过程中，可以通过词性转换来化繁为简，让译文更加精简，如该句可以译为："Our estimates indicate that weaker import prices，including commodities，contributed to half of the undershooting of inflation targets in advanced Asia，and most of the undershooting in emerging Asia."

（4）该句中信息密集，包含多个小句和多个动词如"展望""显示""上涨""逆转""上升""走弱"等。由于英语是形合语言，在汉译英过程中应妥善利用分词结构和主从复句等语法手段，将汉语中的小句之间的逻辑关系显化，便于读者理解译文。

（5）英语中 vigilant 一词的意思是"to give careful attention to a particular problem or situation and concentrates on noticing any danger or trouble that there might be"[①]，名词形式为 vigilance，与多处出现"警惕"意思较为吻合，也比较符合正常场合用语特点。"防护墙"一词在本文中如果直译为"fender wall"，则译文显得非常生硬。参考译文中的用法使用了比喻的修辞手法，指的是灵活的汇率机制可以使得国家免遭输入性通胀的影响。口译学习者在翻译时应充分理解讲话者的意图，通过意译来让译文更加清楚、流畅。

---

① 见柯林斯英语字典网站（https://www.collinsdictionary.com/zh/dictionary/english/vigilant），引用日期：2023 年 8 月 17 日。

➡ 三、口译练习

● （一）英译汉

**Securing a Green Recovery: The Economic
Benefits from Tackling Climate Change**

Kristalina Georgieva, IMF Managing Director

（PBC-IMF High-Level Seminar on Green Finance and
Climate Policy, April 15, 2021）

Good evening! I would like to thank Governor Yi Gang for inviting me here today, and to the People's Bank of China for co-hosting this important event.

......

If we are to achieve a more sustainable and inclusive recovery, we must turn this crisis into opportunity by building greener and more climate-resilient economies.

（1）The existential threat of climate change is one of our most important problems. Left unchecked, it will bring untold disruption. To achieve the goal of reducing climate risks and averting future calamities, action during this decade will be critical.

Which brings me to a second Chinese proverb: "One generation plants the trees; another gets the shade."

The Asia-Pacific region is already experiencing faster-rising temperatures and more weather-related natural disasters than anywhere else—with coastal areas and small island countries being especially affected.

In low-income countries, climate change is already a key driver of rising poverty, accelerating spread of disease, and worsening food insecurity.

The good news is that taking action on climate change now will do more than avoid disasters in the future: by accelerating the historic transformation to greener economies, we also can provide a major boost to the recovery.

In our research, we analyzed how economic policy tools can pave a road toward net zero emissions by 2050, in a matter that supports economic growth, employment and income equality. For illustration, a policy mix of carbon taxes and green investment stimulus could increase the level of global GDP in the next 15 years by about 0.7 percent and create around 12 million new jobs through 2027.

Let us take a closer look at some of the key economic policy tools for climate mitigation.

(a) Carbon Pricing

(2) While there is no one-size-fits-all for countries' policies, there is a growing consensus that carbon pricing is the most efficient and cost-effective approach to curbing emission.

By raising energy prices overall, carbon pricing creates incentives for households and firms to shift towards greener options, promoting energy efficiency. It also boosts green investments, and spurs innovation, by leveling the playing field between renewables and fossil fuels.

Asia is home to the majority of the world's population and has been the main driver of global growth in recent decades. Not surprisingly, it also accounts for almost half of the world's carbon emissions. Yet, new IMF research shows that a moderate and progressive carbon price—starting from a low base but rising steadily—could help countries in the region deliver on their commitments under *the Paris Climate Agreement* over the next 10 years.

(3) In addition, carbon taxes can generate substantial revenues, which could be used to support households, affected by the low carbon transition, and to scale up public investment in health, education, and retraining and re-skilling of displaced workers.

Countries can achieve similar result using other instruments too. China's existing coal tax is a good example, which could eventually be scaled up to curb CO_2 emission.

China is also taking a major step forward by introducing a national carbon emissions trading system for the power sector. It is designed slightly differently from what we see in other countries—instead of a cap on the total emissions a firm can generate, there are limits on emissions relative to a firm's energy output.

Over time, the system can become more comprehensive by: (i) shifting the focus to a cap on total emissions, (ii) gradually adopting more ambitious targets,

(iii) ensuring compliance, (iv) extending it beyond the power sector; and (v) generating revenue from these allocations, which today are free.

A range of other tools, such as "feebate" schemes, that reward efficient practices and discourage high-carbon activities, can contribute to lowering CO_2 emissions in certain sectors as well. In some cases, tighter regulations of emissions and energy efficiency will be needed, along with better green technology policies.

China's continuing reforms towards high-quality, sustainable, and balanced growth can also contribute to lowering carbon emission. (4) Shifting away from investment-heavy to consumption-led growth, and supporting the expansion of services and high-tech sectors—as envisaged in the just-approved 14th Five-Year-Plan—will reduce the energy demand and carbon intensity of growth, thus, making it easier to achieve your climate goals.

These efforts would result in a big cut to emissions—which would be amplified by synchronization across markets. That is why the IMF is advocating for carbon price floors in the world's largest emitters to ensure more substantial climate change mitigation.

(b) Green Financing

The sheer size of the task ahead calls for trillions of dollars in green investment. (5) This suggests, in China as elsewhere, there is room to foster more private-sector green financing by efficiently steering capital from "brown" to green investment, for example, through price signals and regulatory incentives.

Domestically, countries need to set up environmental information disclosures, green finance standard systems, and other support policies to mobilize more private sector investment.

Data has an important role. In a recent survey of 425 investors with $\sim$ \$25 trillion in assets under management, 53 percent cited the poor quality or availability of ESG data and analytics as the biggest barrier to deeper and broader implementation of sustainable investing.

Climate change is in itself a threat to financial stability. Countries and companies—and therefore their banks—face higher risks from extreme weather events and from the transition to a low-carbon economy. Risk management needs to be improved to assess climate-related risks and safeguard financial stability.

Boosting green finance also means ramping up international support for poorer countries—where climate resilience can be a question of life and death, and the price tag can be much higher.

Globally, the average increase in public investment to finance climate adaptation is about 3 percent of GDP per year. But Tonga, for example, will need 14 percent of GDP per year over the next decade.

Vulnerable countries will need more domestic revenue mobilization—but also more external concessional financing, and more help to deal with debt. These challenges have become even more pressing during the pandemic.

Here China is playing an important role—by participating in the recently extended G20 Debt Service Suspension Initiative and in the Common Framework for orderly debt restructuring, and by its support for the IMF's Catastrophe Containment and Relief Trust.

[资料来源：见国际货币基金组织网站（https://www.imf.org/en/News/Articles/2021/04/15/sp041521-securing-a-green-recovery），引用日期：2023 年 8 月 17 日。]

1. 词汇准备

"feebate" schemes	"收费返还"计划
ESG	环境、社会和治理
G20 Debt Service Suspension Initiative	二十国集团"暂缓债务偿付倡议"
Catastrophe Containment and Relief Trust	"控灾减灾信托"

2. 长难句点拨

（1）Existential 的释义是"relating to human existence and experience"[1]，existential threat 就是关系到生死存亡的威胁，在口译过程中可以直接简化为"事关生死存亡"。"Left unchecked, it will bring untold disruption." 该句的前半句是一个省略结构，整句话的完整表述是"If it is left unchecked, climate change will bring untold disruption." "One generation plants the trees; another gets the shade." 对大部分学习者来说这一谚语并不陌生，可以快速想到汉语谚语"前人种树，后人乘凉"。由于谚语翻译在口译中是有一定难度的，因此，口译学习者在日常练习过程中应积累相关表达。

---

① 见柯林斯英语字典网站（https://www.collinsdictionary.com/zh/dictionary/english/credit），引用日期：2023 年 8 月 17 日。

（2）One-size-fits-all 的英语解释是"relating to policies or approaches that are standard and not tailored to individual needs"①，类似于汉语的"放之四海而皆准"这一说法，在不同语境下具体意义有一定的差别，如：a one-size-fits-all monetary policy（一刀切的货币政策）；a one-size-fits-all solution（万全之策）。

（3）该句意群较多，which 引导的定语从句修饰 revenues，affected 这一过去分词短语修饰的对象是 households，be used to 这一部分有 to support 和 to scale up 两个并列的动词不定式短语表示目的，public investment in 的宾语有 health，education 和 retraining and re-skilling 这两个动名词。准确把握意群之间的逻辑关系有助于迅速、准确进行翻译。该句可以尝试译为"此外，碳税能带来可观的收入，可用于支持受低碳转型影响的家庭，并增加对卫生、教育、下岗职工技能再培训的公共投资"。

（4）该句的结构略显复杂，在听力理解过程中如果能厘清句子各个成分之间的关系，翻译起来会事半功倍。该句主语是两个并列的动名词短语 shifting away from …和 and supporting …，谓语是 will reduce，宾语是 demand and carbon intensity of growth，而 making it easier to achieve your climate goals 是结果状语，在主语和谓语之间，插入了 as envisaged in the just-approved 14th Five-Year-Plan 这个短语。对此，在口译过程中不仅要进行语序调整先翻译插入语，再按照主谓宾顺序翻译句子主干，还要根据上下文进行适当的补充，将两个动名词短语 shifting away from … 和 and supporting …的逻辑主语补充，才能让译文更加的流畅、自然。

（5）Private-sector green financing 这个意群最初看起来 private-sector 是 green financing 的定语，但是理解句意后不难发现 private-sector 实际是 green financing 这个动作行为的逻辑主语。green financing 即绿色融资，指的是为了环境利益而进行任何金融活动（贷款、投资、债券等）。在环保话题中，绿色一般表示环境友好，而棕色（也有译为"褐色"）则指代非环境友好，一般表示高污染、高碳（高能耗）和高水耗等，因此，英语中有 brown asset，brown investment 这类表达。该句结构看似并不复杂，但是要准确理解句意则需要把握介词 by 和 through 引导的两个短语之间的关系，该句句意中，这两个短语之间的关系为促进私营部门进行绿色融资的是通过将资本从棕色投资转向绿色投资来实现的，而资本投资转向则是通过价格信号和监管刺激的。

---

① 见柯林斯英语字典网站（https://www.collinsdictionary.com/zh/dictionary/english/credit），引用日期：2023 年 8 月 17 日。

在准确理解意群之间的逻辑关系后，在口译过程中再根据汉语表述习惯进行语序调整，便于理解。

● （二）汉译英

为亚洲经济的持续成功提供政策保障（节选）（下）
国际货币基金组织副总裁　张涛
（亚洲货币政策论坛，2018 年 5 月 25 日）

通常认为，低通胀对低收入家庭是有利的。不过在评估亚洲经济的前景时，还有另一个问题与低收入人群息息相关。这就是普惠金融，也是我今天想谈的最后一个问题。

国际货币基金组织的研究表明，那些降低了收入不平等程度的经济体更有望实现经济的可持续增长。（1）因此，有针对性地推出政策措施，推动普惠金融发展，对减少贫困至关重要。

普惠金融也能提高宏观经济政策的有效性。一些研究表明，普惠金融能够改善利率传导机制，从而使货币政策这一工具更为有效。

在让更多人获得金融服务和提高各类人群可获取的金融产品质量方面，亚太地区各国已经取得长足的进步。

在普惠金融方面，亚洲新兴市场经济体与其他地区的进展是一致的。相比之下，亚洲低收入发展中国家有更多人能获得金融服务。

尽管如此，各国国内的差距，包括贫富差距、城乡差距和两性差距，仍然很大。

（2）例如，在印度最贫困的五分之一成年男性中，仅有约 46% 的人拥有正规的银行账户，而在最富有的五分之一成年男性中，该比例为 79%。当使用移动交易或金融机构贷款等其他指标来衡量时，这种差异更为明显，两类人群的差距分别为相差四倍和相差约三倍。

性别差异依然很大，这在南亚地区尤其如此。在那里，只有不到 40% 的女性拥有银行账户，而男性的这一比率则接近 60%。

我们的研究还显示：与其他地区相比，亚洲各国的普惠金融程度更加参差不齐。（3）一些亚洲国家处在普惠金融的前沿，而其他亚洲国家还只能提供基本的金融服务，其中最大的差异体现在自动提款机的使用和提供正规银行服务等方面。

（4）在许多国家，数字金融服务近年来都有所扩张，包括电子银行、手机银行和移动钱包等。我们看到在孟加拉国、印度尼西亚和蒙古，数字金融服务增长十分迅速。而在太平洋岛国，地域分散是提供金融服务的主要障碍。在萨摩亚，移动产品已深受人们的欢迎，值得大家关注。

（5）有趣的是，在移动银行业务方面，大多数亚太国家落后于撒哈拉以南非洲地区。虽然亚洲在传统银行业基础设施方面处于领先地位，但其移动交易却远远落后于肯尼亚、乌干达、坦桑尼亚和津巴布韦。在这些国家，已有70%以上的民众使用手机银行服务。

显然，亚洲地区推动普惠金融发展的潜力十分巨大。各国可采取以下措施来应对这一问题：

第一，加强个人征信机构、资产登记机构、支付系统和小额信贷机构等基础设施建设，这将降低金融服务的成本。

第二，各国需要投入足够多的资源，使互联网和手机的连接更加便利。

第三，推动一些国家的电信和互联网行业开放，这将有助于降低成本并改善服务。

［资料来源：见国际货币基金组织网站（https://www.imf.org/zh/News/Articles/2018/05/24/sp052518-policies-to-ensure-asia-s-sustained-economic-success），引用日期：2023年8月17日。］

1. 词汇准备

普惠金融	Inclusive Financing
宏观经济政策	macroeconomic policies
货币政策	monetary policy
萨摩亚	Samoa
征信机构	credit bureaus

2. 长难句点拨

（1）汉语是主题突出（topic-prominent）语言，句子中的主语形式灵活。在该句中，主语是两个动词短语"推出政策措施，推动普惠金融发展"，在翻译成英语时不仅要根据英语特点进行词性转换，还应该关注两个动词短语之间的内在逻辑关系，即推出政策措施是为了推动普惠金融发展。在翻译时将两者逻辑关系显化，能使译文更加符合英语习惯，因此，参考译文中将"推出政策措施"处理为偏正短语，将"推动普惠金融发展"处理为表示目的的动词不定式，逻辑关系更加清楚明了。

（2）该句中包含了数字相关的表达，如五分之一（quintile）、四倍（fourfold）。在口译中，数字口译是一大难点，除了要熟悉汉英文在表达数字上的异同，还应该有意识积累数字相关的表达，如倍数、分数、百分比等。尤其要注意的是汉英表述中在表示倍数关系时，存在习惯表达上的差异。汉语表达倍数主要有两种表达方式，即 A 是 B 的 N 倍，或者 A 比 B 大（N−1）倍，但是在英语中 A 是 B 的 N 倍可以译为 A is N times as large as B，也可以译为 A is N times larger than B。

（3）该句比较了处于普惠金融不同阶段的国家，利用 while 引导从句可以体现两类国家之间的弱对比关系。access[①] 在英语中可以表示 the opportunity or right to use sth. or to see sb./sth.，可以用在表示可以获得某项服务的语境下，如 internet access，access to basic financial service。disparity 是表示差异的偏正式的表达，尤指因不公正对待引起的不同和差异。

（4）该段包含一些数字金融（digital finance）的术语，如电子银行（electronic banking）、手机银行（mobile banking），这类术语易于理解，对此可以尝试使用直译策略。

（5）该段涉及一些非洲国家名称，如肯尼亚（Kenya）、乌干达（Uganda）、坦桑尼亚（Tanzania）和津巴布韦（Zimbabwe）。有些口译学习者可能对这些国家没那么熟悉，应注意积累，拓宽百科知识。该句从移动银行业务和传统银行业基础设施两个方面对亚洲国家和撒哈拉以南非洲地区进行了对比，意在突出尽管亚洲国家在传统银行业基础设施领先撒哈拉以南非洲地区，移动银行业务却处于落后状态。在口译过程中，口译学习者应该准确使用逻辑连词，显化逻辑关系，明确传递讲话者的意图，让听众能够更加清楚、明了地理解原文。

---

① 见柯林斯英语字典网站（https://www.collinsdictionary.com/zh/dictionary/english/credit），引用日期：2023 年 8 月 17 日。

➡️ **四、参考译文**

⚫ **（一）口译实践**

1. 英译汉

"数字货币和数字技术"同行学习系列活动之
"央行数字货币及中国的案例"开幕致词
IMF 亚太部主任　克里希纳·斯里尼瓦桑
（2022 年 7 月）

　　大家早上好！西半球的各位晚上好！感谢大家参加今天的"央行数字货币及中国的案例"活动。正如席睿德所言，这是我们在亚太地区举行的有关"数字货币和数字技术"的全新系列活动中的第二场活动。

　　数字货币和数字技术能够带来金融体系的重大变革，并使广大公众深受其益。其中的一些好处包括促进普惠金融，给经济带来新的附加值，降低包括跨境交易在内的各种交易成本等。"数字货币和数字技术"系列活动所涵盖的主题十分广泛，请允许我大体谈一谈。

　　与所有创新一样，我们在这一领域面临的挑战同样也是寻找一种恰当的平衡：既要促进创新，又要维护稳定并保护消费者和投资者。今天我们将详细讨论央行数字货币，但我也想强调我们在加密资产方面的重要发现。例如，近期某大型算法稳定币与支持资产脱钩，引发了加密资产市场的崩溃；而某些从事数字资产银行业务及交易的、杠杆过高的金融机构倒闭，更使加密资产市场的形势雪上加霜——这些事件突显了监管不力导致的风险。随着数字资产规模的增长，若缺乏适当的监管，该行业的系统性风险将增加。

　　这对亚太地区而言尤其具有重大的意义——在亚太地区，很多人将数字金融视为一个机遇，认为其能为经济增长与创新带来了新的动力。随着私人和公共部门数字资产的兴起，亚太地区的一些国家正处于这一领域的最前沿。亚太地区的新型加密资产及相关产品服务快速发展，许多国家的加密资产交易量都走在了世界前列。

政策制定者正积极监测数字金融行业的风险，其中，许多业务仍游离于监管之外，但预计它们会产生广泛的影响。我们可以、也应该互相学习，分享经验。出于这个原因，本"同行学习"系列活动重点介绍了亚太地区各国为发展数字金融提供监管指引的经验。今天的活动将重点介绍中国在央行数字货币和数字人民币方面的经验。

IMF 已经制定了一项富有雄心的议程，以了解金融科技和数字资产对全球经济的影响。IMF 亚太部的目标是：密切跟踪这些快速发展的领域，为成员国提供建议，并与成员国和主要利益相关方开展更密切的合作。特别是，我们将与 IMF 货币与资本市场部合作，努力为小型国家、低收入国家以及新兴市场和发展中国家提供及时的政策建议和能力建设援助。

对此，我们正针对一系列广泛问题开展大量的分析工作。在央行数字货币方面，我想强调：今年早些时候，我们对 36 个亚洲经济体进行了一项调查，以帮助我们了解各国在央行数字货币研究中采取了哪些措施，以及加密资产在其中扮演何种角色。今年晚些时候，我们将发布一份说明文件，总结相关调查结果。不过，请让我现在就与大家分享其中四项主要发现。

首先，我们发现亚太地区正处于央行数字货币探索的最前沿，各方对其兴趣持续上升。虽然尚未有亚洲国家正式启动使用央行数字货币，但中国和印度——世界上人口最多的两个国家——是近期这一领域的领跑者。新加坡等其他经济体在央行数字货币领域的进展也相对领先，日本、韩国、澳大利亚等国也进行了广泛的研究。

其次，各方对央行数字货币感兴趣的背后，存在着若干原因：高收入国家希望提高支付体系的效率和安全性，新兴市场经济体则希望促进普惠金融和金融稳定。一些国家只是单纯不想落后于本地区的其他国家或私人部门。

再次，各国关于采用或探索央行数字货币的决定，与其经济中加密资产使用的迅速增加和监管领域的尝试密切相关。例如，在印度尼西亚、菲律宾和越南，个人在侨汇和投资中更多使用了加密货币，这使政策制定者开始研究技术创新带来的切实好处，包括降低成本和改进支付体系。

最后，虽然各方对央行数字货币都抱有浓厚的兴趣，但实际上，很少有国家有望在短期至中期内发行央行数字货币。该地区的大多数国家都表示感兴趣，从初步的研发工作到推出试点项目进度不一。

我也想借用这个机会强调：除了在央行数字货币方面的工作外，我们还就私人数字资产开展了几项研究，包括对各国采用加密资产的驱动因素和政策措施的影响开展的实证分析。

我们发现，在数字技术渗透率较高、侨汇规模较大、宏观经济基本面较薄弱（如存在高通胀）的国家，加密资产的接受度较高。非正式经济规模、腐败情况、资本管控程度也与较高的加密资产接受度存在正相关。这凸显了妥善监测加密资产业务和完善相关法规的重要性。

我们的研究还表明：加密资产市场推动了美元化，美元稳定币在加密资产市场中对当地货币起到了挤出效应。在通胀率较高、汇率不稳的国家，上述影响更为明显。研究显示，受到监管且由本币支持的私人部门稳定币是零售央行数字货币的一种替代品。

关于政策对加密资产接受度的影响，我们发现加密资产禁令会在短期削弱加密资产业务。但由于此类禁令在执行中存在难度，即使相关法规十分严格，其影响也会逐步减弱。同样有趣的是，当局宣布发行央行数字货币的计划，同样会抑制加密资产业务。

展望未来，IMF 正从事若干分析工作，它们的进展不一。

我们正针对太平洋岛国开展相关分析工作，研究数字货币（包括央行数字货币）的前景，同时建立一个框架帮助这些国家评估采用数字货币的成本收益以及潜在政策影响。

我们还计划开展一系列技术性更强的央行数字货币研究，为我们的能力建设工作提供支持。这包括新兴市场和发展中经济体的央行数字货币基础设施和可选设计方案。其也包括了一个框架，用于决定是否以及如何采用央行数字货币，以及其对货币政策和冲击跨境传导的影响。

鉴于上述问题对我们的成员国和 IMF 都很重要，目前我们在每年的磋商对话中，都会与当局定期讨论数字化问题，而相应的 IMF 工作人员报告也会涵盖这些问题。特别是，第四条款磋商①将重点关注部分国家的数字货币问题——这包括该领域的前沿国家（如部分太平洋岛国；同时，我们也将继续密切关注中国的进展），以及那些可能采用央行数字货币和近期可能遇到其他数字金融问题的国家。

我很高兴今天能邀请到中国人民银行和香港金融管理局的同事和朋友们，以及研究这些问题的国际专家。中国在电子人民币方面的经验和试点项目，可以为数字金融环境快速变化的其他国家提供有益的经验。

我相信本系列活动以及今天关于央行数字货币（尤其是有关中国案例）

---

① 第四条款磋商是指根据 IMF 协定第四条，IMF 每年会向其成员经济体派遣一个工作小组，与所在经济体的政府就当地经济发展情况和政策进行讨论，提出评估意见并撰写报告交 IMF 执董会讨论。

的讨论，将使我们所有人受益匪浅。谢谢！

〔资料来源：见国际货币基金组织网站（https://www.imf.org/en/News/Articles/2022/07/07/sp070722-central-bank-digital-currency-and-the-case-of-china），引用日期：2023 年 8 月 17 日。〕

2. 汉译英

Policies to Ensure Asia's Sustained Economic Success（Excerpt）（Ⅰ）

Zhang Tao，IMF Deputy Managing Director

（Asian Monetary Policy Forum，May 25，2018）

Ladies and gentlemen，

Good morning. It is my honor to be in Singapore for the fifth annual MAS Asian Monetary Policy Forum.

......

Here，I would like to touch upon a key element of a policy to strengthen buffers. This is constant vigilance about inflation. As the central bankers in the room today know only too well，the subdued price increases we have seen in recent years offer no reason to relax. There are unique forces at work that require extra attention.

So let's take a closer look at recent developments.

Our current *Regional Economic Outlook for the Asia-Pacific* analyzed the inflation trends. We saw sharp price declines between 2012 and 2015，when disinflation was broad-based by various inflation measures. Inflation forecasts through 2017 stayed constant or were revised down.

But we now see headline inflation picking up in Australia，Japan，Korea，and some ASEAN-5 economies. That is in line with other advanced economies and emerging markets，reflecting，in part，the recent rise of commodity prices.

Our research has produced three main findings：

First，low inflation has been driven mainly by temporary forces，including imported inflation. Our estimates indicate that weaker import prices，including commodities，contributed to half of the undershooting of inflation targets in advanced Asia，and most of the undershooting in emerging Asia.

Second，the inflation process has become more backward-looking. Expectations are generally well anchored，especially in advanced Asia and economies with inflation-targeting frameworks. Still, the importance of expectations has declined in recent years, with past inflation playing a larger role.

Third, the sensitivity of inflation to slack in labor markets has declined. This is something we have also seen in other emerging market countries outside of Asia. There seems to be a flattening of the Phillips Curve linked to integration in global value chains and automation. These factors weaken labor's bargaining power.

Looking ahead, our findings suggest that inflation may rise in Asia as commodity prices rise and low inflation in advanced economies reverses as monetary policy is normalized. Weaker regional currencies could also become a factor. On the other hand, it is not clear what the long-term impact of technological change will be on prices.

So, central banks should be vigilant about imported inflation, and exchange rate flexibility can help provide useful insulation. It will be important to strengthen monetary policy frameworks and improve central bank communications to increase the role of expectations in driving inflation—and keep those expectations anchored to targets.

[资料来源：见国际货币基金组织网站（https://www.imf.org/zh/News/Articles/2018/05/24/sp052518-policies-to-ensure-asia-s-sustained-economic-success），引用日期：2023 年 8 月 17 日。]

（二）口译练习

1. 英译汉

实现绿色的经济复苏：应对气候变化的经济效益
国际货币基金组织（IMF）总裁　克里斯塔利娜·格奥尔基耶娃
（中国人民银行-国际货币基金组织绿色金融和
气候政策高级别研讨会，2021 年 4 月 15 日）

晚上好！首先，请允许我感谢易纲行长邀请我今天这场活动，感谢中国人民银行与我们承办这场的研讨会。

…………

如果要实现更可持续和更加包容的经济复苏，我们必须转危为机，构建更加绿色、更具气候韧性的经济。

气候变化事关人类存亡，是我们面临的一个最重要的问题。若不加以应对，它将带来无尽的问题。为实现减少气候风险和避免未来灾难的目标，在这10年内采取行动将是至关重要的。这让我想到了第二句中国谚语："前人种树，后人乘凉。"

相比其他地区，亚太地区气温上升更快，气象自然灾害也更多，其中沿海地区和小型岛国受到的影响尤为严重。

在低收入国家，气候变化已成为贫困人口增加、疾病传播加速和粮食不安全加剧的一个主要原因。

好消息是，如果我们现在就立即采取行动应对气候变化，则不仅仅能使我们避免未来的灾难，还能让我们通过加快历史性的绿色经济转型来有力促进经济复苏。

我们的研究分析了经济政策工具可以如何为"到2050年实现零净排放"奠定基础，同时为经济增长、就业和收入平等提供支持。举个例子，如果推出碳税和绿色投资刺激的政策组合，则能在未来15年使全球GDP增速提升约0.7%，并在2027年之前创造约1200万个新就业岗位。

让我们重点谈谈减缓气候变化的一些主要经济政策工具。

（一）碳定价

尽管不存在普遍适用于各国国情的政策，但各方也在日益形成一种共识，即碳定价是最有效、性价比最高的减排方法。

通过上调整体能源价格，碳定价能激励家庭和企业转向更绿色的选择，从而提升能效。它还能为可再生能源和化石燃料建立公平的竞争环境，从而提振绿色投资，刺激创新。

亚洲拥有全世界的大多数人口，是近几十年来全球经济增长的主要引擎。亚太地区自然也占到世界碳排放量的近一半。然而，IMF一项新的研究表明，如果推出温和、累进性的碳价——起点较低，但此后稳步上调——将有助于该地区各国在未来10年内履行其《巴黎气候协定》承诺。

此外，碳税能带来可观的收入，进而可用于支持受低碳转型影响的家庭，并增加对卫生、教育、下岗职工技能再培训的公共投资。

各国也可使用其他手段来实现类似的结果。中国当前的煤炭税就是一个很好的例子：当局最终可推广该制度以抑制二氧化碳排放。

中国也通过为能源部门引入全国碳排放交易制度向前迈出了一大步。该制度的设计与其他国家略有不同——其根据企业的能源产出设置相对的排放限额，而非对企业的总排放量设置上限。

随着时间的推移，该制度可以通过以下方式变得更加全面：①将重点转向设置总排放上限；②逐步采纳更进取的目标；③确保合规；④将其推广至能源部门以外；以及⑤通过分配排放配额（当前免费）获取收入。

一系列其他工具，如奖励高效做法、抑制高排放活动的"收费返还"计划，也有助于降低某些部门的二氧化碳排量。一些情况下，还需要在未来颁布更严格的排放和能效法规，并实施更完善的绿色技术政策。

中国持续推动改革，实现高质量、可持续和平衡增长，这也有助于降低碳排放。正如刚刚通过的"十四五规划"指出，中国持续推动投资驱动向消费驱动型经济增长转型，同时支持服务业和高科技部门扩张，这将降低经济增长的能源需求和碳密度，从而降低实现气候目标的难度。

这些措施将有力削减碳排放量——如果各市场能同步行动起来，则将进一步放大其效果。这正是 IMF 倡导全球最大排放国设置碳价下限的原因，以确保在更大程度上减缓气候变化。

（二）绿色融资

减排任务十分艰巨，需要数万亿美元的绿色投资。这意味着，中国与其他国家一样，存在促进私营部门进行绿色融资的空间，例如，通过价格信号和监管激励这样的措施，有效引导资本从"褐色投资"转向绿色投资。

在国内层面，各国须建立环境信息披露机制、绿色金融标准体系以及其他支持政策，以调动更多私人部门投资。

数据能发挥重要作用。最近一项针对管理资产总规模约为 25 万亿美元的 425 家投资机构的调查显示，53% 的机构认为，环境、社会和治理（ESG）方面的数据和分析质量较差且难以获取，是更深入、更广泛落实可持续投资的最大障碍。

气候变化本身就对金融稳定构成威胁。各国和企业（因此也包括其银行）都面临着更严峻的极端气象灾害和向低碳经济过渡的风险。当局需要改进风险管理，以评估气候相关风险并维护金融稳定。

要促进绿色金融发展，还意味着国际社会需加大对较贫困国家的支持力度——对它们而言，气候韧性可能是一个生死攸关的问题，且支出要高得多。

在全球范围内，每年新增的、用于为适应气候变化提供资金的公共投资平均占到 GDP 的约 3%。然而在汤加，未来 10 年中每年所需的资金约为 GDP 的 14%。

脆弱国家需要调动更多国内收入，同时也须获得更多外部优惠贷款和债务援助。在疫情期间,这些挑战变得更加紧迫。

中国正在这个方面发挥着重要作用——不仅参与了最近延期的二十国集团"暂缓债务偿付倡议"和旨在促进有序债务重组的"债务处置共同框架",并且为 IMF 的"控灾减灾信托"提供了支持。

资料来源:见国际货币基金组织网站(https://www.imf.org/en/News/Articles/2021/04/15/sp041521-securing-a-green-recovery),引用日期:2023 年 8 月 17 日。

2. 汉译英

Policies to Ensure Asia's Sustained Economic Success(Excerpt)(Ⅱ)

Zhang Tao, IMF Deputy Managing Director

(Asian Monetary Policy Forum, May 25, 2018)

Low inflation is generally thought to be good for low-income households. But there is another issue relevant to the poor that is relevant in assessing Asia economic prospects. That issue is financial inclusion—the final topic I would like to focus on today.

IMF research has shown that economies that reduce income inequality are positioned to achieve sustained levels of growth. So, targeted policy action to promote financial inclusion is essential to poverty reduction.

Financial inclusion also enhances the effectiveness of macroeconomic policies. Several studies show that financial inclusion strengthens the interest rate channel, making monetary policy a more effective tool.

Asia-Pacific countries have made considerable progress widening access to financial services and improving the quality of financial products available across population.

Financial inclusion in Asia's emerging markets is in line with other region. But Asia's low-income and developing countries actually show wider accessibility.

Nonetheless, the gaps are significant within countries—between rich and poor, urban and rural, men and women.

For example, in India, only about 46 percent of male adults from the poorest quintile of the population have a formal account. That compares with 79 percent in the richest quintile. This disparity is even more pronounced when measured by use of mobile transactions (a fourfold difference), or borrowing from a financial institution （about a threefold difference）.

Gender disparities also remain significant, especially in South Asia. There, less than 40 percent of women have a bank account compared with nearly 60 percent for men.

Our research also shows a wider range of financial inclusion across Asian countries than within other region. While some Asian countries are at the forefront of financial inclusion, others are only able to provide access to basic financial services. The largest disparity is in access to ATMs or formal banking services.

Digital financial services have expanded recently in many countries, including electronic banking, mobile banking, and mobile money. We have seen notable growth in Bangladesh, Indonesia, and Mongolia. In Pacific island countries, geographical dispersion represents a major obstacle to providing financial services. So it is notable that in Samoa, mobile products have proven popular.

Interestingly, mobile banking is one area where most Asia-Pacific countries lag sub-Saharan Africa. While Asia leads in traditional banking infrastructure, it is far behind Kenya, Uganda, Tanzania, and Zimbabwe in mobile transaction. In those countries, more than 70 percent of the population uses mobile banking services.

Clearly, there is enormous potential to deepen financial inclusion in the Asia. There are several steps that countries can take to address the issue：

First, strengthening such infrastructure as credit bureaus, asset registration, payment systems, and microfinance institutions would lower the costs of financial services.

Second, countries need to allocate adequate resources to expand internet and mobile phone connectivity.

Third, in some countries, liberalization of the telecommunications and internet industries would help bring down cost and improve services. ……

［资料来源：见国际货币基金组织网站（https://www. imf. org/zh/News/Articles/2018/05/24/sp052518-policies-to-ensure-asia-s-sustained-economic-success），引用日期：2023 年 8 月 17 日。]

第三章　世界卫生组织

一、背景阅读

（一）汉语简介

【成立时间】1948 年成立，为联合国专门机构，简称"世卫组织"。

【宗旨】使全世界人民获得尽可能高水平的健康。该组织将健康定义为"身体、精神和社会生活的完美状态"。

【成员】194 个成员和 2 个准成员。

【组织机构】主要为世界卫生大会、执行委员会和秘书处。

【总部】瑞士日内瓦。

【主要负责人】总干事谭德塞（Tedros Adhanom Ghebreyesus，埃塞俄比亚籍），2017 年 7 月 1 日上任，2022 年 5 月 24 日连任，任期至 2027 年。

[资料来源：见中国外交部网站（https://www.mfa.gov.cn/web/gjhdq_676201/gjhdqzz_681964/lhg_681966/jbqk_681968/200704/t20070413_9380001.shtml），引用日期：2023 年 8 月 19 日。]

（二）WMO 英语介绍

1. What is World Health Organization（WHO）？

Founded in 1948, WHO is the United Nations agency that connects nations, partners and people to promote health, keep the world safe and serve the vulnerable—so everyone, everywhere can attain the highest level of health. WHO is champions for healthier, safer lives. WHO's team of 8000 plus professionals includes the world's leading public health experts, including doctors, epidemiologists, scientists and managers. WHO coordinates the world's response to health emergencies, promotes well-being, prevent disease and expands access to health care. By connecting nations, people and partners to scientific evidence they can rely on, WHO strives to give everyone an equal chance at a safe and healthy life.

2. History

In April 1945, during the Conference to set up the United Nations (UN) held in San Francisco, representatives of Brazil and China proposed that an international health organization be established and a conference to frame its constitution convened. On 15 February 1946, the Economic and Social Council of the UN instructed the Secretary-General to convoke such a conference. A Technical Preparatory Committee met in Paris from 18 March to 5 April 1946 and drew up proposals for the Constitution which were presented to the International Health Conference in New York City between 19 June and 22 July 1946. On the basis of these proposals, the Conference drafted and adopted the *Constitution of the World Health Organization*, signed 22 July 1946 by representatives of 51 Members of the UN and of 10 other nation.

The Conference established also an Interim Commission to carry out certain activities of the existing health institutions until the entry into force of the *Constitution of the World Health Organization*. The preamble and Article 69 of the Constitution of WHO provide that WHO should be a specialized agency of the UN. Article 80 provides that the Constitution would come into force when 26 members of the United Nations had ratified it. The Constitution did not come into force until 7 April 1948, when the 26th of the 61 governments who had signed it ratified its signature. The first Health Assembly opened in Geneva on 24 June 1948 with delegations from 53 of the 55 Member States. It decided that the Interim Commission was to cease to exist at midnight on 31 August 1948, to be immediately succeeded by WHO.

3. Organization

WHO remains firmly committed to the principles set out in the preamble to the Constitution. The World Health Assembly is the decision-making body of WHO. It is attended by delegations from all WHO Member States and focuses on a specific health agenda prepared by the Executive Board. The World Health Assembly is held annually in Geneva, Switzerland. The Executive Board is composed of 34 technically qualified members elected for three-year terms. The annual Board meeting is held in January when the members agree upon the agenda for the World Health Assembly and the resolutions to be considered by the Health Assembly. A second shorter meeting takes place in May, as a follow-up to the Health Assembly. Dr Tedros Adhanom Ghebreyesus is the Director-General of WHO, elected by a vote of Member States at the World Health Assembly on 23 May 2017. The Director-General is WHO's chief technical and administrative officer and oversees the policy for the Organization's international health work. Dr Tedros took office for a five-year term on 1 July 2017.

4. What does WHO do?

The World Health Organization leads and champions global efforts to achieve better health for all. By connecting countries, people and partners, WHO strives to give everyone, everywhere an equal chance at a safe and healthy life. From emerging epidemics such as COVID-19 and Zika to the persistent threat of communicable diseases including HIV, malaria and tuberculosis and chronic diseases such as diabetes, heart disease and cancer, WHO brings together 194 countries and works on the frontlines in 150 plus locations to confront the biggest health challenges of our time and measurably advance the well-being of the world's people.

As part of the Thirteenth General Programme of Work, a five-year strategy to improve people's health at the country level, WHO tracks the world's progress toward the three Triple Billion targets, which are to ensure by 2023: One billion more people are benefiting from universal health coverage; One billion more people are better protected from health emergencies; One billion more people are enjoying better health and well-being.

Every day, the experts of WHO are dedicated to creating a world free from disease and addressing the social conditions that influence human health and well-being. There are six key programmatic divisions at the WHO headquarters:

Universal health coverage

Health Emergencies Programme

Access to Medicines and Health Products

Antimicrobial Resistance

Science Division

Data, Analytics and Delivery for Impact

5. Central Terms

（1）Universal health coverage

Universal health coverage means that all people have access to the full range of quality health services they need, when and where they need them, without financial hardship. It covers the full continuum of essential health services, from health promotion to prevention, treatment, rehabilitation and palliative care. Every country has a different path to achieving UHC and deciding what to cover based on the needs of their people and the resources at hand.

（2）COVAX

COVAX is the vaccines pillar of the Access to COVID-19 Tools（ACT）Accelerator. The ACT Accelerator is a ground-breaking global collaboration to accelerate the development, production, and equitable access to COVID-19 tests, treatments, and vaccines. COVAX is co-led by the Coalition for Epidemic Preparedness Innovations（CEPI）, Gavi and the World Health Organization（WHO）, alongside key delivery partner UNICEF. It aims to accelerate the development and manufacture of COVID-19 vaccines and to guarantee fair and equitable access for every country in the world.

WHO has multiple roles within COVAX: It provides normative guidance on vaccine policy, regulation, safety, R&D, allocation, and country readiness and delivery.

［资料来源：见世界卫生组织网站（https://www.mfa.gov.cn/web/gjhdq_676201/gjhdqzz_681964/lhg_681966/jbqk_681968/200704/t20070413_9380001.shtml），引用日期：2023 年 8 月 19 日。］

6. 词汇表 Vocabulary List

Constitution of the World Health Organization	《世界卫生组织组织法》
the Director-General	总干事
universal health coverage	全民健康覆盖
health emergencies programme	卫生紧急项目
access to medicines and health products	获得药品和保健品

antimicrobial resistance	抗菌剂的耐药性
noncommunicable diseases	非传染性疾病
International Health Conference	国际卫生会议
World Health Assembly	世界卫生大会
the community of common health for mankind	人类卫生健康共同体

二、口译实践

（一）英译汉

An Update on the Coronavirus
——Munich Security Conference 2020

Dr. Tedros Adhanom Ghebreyesus Director General, World Health Organization
（February 15, 2020）

Excellencies, distinguished guests, dear colleagues and friends,

Thank you for the opportunity to address you today. And especially my appreciation to my friend Ambassador Ischinger.

Yesterday I was in Kinshasa, in the Democratic of the Congo, meeting with the President and other senior ministers to review progress against the Ebola outbreak and work together on a plan to strengthen DRC's health system so that it never sees another outbreak like this again.

I'd like to thank the President for his leadership, and for his vision of a healthier and safer DRC.

We are finally starting to see the possibility of ending this outbreak, after more than 18 months and the loss of 2,249 lives. In the past week there has been just 1 case of Ebola, compared with 120 cases a week at the peak in April.

（1）This epidemic stands in stark contrast to the previous Ebola outbreak in the western part of DRC in 2018, an area that is relatively stable and peaceful. That outbreak was controlled in just three months.

This experience illustrates a key lesson of history: disease and insecurity are old friends.

(2) It was no coincidence that the 1918 flu pandemic erupted in the middle of the First World War, and killed more people than the First World War itself.

It's no coincidence that the final frontier for eradicating polio is in the most insecure regions of Pakistan and Afghanistan.

It's no coincidence that Ebola has spread in the most insecure region of the DRC.

Without peace, health can be an unattainable dream.

But the opposite can also be true: epidemics have the potential to cause severe political, economic and social instability and insecurity.

Health security is therefore not just the health sector's business. It's everybody's business.

(3) There are three main scenarios in which a coordinated response between the health and security sectors is essential:

First, high-impact epidemics in situations of conflict and insecurity, such as Ebola. In the last few years, 80% of outbreaks requiring an international response have occurred in countries affected by fragility, conflict and insecurity.

Second, the emergence of a pathogen with pandemic potential, moving rapidly from country to country and requiring an immediate and large-scale response in countries.

And third, the deliberate or accidental release of biological agents—a hopefully rare event for which we must nonetheless be prepared.

The second of these three scenarios is what we are seeing now with the outbreak of COVID-19.

Although PHEIC (Public Health Emergency of International Concern) is declared, with 99% of cases in China, this is still very much an emergency for that country. Because in the rest of the world we only have 505 cases and in China we have more than 66000 cases.

Let me be clear: it is impossible to predict which direction this epidemic will take.

What I can tell you is what encourages us, and what concerns us.

(4) We are encouraged that the steps China has taken to contain the outbreak at its source appear to have bought the world time, even though those steps have

come at greater cost to China itself. But it's slowing the spread to the rest of the world.

We're encouraged that outside China, we have not yet seen widespread community transmission.

We're encouraged that the global research community has come together to identify and accelerate the most urgent research needs for diagnostics, treatments and vaccines.

(5) We're encouraged that we have been able to ship diagnostic kits, as well as supplies of masks, gloves, gowns and other personal protective equipment to some of the countries that need it most.

We're encouraged that an international team of experts is now on the ground in China, working closely with their Chinese counterparts to understand the outbreak, and to inform the next steps in the global response.

But we also have concern.

....

Today I have three requests for the international community.

First, we must use the window of opportunity we have to intensify our preparedness.

China has bought the world time. We don't know how much time.

All countries must be prepared for the arrival of cases, to treat patients with dignity and compassion, to prevent onward transmission, and to protect health workers.

WHO is working with manufacturers and distributors of personal protective equipment to ensure a reliable supply of the tools health workers need to do their job safely and effectively.

But we're not just fighting an epidemic; we're fighting an infodemic.

Fake news spreads faster and more easily than this virus, and is just as dangerous.

That's why we're also working with search and media companies like Facebook, Google, Pinterest, Tencent, Twitter, TikTok, YouTube and others to counter the spread of rumors and misinformation.

We call on all governments, companies and news organizations to work with us to sound the appropriate level of alarm, without fanning the flames of hysteria.

（6）Second, this is not a job for health ministers alone. It takes a whole-of-government approach.

But that approach must be coherent and coordinated, guided by evidence and public health priorities.

In many countries, measures have been taken by one part of government without appropriate consultation with the health ministry, or consideration of the impact of these measures.

Now more than ever is the time for us to let science and evidence lead policy.

If we don't, we are headed down a dark path that leads nowhere but division and disharmony.

And third, we must be guided by solidarity, not stigma. I repeat this: we must be guided by solidarity, not stigma.

The greatest enemy we face is not the virus itself; it's the stigma that turns us against each other. We must stop stigma and hate!

Much has been written and said about my praise for China.

（7）I have given credit where it's due, and I will continue to do that, as I would and I did for any country that fights an outbreak aggressively at its source to protect its own people and the people of the world, even at great cost to itself.

It's easy to blame. It's easy to politicize. It's harder to tackle a problem together, and find solutions together.

We will all learn lessons from this outbreak. But now is not the time for recriminations or politicization.

We have a choice. Can we come together to face a common and dangerous enemy? Or will we allow fear, suspicion and irrationality to distract and divide us?

In our fractured and divided world, health is one of the few areas in which international cooperation offers the opportunity for countries to work together for a common cause.

This is a time for facts, not fear.

This is a time for rationality, not rumors.

This is a time for solidarity, not stigma.

I thank you.

[资料来源：见世界卫生组织网站（https://www.who.int/director-general/speeches/detail/munich-security-conference），引用日期：2023 年 8 月 19 日。]

1. 实践解析

本材料是世界卫生组织总干事 Tedors Adhamom Ghebreyesus（谭德塞）于 2020 年 2 月 15 日在德国第 56 届慕尼黑安全会议上的讲话，主题为"新冠肺炎和埃博拉疫情背景下的全球卫生安全"。在演讲中，谭德塞对全球疫情防控形势和存在的问题表达了关切，包括中国确诊病例数量的持续增长、国际社会在提供防控资金方面缺乏紧迫感、谣言和错误信息的出现等。他呼吁国际社会放下自私和仇恨，携手并肩共同寻求解决方案。

本篇讲话逻辑清晰，多用小短句，多用排比、重复，表达口语化，总体难度不大。但准确翻译要对疫情相关背景具有一定了解，如埃博拉病毒；原文灵活的句式表达也可能会给翻译造成一定困难。

Munich Security Conference（MSC）即慕尼黑安全会议，由埃瓦尔德－海因里希·冯·克莱斯特－舒曼森（Ewald Heinrich Von Kleister Schumanson）于 1963 年创办，被誉为安全防务领域的达沃斯论坛。最初被称为"国际防务科学会议（Internationale Wehrkunde Begegnung）"，1992 年更名为"慕尼黑安全政策会议"，2009 年起使用目前的名称。慕尼黑安全会议是各国政要及国际安全领域专家进行独立、非正式交流的重要场合。①

Ambassador Ischinger 即 Wolfgang Ischinger（沃尔夫冈·伊申格尔），曾担任过德国驻美国大使和驻英国大使，还曾任德国外交部副部长，2008 年至 2022 年期间担任慕尼黑安全会议主席。

Infodemic 即信息疫情。"信息疫情的概念有广义与狭义之分。广义的信息疫情指的是信息过载与信息失序导致人们难以发现真正有价值且可靠的信息，从而对个体以及社会安全、经济稳定产生伤害的现象。狭义的信息疫情概念，往往被置于重大公共事件语境中，是伴随社会安全事件、事故灾难、公共卫生事件、自然灾害事件发生的一种次生灾害，尤其是公共卫生事件。"本文中"Infodemic"这个词指代新冠肺炎疫情的信息（主要是假信息）在人际的传播。②

2. 长难句点拨

（1）DRC（The Democratic Republic of the Congo）刚果民主共和国，在正

---

① 参见李超、高瞻《慕尼黑安全会议》，载《国际研究参考》2020 年第 3 期，第 32 页。
② 参见阿嘎尔、庞彦《社交媒体时代的"信息疫情"：概念缘起与防控》，载《情报探索》2020 年第 11 期，第 85 页。

式的外交场合，往往使用标准名称，如朝鲜民主主义人民共和国（Democratic People's Republic of Korea，DPRK），大韩民国（Republic of Korea，ROK），老挝人民民主共和国（Lao Peoples' Democratic Republic，LPDR）。该句中an area that is relatively stable and peaceful是the western part of DRC的同位语。

（2）该段用了三个It was no coincidence that ... 句型来构成排比，原文节奏感强，所表达的语气也非常强烈，因此在口译中应努力实现这些效果。第一句中itself指代第一次世界大战，"killed more people than the First World War itself"即在"一战"期间爆发的流感造成的死亡人数比战争本身造成的死亡人数更多。polio是脊髓灰质炎，俗称"小儿麻痹症"。

（3）该段是典型的总分结构，先总说在三种情况下，健康和安全部门采取协调一致的应对措施非常重要，然后再具体列举和展开说明。对三种情况分别使用三个短语来概括，如果只是字对字直译，则可能会使译文较为生硬。可以适当增补文字，让译文更加流畅。如参考译文中的"第一，当埃博拉这样的造成重大影响的疾病在冲突和不安全局势中发生时""第三，当生物制剂被故意释放或意外泄露时"。对于原文中的抽象名词如fragility、conflict和insecurity，在口译中应灵活进行词性转换，将原文中的后置定语转为汉语中更常用的前置定语"脆弱的、陷入冲突和局势不安全的国家"。

（4）该句是典型的英语长句，意群的切分和理解尤为重要："We are encouraged that//the steps China has taken//to contain the outbreak at its source//appear to have bought the world time, //even though those steps have come//at greater cost to China itself."口译中可以尝试采取顺句驱动的技巧：我们感到欣慰的是，中国政府采取了措施从源头上遏制疫情，为世界赢得了时间，但是这些措施却让中国付出了巨大的代价。

（5）该句中出现了防疫物资词汇：diagnostic kits（检测试剂盒）、gown（防护服）、personal protective equipment（个人防护装备）。新冠肺炎相关的其他防疫物资词汇还包括：医用外科口罩（surgical mask）、诊断器具（diagnostic tool）、护目镜（goggles）、消毒液（disinfectant）、抗菌洗手液（antibiotic hand sanitizer）。

（6）在该段中，谭德塞博士呼吁不仅仅卫生部门要采取措施，整个政府都应协调统一行动，先说明要采取a whole-of-government approach，然后对这种方法进行了进一步阐述：coherent and coordinated，guided by evidence and public health priorities。这里的句意不难理解，主要难点是语言转换，在翻译成汉语时，a whole-of-government approach不宜直译为"全政府方法"，应该结合上下文进行释义（paraphrasing），以免陷入翻译腔。对于方法的具体阐述，也要充分考虑汉语多小句、结构松散的特点。

（7）credit to sb./sth. 即"their qualities or achievements will make people have a good opinion of the person or thing mentioned"①，因此"give credit where it's due"就是实至名归的意思。联系上下文，这里的意思就是"我对中国的称赞是实至名归的"。而 and 后面则是一个长句，其中 any country 后接一个 that 引导的定语从句，意群切分如下："as I would and I did for any country // that fights an outbreak aggressively//at its source //to protect its own people and the people of the world//，even at great cost to itself"。

● （二）汉译英

2022 年世界防治结核病日视频会议上的致辞

国家主席习近平夫人、世界卫生组织结核病和艾滋病防治亲善大使　彭丽媛

（2022 年 3 月 24 日）

尊敬的谭德塞总干事，

女士们，先生们，

朋友们，

大家好！在世界防治结核病日到来之际，很高兴出席世界卫生组织举办的此次会议。结核病是严重威胁人类健康的传染病，终结结核病流行对于维护人类健康福祉、促进全球可持续发展具有重要的意义。

（1）近年来，在世界卫生组织积极推动和国际社会共同努力下，全球结核病防治取得了显著的成果，发病人数和死亡人数都明显下降，结核病已经退出了全球十大死因的行列。（2）中国政府高度重视结核病防治，将这项工作纳入"健康中国"战略，设立专项经费，免费为患者提供检查服务和治疗药品，推广新的诊断技术和新药的应用，结核病患者治愈率保持在百分之九十以上。新冠肺炎疫情发生以来，政府和社会各界积极采取行动，关心、关爱结核病患者，确保治疗不因疫情而中断。

我参与结核病防治工作 10 多年来，走访了不少医疗机构、学校和社区，

---

① 见柯林斯英语字典网站（https://www.collinsdictionary.com/zh/dictionary/english/credit），引用日期：2023 年 8 月 19 日。

看到千千万万名医务工作者和志愿者用爱与行动守护健康，结核病防治离不开他们的真情奉献和默默付出。（3）我始终记得"最美防痨人"，年过九旬的中国医生马玙教授。她从事结核病诊疗、科研和教学工作已经 60 多年，疫情期间仍然从事临床工作，她用精湛的医术和医者情怀，让无数的患者重获健康，重拾希望。她将一辈子奉献给了结核病防治事业，她常说的一句话是："最有效的处方就是爱。"我为世界上有像她一样的医务工作者而感动。

（4）防治结核病更需要倡导全社会的广泛参与。在中国，有 100 多万名志愿者向公众普及结核病防治知识，为患者提供帮扶和支持。他们像和煦的春风，向人们传播关爱和温暖。

女士们，先生们，朋友们，虽然结核病防治已经取得很多成绩，但结核病依然是严重危害公众健康的全球性公共卫生问题。受新冠肺炎疫情影响，结核病防治任务更加艰巨。面对新的挑战，我们必须有信心、有爱心、有恒心。作为世界卫生组织结核病和艾滋病防治亲善大使，我深知结核病防治对人民生命健康十分重要，我将尽心尽力为此做出努力。

（5）在此我呼吁所有人秉持生命至上的理念，全力投入终结结核。我期待各国分享结核病防治的经验，在世界卫生组织的领导下开展富有成效的合作。让我们携手并肩，积极行动，推动联合国 2030 年可持续发展议程健康目标如期实现，共同构建人类卫生健康共同体。

谢谢大家。

［资料来源：见中国国际广播电台网站（https://news.cri.cn/20220324/70efa6c7-ea7a-bd47-7c6e-90d2b739861f.html），引用日期：2023 年 8 月 19 日。］

1. 实践解析

本材料是国家主席习近平夫人、世界卫生组织结核病和艾滋病防治亲善大使彭丽媛应邀在世界卫生组织 2022 年世界防治结核病日视频会议上的致辞。在致辞中，彭丽媛介绍了全球特别是中国结核病防治取得的成果，她呼吁社会广泛参与到结核病防治行动中，也期待各国携手并肩，积极行动，分享结核病防治的经验，开展富有成效的合作。

本材料话题和表达都较为常规，出现了少量健康医疗相关术语，但不会对总体翻译造成很大困难，本材料主要难度在于句子的整合，尤其在于如何拆分重组汉语"一逗到底"的流水句，将其梳理成有逻辑的地道英文。

"健康中国"战略（Healthy China strategy）：2016 年，党中央、发布了国务院《"健康中国 2030"规划纲要》，提出了健康中国建设的目标和任务。

2017 年，习近平总书记在党的十九大报告中提出实施健康中国战略，强调坚持以预防为主，倡导健康文明生活方式，预防控制重大疾病。①

联合国 2030 年 可 持 续 发 展 议 程（2030 Agenda for Sustainable Development）：2015 年 9 月 25 日至 27 日，世界各国领导人在在联合国成立 70 周年之际，通过了 2030 年可持续发展议程，宣布了 17 个可持续发展目标以及 169 个具体目标，并承诺在 2030 年全面执行这一议程。"在世界各地消除贫困与饥饿；消除各个国家内和各个国家之间的不平等；建立和平、公正和包容的社会；保护人权和促进性别平等，增强妇女和女童的权能；永久保护地球及其自然资源。"②

2. 长难句点拨

（1）该句中共包含四个小句，其中"在……共同努力下"是原因，可以通过短语 because of、thanks to 或者 due to 来翻译。"全球结核病防治取得了显著的成果"是努力的结果，译为"The world has made notable progress in the fight against TB"。而"发病人数和死亡人数都明显下降""结核病已经退出了全球十大死因的行列"是显著成果的具体表现，由于主语不同，可以独立译成两个句子。在汉译英过程中，要摆脱汉语原文的束缚，如"退出……行列"，如果逐字翻译，则很难找到合适的动词，不妨将其直接翻译为"结核病不再是全国十大死因"（"TB is no longer among the top 10 global causes of death"）。

（2）"高度重视"属于口译中的高频表达，有多种译法，平时应注意积累，如 attach great importance to、pay close attention to 和 take sth. seriously。该段是典型的政治文本，主要特点为含有一连串的动词，如"纳入""设立""提供"等，在口译过程中首先要把握动词之间的逻辑关系，"设立""提供""推广"这些动词短语其实是"重视结核病防治""纳入'健康中国'战略"后采取的具体措施，而"结核病患者治愈率保持在百分之九十以上"是一系列措施带来的成果。在口译过程中，应灵活使用主动和被动语态，兼用长短句，防止译文生硬、呆板。

（3）在翻译"最美防痨人"这一称号时，切忌直译，要真正理解"美"

---

① 见中国国家健康卫生委员会网站（http://www. nhc. gov. cn/guihuaxxs/jkzcwj/201911/169dc4a5b5c6487586b2b9d612956d7b. shtml），引用日期：2023 年 8 月 19 日。

② 见联合国网站中文版（https://www.un. org/zh/documents/treaty/A-RES-70-1），引用日期：2023 年 8 月 19 日。

的意思，即"为防治肺结核疾病做出突出的贡献的人"。"重获健康，重拾希望"符合汉语常用四字词语的习惯，既对称，也有节奏，但是在翻译成英语时，由于英语更注重简洁，可以直接用 regain health and hope。

（4）第一个小句中出现了多个动词："防治""需要""倡导"和"参与"，这符合汉语动态的特点。而英语倾向多用名词，叙述呈静态，因此在汉译英过程中的常见技巧就是词性转换，用名词或者动名词结构来翻译原文中的动词。但是如果将"倡导全社会的广泛参与"按照字面意思翻译为"advocacy for wide participation of the whole society"，则会让译文显得生硬。可以考虑省略部分动词，以释义为主，如参考译文中"Fighting TB also requires extensive involvement across the social spectrum."

（5）"人民至上，生命至上"（put people and their lives first）是我国在抗击新冠肺炎疫情时反复强调的理念。对此，应重点学习和记忆，这样，今后遇到类似的语境就可以灵活使用。鉴于 2022 年世界防治结核病日的宣传主题是 Invest to End TB and Save Lives，直接使用宣传主题更加契合语境。

➡ 三、口译练习

● （一）英译汉

COVID-19 Vaccine Development, Strategy and Implementation
——Opening Remarks at the Vaccines and Global Health Symposium (Excerpt)

Dr Tedros Adhanom Ghebreyesus, Director-General of the World
Health Organization

(February 23, 2021)

Good morning and good afternoon to all of you, and thank you for the invitation to speak to you.

I'm very glad to be back at Columbia, albeit virtually.

……

Before the COVID-19 pandemic struck, people would often ask me what kept me awake at night. I would answer without hesitation: a global pandemic of a respiratory virus.

The COVID-19 pandemic has demonstrated that indeed, the world was not prepared.

More than 110 million cases of COVID-19 have now been reported to WHO from around the world, and more than 2.5 million people have lost their lives.

But we do see signs of hope. Globally, the number of reported cases has now declined for six consecutive weeks, and the number of deaths has declined for three weeks in a row.

This trend is a reminder that even though we are discussing vaccines today, COVID-19 can be suppressed and controlled with proven public health measures.

And indeed, that is exactly what many countries have done.

We must remember that although this is a global pandemic, not all countries have responded in the same way, and not all countries have been affected in the same way.

One of the greatest tragedies of the pandemic is that since it started, the whole world has had the tools to control it, but not all countries have used them effectively.

It's important to emphasize that even as vaccines start to roll out around the world, vaccines will complement, and not replace, the public health measures that we know work.

But there is no question that vaccines are the shot in the arm we all need, literally and metaphorically.

(1) The development and approval of safe and effective vaccines less than a year after the emergence of a new virus is an incredible scientific achievement that must change our expectations for what is possible in future vaccine development.

I would like to pay tribute to the researchers, trial participants, and public-private partnerships that have made this possible.

The lightning speed at which COVID-19 vaccines have been developed is no accident. In fact, it has been years in the making.

......

Much of the work done on developing vaccines for MERS laid the groundwork for the development of vaccines against the new coronavirus, SARS-CoV-2.

As you know, on New Year's Eve 2019, WHO was notified of a cluster of cases of pneumonia of unknown cause in Wuhan, China.

Within two weeks, Chinese researchers identified a novel coronavirus as the cause of the outbreak, and sequenced and published its genome.

The same week, WHO held the first of a series of calls of the Global Coordination Mechanism for Research and Development.

Then in February last year, WHO brought together more than 300 leading researchers from around the world, in line with the R&D Blueprint, to identify and accelerate a research road map for COVID-19.

(2) By April, WHO had published a range of products to guide vaccine development, including target product profiles, core protocols for vaccine trials, animal models, assays and more.

And we have continued to track vaccine development globally.

(3) Most recently, WHO has provided emergency use listing for three vaccines, including the Pfizer-BioNTech vaccine and two versions of the AstraZeneca vaccine.

WHO emergency use listing gives the green light for COVAX to buy vaccines, and enables countries to expedite their own regulatory approval to import and roll out vaccines.

But as we often say, it's not vaccines that save lives, it's vaccination.

Since the beginning of the pandemic, we knew that vaccines would be a vital tool for controlling it.

But we also knew from experience that the equitable distribution of vaccines would not just happen.

Antiretrovirals for HIV were first approved in 1996, but more than a decade passed before the world's poor got access to them.

In the same way, when the H1N1 pandemic erupted in 2009, vaccines were developed but by the time the poor got access, the pandemic was over.

So in April last year, with support from France, Germany, the European Commission and a coalition of partners including Gavi, CEPI and others, WHO launched the Access to COVID-19 Tools Accelerator.

(4) The aims of the ACT Accelerator were twofold: to facilitate the rapid development of vaccines, diagnostics and therapeutics for COVID-19, and to distribute them equitably.

The first objective has been achieved; the second is in jeopardy.

At the beginning of the year, I issued a call to action to ensure that vaccination of health workers and older people is underway in all countries within the first 100 days of this year.

So far, more than 210 million doses of vaccine have been administered globally.

......

But many countries are yet to administer a single dose.

We understand that governments have an obligation to protect their own people.

But the best way to do that is by suppressing the virus everywhere at the same time.

The more the virus circulates, the more opportunity it has to mutate in ways that could render vaccines less effective. We could end up back at square one.

And in our interconnected world, the longer the pandemic persists anywhere, the longer global trade and travel will be disrupted, and the longer the recovery will take.

Vaccine equity is not just a moral imperative; it's an economic and strategic imperative. It's in every country's own best interests.

(5) WHO and our partners in the ACT Accelerator have laid the groundwork. We have created a dose-sharing mechanism, set up rapid processes for emergency use listing, set up indemnification and no-fault compensation mechanisms and completed readiness assessments in almost all countries.

Through our 150 country offices, we have been working closely with countries to prepare them to roll out vaccines as rapidly as possible.

This is great news, but we still face significant challenges to realizing the promise of the ACT Accelerator and COVAX.

First, we still face a financing gap of at least 22.9 billion dollars for the ACT Accelerator this year.

Last week, G7 countries committed 4.3 billion U. S. dollars in new funding, and several countries committed to sharing doses with COVAX.

This is very welcome, but we need all countries to step up.

(6) The longer this gap goes unmet, the harder it becomes to understand why, given this is a tiny fraction of the trillions of dollars that have been mobilized for stimulus packages.

Second, we call on all countries to respect COVAX contracts and not compete with them.

Some countries continue to sign bilateral deals while other countries have nothing.

We continue to hear about high-income countries that express support for COVAX in public, but in private enter contracts that undermine it, by offering higher prices and reducing the number of doses COVAX can buy.

And third, we need an urgent scale-up in manufacturing to increase the volume of vaccines.

That means innovative partnerships including tech transfer, licensing and other mechanisms to address production bottlenecks.

None of these challenges is insurmountable.

The world has already proven that in the face of an unprecedented threat, we can do unprecedented things.

With proven public health measures, rapid diagnostics, oxygen and dexamethasone and vaccines, we have all the tools we need to bring the pandemic under control.

Whether we do is not a test of science; it's a test of character.

Thank you.

［资料来源：见世界卫生组织网站（https://www.who.int/director-general/speeches/detail/who-director-general-s-opening-remarks-at-the-vaccines-and-global-health-symposium-covid-19-vaccine-development-strategy-and-implementation），引用日期：2023 年 8 月 19 日。］

1. 词汇准备

the Global Coordination Mechanism for Research and Development

全球研发协调机制

core protocols for vaccine trials	疫苗试验的核心方案
animal models	动物模型
Pfizer-BioNTech vaccine	辉瑞/BioNTech 新冠疫苗
the AstraZeneca vaccine	阿斯利康新冠疫苗
antiretroviral	抗逆转录病毒
Gavi	全球疫苗免疫联盟
CEPI	流行病预防创新联盟

dexamethasone   地塞米松

2. 长难句点拨

（1）该句中出现了一些关于疫苗开发的术语，如 target product profiles（目标产品概况）、core protocols for vaccine trials（疫苗试验的核心方案）、animal models（动物模型）、assays（分析），除此之外，疫苗开发相关的其他词汇还有：virus isolation（病毒分离）toxicity testing（毒性试验）preclinical research（临床前研究）clinical trials（临床试验）clinical trial and application of vaccines（疫苗临床试验和上市使用）safety and efficacy studies（有效性和安全性研究）。

（2）该句中出现了获得世卫组织紧急使用授权的三款新冠肺炎疫苗，有些同学可能对制药公司或者疫苗名称不太熟悉，除了 Pfizer（辉瑞）、AstraZeneca（阿斯利康），一些世界知名的制药公司如 Abbvie（艾伯维）、Novartis（诺华）、Johnson&Johnson（强生）、Roche（罗氏）、Bristol-Myers Squibb（百时美施贵宝）、Merck Sharp & Dohme（默沙东）、AstraZeneca（阿斯利康）和 Glaxo Smith Kline（葛兰素史克）也应该注意积累。

（3）ACT Accelerator 即 Access to COVID-19 Tools Accelerator 获取 COVID-19 工具，这是一个具有开创性的全球合作项目，旨在加速 COVID-19 检测工具、治疗方法和疫苗的研发、生产和公平获取。therapeutic（治疗的）、therapeutics（疗法，治疗学）、diagnostic（诊断的）、diagnostics（诊断，诊断学）；in jeopardy（处于危险境地，受到威胁）。

（4）该句中包含了获取疫苗的一些术语，如 dose-sharing mechanism（疫苗共享机制）emergency use listing（紧急使用列表流程）indemnification and no-fault compensation mechanism（补偿和无过错赔偿机制）readiness assessments（准备情况评估）。

（5）该句中包含了获取疫苗的一些术语，如 dose-sharing mechanism（疫苗共享机制）、emergency use listing（紧急使用列表流程）、indemnification and no-fault compensation mechanism（补偿和无过错赔偿机制）、readiness assessments（准备情况评估）。

（6）fraction 的英文解释是"a tiny amount or proportion of sth."①。该句包

---

① 见柯林斯英语字典网站（https://www.collinsdictionary.com/zh/dictionary/english/faction），引用日期：2023 年 8 月 19 日。

含了 the more …, the more … 句型和 given 引导的原因状语从句, given 从句主要是解释 why 的内容。参考译文中该句可以译为: "这一资金缺口持续时间越长, 就越难以让人理解, 因为与国家为刺激经济动辄动用的数万亿美元相比, 这只是一个零头而已。"

(二) 汉译英

团结合作战胜疫情 共同构建人类卫生健康共同体
——在第 73 届世界卫生大会视频会议开幕式上的致辞 (节选)

中华人民共和国主席　习近平

(2020 年 5 月 18 日)

大会主席先生,

世界卫生组织总干事先生,

各位代表:

首先, 我认为, 在人类抗击新冠肺炎疫情的关键时刻举行这次世卫大会, 具有十分重要的意义!

人类正在经历第二次世界大战结束以来最严重的全球公共卫生突发事件。新冠肺炎疫情突如其来, 现在已波及 210 多个国家和地区, 影响 70 多亿人口, 夺走了 30 余万人的宝贵生命。在此, 我谨向不幸罹难者表示哀悼! 向他们的家属表示慰问!

人类文明史也是一部同疾病和灾难的斗争史。(1) 病毒没有国界, 疫病不分种族。面对来势汹汹的新冠肺炎疫情, 国际社会没有退缩, 各国人民勇敢前行, 守望相助、风雨同舟, 展现了人间大爱, 汇聚起同疫情斗争的磅礴之力。

经过艰苦卓绝努力, 付出巨大代价, 中国有力扭转了疫情局势, 维护了人民生命安全和身体健康。中方始终本着公开、透明、负责任的态度, 及时向世卫组织及相关国家通报疫情信息, 第一时间发布病毒基因序列等信息, 毫无保留同各方分享防控和救治经验, 尽己所能为有需要的国家提供了大量支持和帮助。

主席先生!

现在, 疫情还在蔓延, 防控仍需努力。我愿提出以下建议。

第一, 全力搞好疫情防控。这是当务之急。我们要坚持以民为本、生命至上，科学调配医疗力量和重要物资，在防护、隔离、检测、救治、追踪等重要领域采取有力举措，尽快遏制疫情在全球蔓延态势，尽力阻止疫情跨境传播。(2) 要加强信息分享，交流有益经验和做法，开展检测方法、临床救治、疫苗药物研发国际合作，并继续支持各国科学家们开展病毒源头和传播途径的全球科学研究。

第二，发挥世卫组织领导作用。在谭德塞总干事带领下，世卫组织为领导和推进国际抗疫合作作出了重大贡献，国际社会对此高度赞赏。当前，国际抗疫正处于关键阶段，支持世卫组织就是支持国际抗疫合作、支持挽救生命。中国呼吁国际社会加大对世卫组织政治支持和资金投入，调动全球资源，打赢疫情阻击战。

第三，加大对非洲国家支持。发展中国家特别是非洲国家公共卫生体系薄弱，帮助他们筑牢防线是国际抗疫斗争重中之重。我们应该向非洲国家提供更多物资、技术、人力支持。中国已向50多个非洲国家和非盟交付了大量医疗援助物资，专门派出了5个医疗专家组。在过去70年中，中国派往非洲的医疗队为两亿多人次非洲人民提供了医疗服务。目前，常驻非洲的46支中国医疗队正在投入当地的抗疫行动。

第四，加强全球公共卫生治理。人类终将战胜疫情，但重大公共卫生突发事件对人类来说不会是最后一次。要针对这次疫情暴露出来的短板和不足，完善公共卫生安全治理体系，提高突发公共卫生事件应急响应速度，建立全球和地区防疫物资储备中心。(3) 中国支持在全球疫情得到控制之后，全面评估全球应对疫情工作，总结经验，弥补不足。这项工作需要科学专业的态度，需要世卫组织主导，坚持客观公正原则。

第五，恢复经济社会发展。(4) 有条件的国家要在做好常态化疫情防控的前提下，遵照世卫组织专业建议，有序开展复工、复产、复学。要加强国际宏观经济政策协调，维护全球产业链供应链稳定畅通，尽力恢复世界经济。

第六，加强国际合作。人类是命运共同体，团结合作是战胜疫情最有力的武器。(5) 这是国际社会抗击艾滋病、埃博拉、禽流感、甲型H1N1流感等重大疫情取得的重要经验，是各国人民合作抗疫的人间正道。

主席先生！

中国始终秉持构建人类命运共同体理念，既对本国人民生命安全和身体健康负责，也对全球公共卫生事业尽责。

…………

我呼吁，让我们携起手来，共同佑护各国人民生命和健康，共同佑护人类共同的地球家园，共同构建人类卫生健康共同体！

谢谢大家。

［资料来源：见中国中央政府网站（https://www.gov.cn/gongbao/content/2020/content_5515270.htm），引用日期：2023 年 8 月 19 日。］

1. 词汇准备

基因序列	genome sequence
传播途径	transmission routes
公共卫生安全治理体系	the governance system for public health security
重大公共卫生突发事件	a major health emergency
常态化疫情防控	regular epidemic prevention and control

2. 长难句点拨

（1）汉语句子使用了对仗、排比和比喻的修辞手法，如"守望相助、风雨同舟"，鉴于口译即时性的要求，口译学习者在语言转换中以传递意义为主，对于一些意象如"风雨""舟"，如果在短时间内想不到合适的翻译策略，不妨省略，翻译出"齐心协力、共同面对困难"的意思。同时，在口译过程中，还要考虑目标读者的文化背景和语言习惯，以确保译文更贴近目标读者的理解。如"汇聚起同疫情斗争的磅礴之力"，此处强调的是"各国步调一致，共同抗疫疫情"，可以将其处理为"synergy"。

（2）该句中信息点比较密集，使用了多个并列的动词和名词短语，如"加强信息分享""交流有益经验和做法"等。在口译中应使用适当的连接词来连接并列成分。除此之外，该句中还包含一些新冠肺炎相关的专业词语，如检测方法（testing method）、临床救治（clinical treatment）、疫苗药物研发（vaccine and medicine research and development）、传播途径（transmission routes）等，对于术语积累有一定要求。

（3）该句的难点在句意整合。汉语中的动词没有形态变化的约束，也不区分谓语和非谓语动词，可以多个动词连用，如该句中的"支持""评估""总结""弥补"，看似是并列关系，但是在翻译成英语时应充分考虑英语的特点，即英语经常通过动词的派生、转化，或者采用非动词的形式（名词、形容词、介词）来表达动词含义。以该句为例，如果抛弃原文中"副词＋动词"的结构，译文的句子结构更加简洁："China supports the idea of a comprehensive review of …"，再利用动词不定式引出"总结经验，弥补不足"作为目的状语，让逻辑关系更加清晰。后半句"需要科学专业的态度，需要世卫组织主导，坚持客观公正原则"这三个动词短语的主语都是"这项工作"，故可将其合并成一个英语句子，其中将"客观公正原则"处理成方式状语。

（4）该句的翻译难点是在把握句子逻辑的同时，确保英语译文连贯、简洁。该句包含两个条件限定："在做好常态化疫情防控的前提下"和"遵照世卫组织专业建议"，其中"遵照"可以译为"in compliance/accordance with"或者"in observance of"，而"在 … 前提下"不妨用 while 从句引出，以减轻记忆负担。"复工、复产、复学"是并列结构，通过重复动词"复"形成排比，增强气势。但是英语动词忌重复，往往会将重复的动词省略，因此，"复工、复产、复学"可以合并译为"reopen businesses and schools"。

（5）该句中列举多了多种疾病名称，既考察口译学习者的专业词汇掌握情况，也考察汉译英过程中对并列结构的处理。该句中两个小句看上去是并列结构："这是……重要经验"和"这是……人间正道"，但在翻译时，第二句要采取更加灵活的处理方式。"人间正道"这个词本意是"正确的规律"，此处使用这个词语意在强调只有国际社会通力合作才能战胜疫情，因而在翻译中不必过分纠结"正道"这个比喻意象，而应该突出真实意图。

➡ 四、参考译文

● （一）口译实践

1. 英译汉

新冠肺炎最新进展
——在慕尼黑安全会议上的讲话
世卫组织总干事　谭德塞博士
（2020 年 2 月 15 日）

诸位阁下，尊敬的各位来宾，亲爱的同事和朋友们，

感谢今天有机会向各位发表演讲。特别是感谢我的朋友 Ischinger 大使。

昨天，我在刚果民主共和国金沙萨市会见了该国总统和各位高级部长，回

顾了抗击埃博拉疫情的进展，并共同制订了一项计划，以加强刚果民主共和国的卫生系统，使其再也不会遭遇类似的疫情。

我要感谢刚果民主共和国总统的领导，以及他对一个更健康、更安全的刚果民主共和国的愿景。

历经 18 个多月和 2249 人丧生之后，我们终于开始看到，这场疫情可能即将结束。过去一周，只有 1 例埃博拉病例，而在 4 月份的高峰期，每周就有 120 例。

这次流行疫情与 2018 年在刚果民主共和国西部暴发的埃博拉疫情形成了鲜明的对比。该地区相对稳定与和平，那次疫情仅用了三个月就得到了控制。

这一经历揭示了一个重大历史教训：疾病与不安全局势难解难分。

1918 年在第一次世界大战期间暴发大流行性流感，死亡总人数超过第一次世界大战死亡人数，这绝非巧合。

消灭脊髓灰质炎的最终前线位于巴基斯坦和阿富汗最不安全的地区，这也绝非巧合。

埃博拉在刚果民主共和国最不安全的地区传播亦非巧合。

没有和平，健康就是一个无法企及的梦想。

反之亦然。流行病有可能导致严重的政治、经济和社会不稳定和不安全状况。

因此，健康保障不仅是卫生部门的事务，也是每个人的要务。

在以下三种主要情况下，卫生部门与安全部门采取协调一致的应对措施至关重要：

第一，在冲突和不安全局势中，埃博拉等流行病造成重大影响。在过去几年中，80% 需要国际应对的疫情发生在脆弱的、陷入冲突和局势不安全的国家中。

第二，出现了某种可能会引发大流行病的病原体，而且这种病原体从一个国家迅速传播到另一个国家。这需要各国立即采取大规模应对措施。

第三，故意释放或意外泄露生物制剂。但愿这是一种罕见事件，尽管如此，我们仍必须为此做好准备。

目前，2019 年新型冠状病毒病疫情是这三种情况中的第二种。

世卫组织已宣布本次疫情为国际关注的突发公共卫生事件。99% 的病例发生在中国，所以在很大程度上，这仍然是中国的紧急突发事件。在世界其他地方，仅有 505 个病例，而在中国，病例总数超过 66000 例。

我要明确指出，无法预测这一流行病将朝哪个方向发展。

我能告诉各位的是，什么让我们感到欣慰，什么令我们感到担忧。

我们感到欣慰的是，中国从源头上遏制疫情的措施虽给中国本身带来了巨大的代价，但看来为世界争取了时间，减缓了病毒向世界其他地区传播的速度。

我们感到欣慰的是，在中国以外，我们并没有看到广泛的社区传播。

我们感到欣慰的是，全球研究界汇聚一道，努力确定并快速满足诊断工具、疗法和疫苗等最迫切的研究需求。

我们感到欣慰的是，我们能够向一些最需要的国家运送诊断试剂盒，以及口罩、手套、防护服和其他个人防护装备。

我们感到欣慰的是，一个国际专家小组目前已抵达中国，正与中国同行密切合作，了解疫情，并协助制订全球后续应对措施。

但我们也有担忧。

…………

今天，我对国际社会提出三项请求。

首先，必须善用我们目前的机会之窗加强防范。

中国为世界争取了时间。但我们不知道争取了多少时间。

所有国家都必须为疫情的到来做好准备，以尊重和同情的方式对待病人，防止疾病继续传播，并保护卫生工作者。

世卫组织正在与个人防护装备的制造商和经销商合作，确保提供可靠装备给卫生工作者，确保他们安全有效完成工作。

我们抗击的不只是流行病，我们还在抗击"谣言疫情"。

假新闻比这一病毒传播得更快、更容易，但同样危险。

我们为此与搜索引擎和媒体公司合作，例如与脸书、谷歌、拚趣、腾讯、推特、抖音、YouTube 以及其他公司一道，对抗谣言和虚假信息的传播。

我们呼吁所有政府、公司和新闻机构与我们合作，发出恰当的警报，而不是煽动歇斯底里的狂焰。

其次，这不仅仅是卫生部长的工作，而需要政府各部门统一应对。

但政府各部门必须协调一致，统一应对，以证据为基础，并根据公共卫生重点开展工作。

在许多国家，政府某些部门在没有与卫生部进行恰当协商的情况下就采取了措施，而且并未考虑到这些措施的影响。

我们现在比以往任何时候都更需要以科学和证据指导政策。

如果我们不这样做，我们将陷入分裂和不和，迈向黑暗的深渊。

第三，我们必须团结一致，而不是污名化。我再说一遍：我们必须团结一致，而不是污名化。

我们面临的最大敌人不是这一病毒本身，而是导致人们对立的污名化。我们必须停止污名化和仇恨！

有很多人评论我称赞中国。

我对中国的称赞是实至名归的，我还将继续赞扬中国。我会称赞任何从源头上大力抗击疫情从而保护本国人民以及世界人民，甚至不惜付出巨大代价的国家。

指责很容易，政治化也很容易。而一起解决一个问题，一道寻找解决方案则很艰难。

我们都将从这次疫情中吸取教训。但现在不是相互指责或政治化的时候。

我们需要作出选择。我们能够携手并肩对付一个共同且危险的敌人吗？还是我们任由恐惧、怀疑和非理性左右，四分五裂？

在我们这个支离破碎的世界中，卫生是少有的能让各国为一项共同事业开展国际合作和共同奋斗的一个领域。

此时此刻，需要事实，而非恐惧。

此时此刻，需要理性，而非谣言。

此时此刻，需要团结，而非污名化。

谢谢大家。

［资料来源：见世界卫生组织网站（https://www. who. int/director-general/speeches/detail/munich-security-conference），引用日期：2023 年 8 月 19 日。］。）

2. 汉译英

Video Conference Address on World TB Day 2022
PENG Liyuan，Wife of Chinese President XI Jinping and
World Health Organization (WHO) Goodwill Ambassador for
Tuberculosis (TB) and HIV/AIDS
(March 24，2022)

Director-General Dr. Tedros Adhanom Ghebreyesus,

Ladies and gentlemen,

Dear friends,

Greetings to you all! On the occasion of World TB Day, it gives me great pleasure to attend this event held by the WHO. TB is an infectious disease that poses a serious threat to human health. Ending TB is of great significance for people's health and well-being and for sustainable development across the globe.

In recent years, thanks to the hard work of the WHO and the joint efforts of the international community, the world has made notable progress in the fight against TB. The number of TB instances and deaths have dropped markedly. TB is no longer among the top 10 global causes of death. The Chinese government takes TB prevention and treatment very seriously, and has incorporated it into the Healthy China strategy. Special funds have been set up; free follow-up examination and anti-TB drugs are provided to patients, and more is being done to promote new diagnostic technologies and medicines. As a result, the TB cured rate has been kept above 90 percent. Even during the COVID-19 pandemic, the government and various social sectors have taken active steps to care for TB patients and ensure their uninterrupted treatment.

Since I joined the anti-TB endeavor more than a decade ago, I have visited many medical facilities, schools and communities, and I have witnessed tens of thousands of medical workers and volunteers, serving as defenders of health with love and action. The fight against TB could not be won without their silent yet complete dedication. Among them is Professor Ma Yu. This Chinese doctor in her 90s has been recognized as one of the "Most Outstanding Figures in Anti-TB Fight". She has been engaged in TB diagnosis, treatment, research and teaching for more than 60 years, and has been doing clinical work even during the pandemic. With exceptional expertise and work ethic, she has helped countless patients regain health and hope, devoting a lifetime to fighting TB. Her motto is "Love is the best prescription." I am deeply touched by Professor Ma and many other medical workers like her around world.

Fighting TB also requires extensive involvement across the social spectrum. In China, more than one million volunteers are working to raise public awareness of TB prevention and treatment, and to help and support TB patients. They spread love and care like the spring breeze.

Ladies and gentlemen,

Friends,

Although much has been accomplished in TB prevention and treatment, the disease remains a global issue, posing serious danger to public health. The COVID-19 pandemic has further complicated the anti-TB efforts. We must rise to the new challenges with confidence, love, and tenacity. As WHO Goodwill Ambassador for TB and HIV/AIDS, I know full well how important fighting TB is to people's life and health. I will do all I can for this great cause.

Here, I call on everyone to Invest to End TB and Save Lives. I hope that countries will share their experience in fighting TB and, under the leadership of the WHO, carry out fruitful cooperation. Let us stand side by side and work actively to attain the health-related goals of the 2030 Agenda for Sustainable Development as scheduled, and jointly build a global community of health for all.

Thank you.

［资料来源：见中国国际广播电台网站（https://news. cri. cn/20220324/70efa6c7-ea7a-bd47-7c6e-90d2b739861f. html），引用日期：2023 年 8 月 19 日。］

（二）口译练习

1. 英译汉

COVID-19 疫苗开发、战略和实施
——在疫苗与全球卫生研讨会上的讲话（节选）
世卫组织总干事　谭德塞博士
（2021 年 2 月 23 日）

你们好。感谢你们邀请我参会和讲话。

我很高兴在网上再次回到哥伦比亚大学。

…………

在新冠肺炎大流行疫情暴发之前，人们经常会问我什么事情让我晚上睡不着觉。我总是毫不犹豫地回答：呼吸道病毒的全球大流行。

新冠肺炎大流行显示，世界的确没有做好准备。

目前，全世界向世卫组织报告了 1.1 亿多例新冠肺炎病例，250 多万人丧生。

但我们现在确实也看到了希望迹象。在全球范围内，报告病例数已经连续六周下降，死亡人数连续三周下降。

这一趋势提醒我们，尽管今天讨论疫苗问题，但我们可以采取行之有效的公共卫生措施抑制和控制新冠肺炎。

事实上，许多国家就是这样做的。

我们必须指出的是，虽然这是全球大流行病，但并非所有国家都以同样方式应对，也并非所有国家都受到了同样的影响。

这场大流行最大的一个悲剧是，自疫情开始以来，全世界虽有控制疫情的工具，但并非所有国家都有效利用了这些工具。

必须强调指出的是，即使开始在世界各地推出疫苗，疫苗只是补充而不是取代我们所熟悉的有效公共卫生措施。

毫无疑问，我们都需要接种疫苗。

在新病毒出现不到一年内开发并批准了安全有效的疫苗是一项惊人的科学成就，这将改变我们对今后疫苗开发工作的预期。

我要向对此做出贡献的研究人员、参与试验者和公私伙伴关系表示敬意。

新冠肺炎疫苗研发迅速取得成果不是偶然的。事实上，已有多年积淀。

…………

在开发 MERS 疫苗方面所做的许多工作为研制新型冠状病毒 SARS – CoV –2疫苗奠定了基础。

众所周知，2019 年 12 月 31 日，中国向世卫组织通报了武汉发生的一组不明原因肺炎病例。

在短短两周内，中国研究人员发现是一种新型冠状病毒造成了此次疫情，并测定和公布了这一病毒的基因组序列。

同一周，世卫组织全球研发协调机制开始了一系列活动。

去年 2 月，世卫组织根据研发蓝图召集了世界各地 300 多名顶尖研究人员，以确定并加速落实新冠肺炎研究路线图。

到了 4 月，世卫组织已发表了一系列指导疫苗开发的文件，包括目标产品概况、疫苗试验的核心方案、动物模型、分析等。

我们继续跟踪全球疫苗开发动态。

最近，世卫组织将辉瑞－生物科技疫苗和两版阿斯利康疫苗列入了紧急使用清单。

世卫组织紧急使用清单为 COVAX 机制购买疫苗开了绿灯，并有助于各国加快本国监管部门对疫苗进口和接种的批准程序。

我们常说，拯救生命的不是疫苗，而是疫苗接种。

自大流行刚开始，我们就知道疫苗是控制大流行疫情的重要工具。

但经验也告诉我们，可能会有疫苗公平分配问题。

艾滋病毒抗逆转录病毒药物于1996年首次获得批准，但10多年后，世界各地贫困人群才获得这些药物。

同样，2009年H1N1病毒大流行后，疫苗研制成功，但当穷人获得疫苗时，大流行疫情已结束。

因此，去年4月，在法国、德国、欧盟委员会以及全球疫苗免疫联盟和流行病防范创新联盟等合作伙伴的支持下，世卫组织发起了"获取新冠肺炎工具加速计划"。

这项加速计划的两项目标是：促进迅速开发并公平分配新冠肺炎疫苗、诊断试剂和治疗工具。

第一个目标已实现；但第二个目标仍有问题。

今年初，我发出一项行动呼吁，吁请在今年头100天内，为所有国家的卫生工作者和老年人接种疫苗。

迄今为止，全球已接种了超过2.1亿剂疫苗。

…………

但许多国家尚未能开始接种疫苗。

我们理解，政府有义务保护本国人民。

但保护本国人民的最佳方式是同时在各地抑制这一病毒。

病毒传播得越多，就越有机会发生变异，进而降低疫苗效果。我们可能会回到原点。

在相互关联的世界中，大流行疫情在任何地方持续时间越长，全球贸易和旅行受到干扰的时间就越长，复苏的时间也就越长。

公平分享疫苗不仅符合道德要求，而且是经济和战略需要。这符合每个国家自身的最佳利益。

世卫组织和ACT加速计划的合作伙伴已为公平分享疫苗奠定了基础。我们建立了疫苗共享机制，确定了紧急使用列表流程，设立了补偿和无过错赔偿机制，并完成了对几乎所有国家准备情况的评估工作。

通过我们的150个国家办事处，我们与各国密切合作，为尽快推出疫苗做好准备。

这是好消息，但我们在实现ACT加速计划和COVAX机制的期望方面仍然面临重大挑战。

首先，ACT加速计划今年仍有至少229亿美元的资金缺口。

上周，七国集团成员国承诺提供 43 亿美元的新资金，有几个国家承诺与 COVAX 分享疫苗剂量。

我们对此非常欢迎，但所有国家都需要做出努力。

这一资金缺口持续时间越长，就越难以让人理解。与国家为刺激经济动辄动用的数万亿美元相比，这只是一个零头而已。

第二，我们呼吁所有国家履行 COVAX 合同，不要损害这些合同。

一些国家仍在签署双边协议，而另一些国家则一无所有。

高收入国家继续公开表示支持 COVAX，但私下签署的协议损害了 COVAX 机制，以更高的价格购买疫苗，致使 COVAX 可以购买的剂量减少。

第三，我们需要紧急扩大生产规模，以增加疫苗剂量。

为此需要建立新颖的伙伴关系，包括建立技术转让、发放许可和其他机制，以解决生产瓶颈问题。

这些挑战都不是无法克服的。

世界的行动已证明，面对前所未有的威胁，我们可以有前所未有的创举。

我们拥有控制大流行所需的所有工具，例如行之有效的公共卫生措施、快速诊断试剂、氧气和地塞米松以及疫苗等。

我们是否这样做不是科学考验，而是性格考验。

谢谢大家。

[资料来源：见世界卫生组织网站（https://www.who.int/director-general/speeches/detail/who-director-general-s-opening-remarks-at-the-vaccines-and-global-health-symposium-covid-19-vaccine-development-strategy-and-implementation），引用日期：2023 年 8 月 19 日。]

2. 汉译英

Fighting COVID-19 Through Solidarity and Cooperation
Building a Global Community of Health for All

Statement at Virtual Event of Opening of the 73rd World Health Assembly

H. E. XI Jinping President of the People's Republic of China

((Excerpt) May 18, 2020)

President of the World Health Assembly,

Director General of the World Health Organization,

Dear Delegates,

To begin with, I wish to say that it is of significant importance for this World

Health Assembly to be held at such a critical moment as the human race battles this novel coronavirus.

What we are facing is the most serious global public health emergency since the end of World War Ⅱ. Catching the world by surprise, COVID-19 has hit over 210 countries and regions, affected more than seven billion people around the world and claimed over 300000 precious lives. I mourn for every life lost and express condolences to the bereaved families.

The history of human civilization is one of fighting diseases and tiding over disasters. The virus does not respect borders. Nor is race or nationality relevant in the face of the disease. Confronted by the ravages of COVID-19, the international community has not flinched. The people of all countries have tackled the virus head on. Around the world, people have looked out for each other and pulled together as one. With love and compassion, we have forged extraordinary synergy in the fight against COVID-19.

In China, after making painstaking efforts and enormous sacrifice, we have turned the tide on the virus and protected the life and health of our people. All along, we have acted with openness, transparency and responsibility. We have provided information to WHO and relevant countries in a most timely fashion. We have released the genome sequence at the earliest possible time. We have shared control and treatment experience with the world without reservation. We have done everything in our power to support and assist countries in need.

Mr. President,

Even as we meet, the virus is still raging, and more must be done to bring it under control. To this end, I want to make the following proposals:

First, we must do everything we can for COVID-19 control and treatment. This is a most urgent task. We must always put the people first, for nothing in the world is more precious than people's lives. We need to deploy medical expertise and critical supplies to places where they are needed the most. We need to take strong steps in such key areas as prevention, quarantine, detection, treatment and tracing. We need to move as fast as we can to curb the global spread of the virus and do our best to stem cross-border transmission. We need to step up information sharing, exchange experience and best practice, and pursue international cooperation on testing methods, clinical treatment, and vaccine and medicine research and development.

We also need to continue supporting global research by scientists on the source and transmission routes of the virus.

Second, the World Health Organization should lead the global response. Under the leadership of Dr. Tedros, WHO has made a major contribution in leading and advancing the global response to COVID-19. Its good work is applauded by the international community. At this crucial juncture, to support WHO is to support international cooperation and the battle for saving lives as well. China calls on the international community to increase political and financial support for WHO so as to mobilize resources worldwide to defeat the virus.

Third, we must provide greater support for Africa. Developing countries, African countries in particular, have weaker public health systems. Helping them build capacity must be our top priority in COVID-19 response. The world needs to provide more material, technological and personnel support for African countries. China has sent a tremendous amount of medical supplies and assistance to over 50 African countries and the African Union. Five Chinese medical expert teams have also been sent to the African continent. In total, in the past seven decades, over 200 million people in Africa have received care and treatment from Chinese medical teams. At present, 46 resident Chinese medical teams are in Africa helping with COVID-19 containment efforts locally.

Fourth, we must strengthen global governance in the area of public health. We human beings will eventually prevail over the coronavirus. Yet this may not be the last time a major health emergency comes knocking at our door. In view of the weaknesses and deficiencies exposed by COVID-19, we need to improve the governance system for public health security. We need to respond more quickly to public health emergencies and establish global and regional reserve centers of anti-epidemic supplies. China supports the idea of a comprehensive review of the global response to COVID-19 after it is brought under control to sum up experience and address deficiencies. This work should be based on science and professionalism, led by WHO and conducted in an objective and impartial manner.

Fifth, we must restore economic and social development. While working on an ongoing basis to contain the virus, countries where conditions permit may reopen businesses and schools in an orderly fashion in observance of WHO's professional recommendation. In the meantime, international macroeconomic policy coordination should be stepped up and the global industrial and supply chains be kept stable and unclogged if we are to restore growth to the world economy.

Sixth, we must strengthen international cooperation. Mankind is a community with a shared future. Solidarity and cooperation is our most powerful weapon for defeating the virus. This is the key lesson the world has learned from fighting HIV/AIDS, Ebola, avian influenza, influenza A（H1N1）and other major epidemics. And solidarity and cooperation is a sure way through which we, the people of the world, can defeat this novel coronavirus.

Mr. President,

China stands for the vision of building a community with a shared future for mankind. China takes it as its responsibility to ensure not just the life and health of its own citizens, but also global public health.

......

To conclude, I call on all of us to come together and work as one. Let's make concerted efforts to protect the life and health of people in all countries. Let's work together to safeguard planet Earth, our common home. Let's work together to build a global community of health for all!

Thank you.

［资料来源：见中国时报网（https://language. chinadaily. com. cn/a/202005/19/WS5ec3 3e74a310a8b2 41156a8a. html.)，引用日期2023 年 8 月 19 日。]

第四章　世界气象组织

一、背景阅读

（一）汉语简介

【成　立】《世界气象组织公约》于 1950 年正式生效，世界气象组织随之宣告成立。

【宗　旨】促进设置站网方面的国际合作，以进行气象、水文以及与气象有关的地球物理观测，促进设置和维持各种中心以提供气象和与气象有关的服务；促进建立和维持气象及有关信息快速交换系统；促进气象及有关观测的标准化，确保以统一的规格出版观测和统计资料；推进气象学应用于航空、航海、水利、农业和人类其他活动；促进业务水文活动，增进气象与水文部门间的密切合作；鼓励气象及有关领域内的研究和培训，帮助协调研究和培训中的国际性问题。

【成　员】现有国家会员 187 个，地区会员 6 个。

【负责人】主席亚德里安（Dr. Gerhard Adrian，德国籍），2019 年当选，任期至 2023 年。秘书长塔拉斯（Petteri Taalas，芬兰籍），2019 年连任，任期至 2023 年。

【总部】瑞士日内瓦。

【组织机构】最高权力机构是世界气象大会，每 4 年召开一次，4 年期间召开一次特别大会。还设有执行理事会、区域协会、技术委员会和秘书处。

【双方合作情况】中国是世界气象组织创始国之一。中华人民共和国于 1972 年恢复在世界气象组织的合法席位。中国香港和中国澳门是地区会员。自 1973 年起，中国一直是世界气象组织执行理事会成员。中国与世界气象组织关系良好，世界气象组织历届主席、秘书长及高级官员均多次访华，受到中国国家领导人的接见。

[资料来源：见中国外交部网站（https://www.mfa.gov.cn/web/gjhdq_676201/gjhdqzz_681964/sjqx_685760/gk_685762/），引用日期2023年8月19日。]

（二）WMO 英语介绍

1. What is WMO?

The World Meteorological Organization（WMO）is an intergovernmental organization with a membership of 193 Member States and Territories. As a specialized agency of the United Nations, WMO is dedicated to international cooperation and coordination on the state and behaviour of the Earth's atmosphere, its interaction with the land and oceans, the weather and climate it produces, and the resulting distribution of water resources.

WMO facilitates and promotes：

➢ The establishment of an integrated Earth System observation network to provide weather, climate and water-related data；

➢ The establishment and maintenance of data management centers and telecommunication systems for the provision and rapid exchange of weather, climate and water-related data；

➢ The creation of standards for observation and monitoring in order to ensure adequate uniformity in the practices and procedures employed worldwide and ascertain the homogeneity of data and statistics；

➢ The provision of weather, climate and water-related services—through the application of science and technology in operational meteorology and hydrology—to reduce disaster risks and contribute to climate change adaptation, as well as for sectors such as transport, water resource management, agriculture, health, energy and other areas；

➢ Activities in operational hydrology as well as closer cooperation between National Meteorological and Hydrological Services in states and territories where they are separate；

➢ The coordination of research and training in meteorology and related fields

2. History

The World Meteorological Organization originated from the International Meteorological Organization (IMO), the roots of which were planted at the 1873 Vienna International Meteorological Congress. Established by the ratification of the WMO Convention on 23 March 1950, WMO became the specialized agency of the United Nations for meteorology (weather and climate), operational hydrology and related geophysical sciences a year later.

3. Institutions

(1) The Secretariat

The Secretariat, headquartered in Geneva, is headed by the Secretary-General. The Executive Office comprises the Secretary-General, Deputy Secretary-General and Assistant Secretary-General.

The Secretary-General of WMO is appointed by the World Meteorological Congress for a four-year term with a maximum tenure of 8 years. The Secretary-General is responsible for the overall technical and administrative work of the Secretariat. The Secretary-General has the responsibility to appoint all Secretariat staff, including the Deputy Secretary-General and the Assistant Secretary-General, in accordance with regulations established by Congress, and with the approval of the Executive Council.

Gerhard Adrian was elected by the Eighteenth World Meteorological Congress in 2019 for a four-year term beginning immediately after the closure of the Congress.

(2) The World Meteorological Congress

The World Meteorological Congress is the supreme body of WMO. The Executive Council implements its decisions, while six Regional Associations are responsible for the coordination of meteorological, hydrological and related activities within their respective Region.

(3) Board of Directors

In June 2019, the World Meteorological Congress approved a reform of the WMO governance and a vision for 2030 as well as other changes that called for an overhaul of the structure of the Secretariat. One of the most important changes implemented thus far is the creation of a Board of Directors. The Board, composed of senior Directors, meets once a month to discuss overall progress towards achieving departmental targets and overall organizational objectives and goals.

4. 词汇表 Vocabulary List

meteorology	气象状态，气象学
hydrology	水文学，水文地理学
geophysical	地球物理学的
weather forecast	天气预报
natural hazards	自然灾害
World Meteorological Congress	世界气象大会

➡ 二、口译实践

● (一) 英译汉

Early Warning and Early Action
Hydrometeorological and Climate information for Disaster Risk Reduction
Statement by Petteri Taalas, WMO Secretary-General for World

Meteorological Day

(March 23, 2022)

Greetings from the World Meteorological Organization secretariat in Geneva.

The top priority of WMO is to protect lives and livelihoods from weather, climate and water extremes.

Every minute of every day of the year.

I am therefore very happy that the theme of World Meteorological Day 2022 is "Early Warning and Early Action".

(1) It celebrates the great achievements of national meteorological and hydrological services in improved early warning systems. It also highlights the vital work of the disaster risk reduction community in making sure that these early warnings lead to early action.

（2）But we cannot be complacent. We face many challenges, especially in making sure that early warnings reach the last mile to the most vulnerable who need them most.

Climate change is already very visible through more extreme weather in all parts of the world. （3）We are seeing more intense heatwaves and drought and forest fires. We have more water vapor in the atmosphere, which leads to extreme rainfall and deadly flooding. The warming of the ocean fuels more powerful tropical storms and rising sea levels increase the impacts.

We expect this negative trend to continue. （4）Greenhouse gas concentrations are at record levels, locking in climate change to continue for decades to come, melting of glaciers and sea level rise up to centuries.

In addition to climate change mitigation, climate change adaptation is a top priority. Early warning systems are a powerful way to adapt.

Last year, WMO published a report on disaster statistics for the past 50 years. It showed that there were more than 11000 disasters linked to weather, climate and water-related hazards, almost equal to one disaster per day. There were 2 million deaths—or 115 per day.

The number of disasters has increased five-fold in the past 50 years. And the economic cost has soared.

But the good news is that the number of casualties has fallen dramatically. We are better than ever before at saving lives.

Supercomputers, satellites and advances in science have greatly increased the accuracy of our forecasts. Mobile phone alerts and weather apps can reach even remote areas.

（5）WMO is promoting impact-based forecasting, of what the weather will be and what it will do. That is needed to enhance the preparedness and early action of various user and customer groups, who are dependent on weather.

But much more remains to be done. Only half of the 193 Members of WMO have multi-hazard early warning systems in place. There is also a major need to enhance the impact-based forecasting skills of a large fraction of Members.

There are severe gaps in weather and hydrological observing networks in Africa, some parts of Latin America and in Pacific and Caribbean island. This undermines forecasts local and globally.

WMO has therefore created a financing mechanism known as SOFF (The Systematic Observation Financing Facility) to drive investment in the basic observing system and fill data gaps.

WMO is an implementing partner in the Climate Risk and Early Warning Systems Initiative (CREWS), which builds resilience among vulnerable countries and communities.

(6) WMO is spearheading a new water and climate coalition to focus more attention on water-related hazards and shortages. We have highly successful programs and projects on tropical cyclones, coastal inundation, floods and drought.

In Geneva, we have joined forces with the UN Office for Disaster Risk Reduction to form a centre of excellence on climate change and disasters.

WMO has been developing a support mechanism to provide reliable and authoritative information to the UN humanitarian agencies to be able to optimize the humanitarian aid before and after a weather-related disaster. We are working together with financing institutions like the World Bank, European Union, UNDP, Green Climate Fund, to allocate more funding to early warning services and to ensure sustainability of the investments.

And of course, WMO is committed to the 2030 international agenda on climate action, sustainable development and disaster risk reduction.

WMO's vision is that "by 2030, we see a world where all nations, especially the most vulnerable, are more resilient to the socioeconomic consequences of extreme weather, climate, water and other environmental events".

Early warnings work. They must work for everyone. They must lead to early action.

I wish you all a happy World Meteorological Day.

[资料来源：见英文巴士网站（https://www.en84.com/13115.html），引用日期：2023年8月19日。]

1. 实践解析

本材料是世界气象组织（WMO）秘书长 Petteri Taalas（佩特里·塔拉斯）在 2022 年 3 月 23 日世界气象日上发表的讲话。他在致辞中提到，气候变化已经在全球各地导致更加极端的天气，如高温、干旱、森林火灾、极端降雨等，强调气候变化适应是当务之急，"早期预警和早期行动"对于灾害风险减轻有重大作用。他认为，虽然早期预警取得了一些成就，但仍面临不少挑战，特别是确保警报能够传达到最需要的最脆弱人群方面。最后，他强调了 WMO 对2030 年气候行动、可持续发展和减灾国际议程的承诺，希望到 2030 年，各国更有能力抵御极端天气、气候、水和其他环境事件的社会经济影响。

材料中长短句交错，作为节日致辞，含有不少口语化表达；材料涉及部分天气气象相关术语，但总体难度适中。

Climate change mitigation and adaptation 即气候变化减缓和气候变化适应。人类在面对气候变化问题时，需要双管齐下，既要采取措施遏制全球变暖，也要采取措施适应气候变化的影响。气候变化减缓策略是指"采取措施，减缓或阻止化石燃料相关碳排放的增加，以应对根本性的问题"。气候变化适应策略指"开展适应工作，帮助民众和政府抵御并尽可能减少气候变化已经造成的破坏"。[①]

Climate Risk and Early Warning Systems Initiative（CREWS）即气候风险与预警系统倡议，2015 年在巴黎举行的联合国气候变化大会上被提出。该倡议由法国牵头，澳大利亚、德国、卢森堡和荷兰等联合发起，可以强化多灾种预警系统，已应用于非洲和太平洋地区的 19 个国家，包括最容易遭受热带气旋和洪水的最不发达国家和小岛屿发展中国家。[②]

Systematic Observations Financing Facility（SOFF）即系统观测融资机制，该机制由世界气象组织、开发计划署和环境规划署于 2021 年年底在英国格拉斯哥举行的气候变化大会上建立的，旨在"通过提供赠款融资和技术援助，来支持小岛屿发展中国家和最不发达国家，以便根据国际商定的全球基本观测网持续收集地面天气和气候观测资料，并进行国际交流，同时帮助其他发展中国家评估如何满足全球基本观测网的要求"[③]。

Tropical Cyclones（TC）即热带气旋，是在热带或副热带洋面上生成的低压涡旋，是热带低压、热带风暴、台风、飓风的统称。我国使用国际热带气旋名称和等级标准，热带气旋中心附近的平均最大风力小于 8 级则被称为热带低压，8～9 级被称为热带风暴，10～11 级被称为强热带风暴，12 级以上被称

---

① ［英］亚当·贝苏迪:《什么是减缓，什么是适应?》，载《金融与发展》2021 年第 3 期，第 46页。

② 见联合国网站（https://www.un.org/zh/climatechange/climate-solutions/early-warning-systems.），引用日期：2023 年 8 月 19 日。

③ 见联合国网站（https://news.un.org/zh/story/2022/06/1105412），引用日期：2023 年 8 月 19日。

为台风。①

2. 长难句点拨

（1）部分口译学习者可能对该句中 meteorological 和 hydrological 比较陌生，建议在学习时和名词形式一起记忆：meteorology（气象学）、meteorological（与气象学有关的、气象的水文学）、hydrology（水文学、水文地理学）、hydrological（水文学的）。该句的抽象名词比较多，翻译时可能会对理解造成一定的困难，尤其是后半句信息比较密集，要能够准确理解介词 of 和 in 的作用。英语和汉语的一大差异就是英语偏"静态"，习惯使用名词尤其是抽象名词，而汉语偏"动态"，往往一个汉语句子中有多个动词。因此，在将该句翻译为汉语时，要灵活增补动词，与名词组成动宾结构，让译文更加符合汉语的特点，如将 the great achievements 翻译为"取得的巨大成就"，the vital work 译为"开展的重要工作"。

（2）complacent 一词的英文解释是"very pleased with themselves or feels that they do not need to do anything about a situation，even though the situation may be uncertain or dangerous"②，暗含不赞成这种态度的意味，此处可以译为"沾沾自喜"。the last mile 从字面不难猜测这个短语的原意是指"长途跋涉中的最后一段里程"，由此引申出了"办成一件事最终的、最关键性的步骤"这个意思。该句在处理的时候建议直译，让听众可以更加直观地理解。

（3）该句连续使用了"We are seeing…""We have…"这样的句式来强化语气，突出极端天气的严重性。口译学习者在翻译过程中不仅要传递忠实于原文的信息，还应该还原原文的语气和效果。英语原文是通过长句和类似排比的结构来实现，在将其翻译成汉语时要考虑汉语的特点，翻译成一连串的短句，反而更有气势。Heatwave、drought、forest fires（也有一些演讲中用wildfires）、tropical storm、rising sea levels、tropical cyclones、coastal inundation 这些词汇都是描述气候变化或者极端天气的高频词，口译学习者应该熟记并掌握。

（4）该句在翻译过程中首先要理解各个成分之间的关系：Greenhouse gas

---

① 见知网百科（https://xuewen.cnki.net/read-R2017030020000007.html），引用日期：2023 年 8 月19 日。

② 见柯林斯英语字典网站（https://www.collinsdictionary.com/zh/dictionary/english/complacent），引用日期：2023 年 8 月 19 日。

concentrations are at record levels 是句子核心成分，而 locking 引导的短语和 melting 引导的短语实际是动名词短语作结果状语，表明温室气体浓度高导致的后果。部分口译学习者的理解难点可能是词组 lock in，一般用法是 lock sb. in，表示锁住某人。但是在该句中显然不同，理解气候变化的原理，有助于理解这句话的意思。参考译文中，该句可理解为现在人类排放了大量的二氧化碳到大气中，导致大气里温室气体浓度创了新的纪录，这会导致未来几十年气温持续上升。原文中的 lock in 大致意思为提前锁定了结果，在翻译的时候传递相近的意思即可。at record levels 意为达到创纪录的水平，这个短语是表示数字相关表达中的高频词汇，口译学习者应该熟记。

（5）该句中 impact-based forecasting 可能会对于听力理解有一定障碍，直译也比较拗口，但是紧接着的同位语"of what the weather will be and what it will do"实际就是在解释什么是"基于影响的预测"。由于原文自带了解释成分，因此，即使直译也不会造成理解上的困难。第二句"That is needed to enhance the preparedness and early action of various user and customer groups, who are dependent on weather."是典型的长句，翻译时进行的必要的切分和语序调整，不仅是为了让译文更地道，也是为了减轻译文输出译文时的记忆负担。翻译抽象名词 preparedness 和 early action 要进行适当的增补，便于听众理解。

（6）spearhead 作动词时，英文释义是"to serve as leader or leading element of sth."①，在此处可以根据搭配译为"领导……联盟"。在汉译英的有些句式中可以灵活使用 spearhead。该句中也出现了"热带气旋""海岸洪涝""洪水""干旱"等气候话题高频词，应该重视积累高频词。

[资料来源：见新浪网（https://k.sina.com.cn/article_2096315820_7cf33dac001016ys5.html），引用日期：2023 年 8 月 19 日。]

---

① 见韦氏词典网站（https://www.merriam-webster.com/dictionary/spearhead，引用日期：2023 年 8 月 19 日。

（二）汉译英

开放咨询平台第三次高级会议
中国气象局副局长　余勇
（2022 年 6 月 20 日）

谢谢主持人先生。

新的白皮书更好地阐述了我们气象水文部门的未来的使命与责任。（1）中国气象局是中国气象服务的主体，负责为政府防灾减灾提供决策服务，为公众提供气象预报和灾情天气警报服务，为经济社会发展和各行各业提供专业、专项气象服务，承担着中国气象事业发展政策的制定职责、履行气象服务监管义务。

今年 4 月，中国政府印发了《气象高质量发展纲要（2022—2035 年）》，明确了中国气象发展的思路和目标。

（2）中国气象局正按照监测精密、预报精准、服务精细的要求，推进气象服务的数字化、智能化转型，重点聚焦 4 个领域的服务：

（3）一是面向生命安全，健全分灾种、分重点行业的气象灾害监测预报预警体系。开展气象灾害风险普查，发展基于影响的预报和风险的预警，推进建立以气象预警为先导的联动机制。

（4）二是面向生产发展，实施"气象＋"赋能行动，强化农业、海洋、交通等敏感行业的精细化、专业化气象服务。

（5）三是面向美好生活，强化服务供给。建立覆盖城乡的气象服务体系，推进公共建筑均等化，开展公众个性化、定制式的气象服务。

四是面向生态良好，加强气候变化的监测评估。强化生态系统保护和修复气象保障，推进气象资源合理开发利用。

今年 6 月，中国气象局发布了《促进气象产业健康持续发展》的文件，强化气象服务市场的培育，引导社会力量有序开展气象服务。一是优化政策环境，分级、分类推动气象数据资源的有序开放。二是加强规范引领，完善气象服务社会监督和评价体系，营造公平竞争的市场环境。三是加强与私营气象企业的合作交流，建立健全政府购买气象服务的机制，鼓励私营企业参与气象服务。所以我们建议 WMO 在推进公司合作伙伴关系中，以维护全球公共利益为最高准则，以会员能力的共同进步为追求，制定国家气象水文部门和私营气象服务企业共同遵守的国际规则，正确引导和规范，使私营企业参与项目服务，共同提高全球项目能力。

谢谢大家。

[资料来源：见 VIMEO 视频网站（https://vimeo.com/726713916），引用时间：2023 年 8 月 19 日。]

1. 实践解析

本材料是中国气象局副局长余勇（YU Yong）于 2022 年 6 月 20 日参加世界气象组织（WMO）开放咨询平台（Open Consultative Platform，OCP）第三次高级别圆桌会议的讲话。本次会议以线上线下结合的方式召开，来自世界气象组织、中国气象局、英国气象局、日本气象厅的高级别官员和专家参加会议。余勇表示，中国气象局作为中国气象服务的主体，负责为政府防灾减灾提供决策服务，为公众提供气象预报和灾害性天气预报预警服务，为经济社会发展和各行业提供专业专项气象服务。余勇还介绍了中国气象局在促进气象产业健康可持续发展方面的做法，并建议 WMO 在推进公私合作伙伴关系中要以维护全球公共利益为最高准则，以共同提升会员能力为追求，制定国家气象水文部门和私营气象服务企业共同遵守的国际规则，正确引导和规范企业参与气象服务，提升全球气象服务能力。

本材料有一定难度，涉及《气象高质量发展纲要（2022—2035 年）》《促进气象产业健康持续发展》等文件的具体措施，内容专业。材料用词风格也偏正式严谨，需要仔细分析斟酌。

《气象高质量发展纲要（2022—2035 年）》即 *The 2022 to 2035 Guideline on Fostering High-Quality Meteorological Development*。2022 年 4 月 28 日，国务院印发《气象高质量发展纲要（2022—2035 年）》，纲要的发展目标包括："到 2025 年，气象关键核心技术实现自主可控，现代气象科技创新、服务、业务和管理体系更加健全；到 2035 年，气象关键科技领域实现重大突破，以智慧气象为主要特征的气象现代化基本实现。"[①]

基于影响的预报和风险的预警即 impact-based forecast and risk warnings，是指"在结合区域内气象水文地质发展趋势、防灾减灾救灾基础设施、水文地质灾害风险、致灾因子强度及持续时间等多方面因素基础上的灾害预报和预

---

① 见中国人民政府网（https://www.gov.cn/zhengce/content/2022-05/19/content_5691116.htm），引用日期：2023 年 8 月 19 日。

警"，它需要气象、水文、地质、应急等多方紧密合作，不仅说明"天气会如何变化"，而且从影响出发，说明"天气变化会影响到什么"，信息分析结果能够帮助决策者和公众更有针对性地做好灾害应对准备工作。①

"气象＋"赋能行动即 the "Met Plus" empowering action plan。国务院印发的《气象高质量发展纲要（2022—2035年）》指出，"实施'气象＋'赋能行动，推动气象服务深度融入生产、流通、消费等环节。提升能源开发利用、规划布局、建设运行和调配储运气象服务水平。强化电力气象灾害预报预警，做好电网安全运行和电力调度精细化气象服务。积极发展金融、保险和农产品期货气象服务。健全相关制度政策，促进和规范气象产业有序发展，激发气象市场主体活力"②。

2. 长难句点拨

（1）气象服务即 meteorological service，也可以缩写为 met service。该句是典型的汉语流水句（run-on sentences）。吕叔湘在《汉语语法分析问题》中首次提出了"流水句"这个概念，指出"汉语口语里特多流水句，一个小句接一个小句，很多地方可断可连"③。在处理该句时，应仔细分析小句之间的逻辑关系，其中"中国气象局是中国气象服务的主体"是意思完整的独立小句，指出了中国气象局的定位；而"负责为政府防灾减灾提供决策服务，为公众提供气象预报和灾情天气警报服务，为经济社会发展和各行各业提供专业、专项气象服务"这一系列小句是并列关系，具体阐述中国气象局针对不同的群体提供了什么样的服务；"承担着中国气象事业发展政策的制定、行使气象服务监管职责"则是基于前文的阐述，对气象局的作用进行提纲挈领的概括。因此，在口译过程中应该灵活利用语法结构和增加连词，显化逻辑。

（2）该句包含两个难点。首先是句式选择，因为原文中有"按照……要求"这个表达，口译学习者可能会受到原文的影响直译为"according to/based on the requirements of …"，导致译文比较生硬。第二个难点在于三个并列的四字词语"检测精密""预报精准"和"服务精细"，口译学习者可能会更加关注"精密""精准"和"精细"的意义差别及如何在翻译中体现这种差别。

① 吴大明：《国外基于影响的灾害预报与预警经验做法及借鉴意义》，载《中国减灾》2023年第3期，第58页。

② 见中国中央人民政府网（https://www.gov.cn/zhengce/content/2022-05/19/content_5691116.htm），引用日期：2023年8月19日。

③ 吕叔湘：《汉语语法分析问题》，商务印书馆1979年版，第27页。

在实际的口译过程中应该在语篇中理解三个词的具体意思，并充分考虑与名词的搭配。该句在翻译时建议省略"按照……要求"这个结构，将三个并列的四字词语处理为句子的谓语，再灵活运用语法手段来连接剩下的两个小句。该句可以译为："CMA strives to achieve sophisticated monitoring, precise forecasting, and a tailored service to promote the digital and smart transformation of met service with focus in four areas in particular."

（3）该句是正式发言中常见的类型，特点是句子没有主语，含有一连串的动词短语。这类句型有两种处理方法：一种是补充隐含主语"we"或者"CMA"；另一种是使用被动语态。该句选择被动句更加便捷，因为动词短语中又包含了信息密集的修饰语，利用被动句可以用动词不定式把动词短语引出，减轻记忆负担。除此之外，该句中包含的"健全……体系，开展……普查，发展……预警，推进……联动机制"看似是并列关系，但是在翻译过程中应厘清逻辑关系，体现句子层次。该句的参考译文为："First, safeguarding lives. Efforts will be made to improve the met hazard monitoring and early warning system to target specific hazards and key sectors, and to conduct reviews of hazard risks to develop impact-based forecast and risk warnings, so as to have in place a warning-led chain mechanism."

（4）该句中出现了"'气象+'赋能行动"（The "Met Plus" empowering action plan）这一表达，口译学习者应仔细了解相关背景知识，揣摩术语的翻译策略，并让这种策略成为可迁移的技巧。近年来，出现了"互联网+"（Internet plus）、"人工智能+"（AI plus）、"电子商务+"（e-commerce plus）等一系列类似表达，本质都是鼓励一个行业在深度发展之后，进行变革和创新，与其他产业融合。

（5）该句中的"公共建筑均等化"可能会对翻译造成一定的困难，因为英语中似乎没有一个完全对应的单词。实际上，"均等化"的本质是城市和乡村之间享受同样的权利，城市和农村在公共建筑使用上没有过大差距，没有过大的差距。因此，此处可以考虑翻译为"universal accessibility"。个性化一般译为"personalized"，而定制服务则译为"tailor-made service"。该句也包含多个动词短语，在口译的过程中要准确把握几个短语之间暗含的逻辑关系，让译文更加符合英语"形合"的特点。

三、口译练习

（一）英译汉

The Ocean, Our Climate and Weather

Statement by WMO Secretary-General Petteri Taalas for World Meteorological Day
(March 22, 2021)

World Meteorological Day in 2021 is devoted to the theme "the ocean, our climate and weather". It celebrates WMO's focus in connecting the ocean, climate and weather within the Earth System.

Our changing climate is warming the ocean, having a profound effect on our weather. (1) The WMO's annual *State of the Global Climate* report, shows that 2020 was one of the three warmest years on record, despite La Nina cooling in the Pacific Ocean. The past decade from 2011-2020 was the warmest on record.

Ocean heat is at record levels, ocean acidification is continuing. Sea ice is melting. The rate of sea level rise has accelerated.

During the past year, we have seen prolonged droughts that extended fire seasons throughout the world. Devastating wildfires in Australia, for example, were linked to ocean temperatures influencing drier seasonal climate pattern.

(2) Warm ocean temperatures helped fuel a record Atlantic hurricane season, and unusually intense tropical cyclones in the Indian and South Pacific Ocean. The storm surge damage in these areas demonstrated the power of the ocean and its devastating impact on coastal communities.

Non-tropical ocean storms continued to wreak havoc aboard ships, with additional losses of life and cargo at sea.

In 2020, the annual Arctic sea ice minimum was among the lowest on record. Polar communities suffered abnormal coastal flooding, and sea ice hazards as a result of melting ice.

(3) In view of this, the WMO community has a major stake in supporting

research, observations, predictions, and services for the ocean as much for as the atmosphere, land, and cryosphere.

(4) Major gaps in data over the ocean hinder our ability to accurately forecast weather at extended time scales and, more so, sub-seasonal to seasonal. The WMO Data Conference in November 2020 recognized major gaps in data, particularly over the ocean. It highlighted the need for free and open access to Earth system data, to maximize the overall economic impact of these data.

WMO has a large number of partnerships, including with the UNESCO's Intergovernmental Oceanographic Commission, to better understand, observe, and predict the ocean as part of our Earth System.

With more than 40% of the global population living within 100km of the coast, there is an urgent need to keep communities safe from the impacts of coastal hazards. WMO and its Members work to support coastal management and resilience and strengthen Multi Hazard Early Warning Systems.

Nearly 90% of world trade is carried across the sea and is exposed to the dangers of extreme maritime weather. WMO partners with the International Maritime Organization and the International Hydrographic Organization to provide standardized information, forecasts and warnings to ensure the safety of life and property at sea.

The coming Decade will be a critical one for addressing ways to adapt and mitigate to climate change impacts. WMO is helping in this effort, as a designated Nominator for the Earth Shot Prize (2021 to 2030), seeking solutions for urgent environmental challenges, including the ocean and climate.

This year is also important for the WMO to mark the start of *the United Nations Decade of Ocean Science for Sustainable Development* (2021-2030). WMO is committed to contributing with much of its work integral for the "safe ocean" "predicted ocean" and "transparent ocean" goals of the Decade.

Together with partners, WMO is striving to strengthen the Earth System Science to services.

To understand our weather and climate, we must understand our ocean. We will continue working towards this, to protect vulnerable communities and in support of *the Sendai Framework for Disaster Risk Reduction*, the *United Nations Sustainable Development Goals* (*SDGs*), *the Paris Climate Change Agreement*, and *SAMOA Pathway*.

WMO is leading several important global initiatives during the coming year to address priorities of our members:

(5) The importance of enhancing the global basic observing network and putting in place an innovative financing facility SOFF to ensure systematic weather and climate observations especially for LDCs and SIDs.

Secondly, we are creating a water and climate coalition for accelerating action on SDG 6, which is related to water.

And thirdly, we would like to ensure enhanced the Multi Hazard Early Warning System and services of all our Member Countries.

I wish you all a happy World Meteorological Day.

[资料来源：见英文巴士网（https://www.en84.com/11003.html），引用日期：2023 年 8 月 19 日。]

1. 词汇准备

State of the Global Climate report	《全球气候状况报告》
La Nina	拉尼娜现象
storm surge	风暴潮、暴潮
WMO Data Conference	WMO 数据会议
United Nations Intergovernmental Oceanographic Commission	
	政府间海洋学委员会
Decade of Ocean Science for Sustainable Development (2021—2030)	
	联合国海洋科学促进可持续发展十年（2021—2030）
Sendai Framework for Disaster Risk Reduction	《仙台减少灾害风险框架》
SAMOA Pathway	《萨摩亚途径》

2. 长难句点拨

（1）该句主要涉及气象术语，应理解并记忆常见术语。La Nina 就是拉尼娜现象，指的是赤道太平洋中部和东部洋面温度的大尺度降温，并伴有热带大气环流（即风、气压和降雨量）的变化。拉尼娜现象对天气和气候的影响通常与厄尔尼诺（El Nino）相反，与热带太平洋中部和东部海洋表面温度变暖相关，平均每 2～7 年发生一次，通常持续 9～12 个月。厄尔尼诺是厄尔尼诺南方涛动（ENSO）的温暖阶段，当太平洋既没有出现厄尔尼诺现象，也没有出现拉尼娜现象时，我们称其处于 ENSO 中性状态。[1]

（2）storm surge（风暴潮），也称"风暴增水""风暴海啸""气象海啸"或"风潮"，"是由风暴引起的水位异常上升。热带气旋或中纬度强风暴中的强风是其主因"[2]。该句描述了温度升高带来的一系列极端天气，在口译时应注意选择动词，展现原文中的效果。该句可以译为：温暖的海洋温度助推大西洋飓风季创了纪录，并使印度洋和南太平洋上的热带气旋异常强烈。这些区域的风暴潮破坏显示了海洋的威力及其对沿海地区的破坏性影响。

（3）该句中出现了多个并列名词，应注意判断其中的逻辑关系，其中ocean、atmosphere、land、cryosphere 是 research、observations、predictions、services 的对象，翻译时应根据汉语表述习惯调整语序。英语 stake 一词的英文释义是"an interest or share in an undertaking or enterprise"[3]，即（在计划等中的）重大利害关系。一个与 stake 相关的词组是 at stake（成败难料、有风险）。在翻译该句时应充分考虑语境和讲话者的意图，不建议直译为"世界气象组织在支持……研究方面有重大利益关系"，可以处理得更灵活一点，如"WMO在支持海洋、大气、陆地和冰冻圈的研究、观测、预测和服务方面肩负着重大责任"。

（4）seasonal 意为季节性，季节预报是指未来三个月或以上的预报，它属于长期的天气预报。sub-seasonal 即次季节，次季节预测通常指提前 2～6 周预测一周或几周海洋和大气平均状态。sub 是英语中常见的前缀，一般翻译为"次""亚"，如 tropics（热带）、subtropics（亚热带的）；atomic（原子的）、subatomic（亚原子的）；continent（大陆）、subcontinent（次大陆）。该句是典型的抽象名词做主语，可能会对理解造成一定的障碍。在翻译时，要进行灵活的词性转换，如该句也可译为：严重缺乏海洋数据阻碍了我们在更长时间尺度上准确预测天气的能力，尤其是对次季节到季节性的预测。

（5）该句其实是上文中提到的世界气象组织下一年的优先事项中的一项，

---

① 见世界气象组织网站（https://public. wmo. int/zh-hans/media/%E6%96%B0E9%97%BB%E9%80%9A%E7%A8%BF/wmo%E6%9C%80%E6%96%B0%E9%80%9A%E6%8A%A5%EF%BC%9A%E9%92%88%E5%AF%B9%E5%8E%84%E5%B0%94%E5%B0%BC%E8%AF%BA%E7%8E%B0%E8%B1%A1%E5%81%9A%E5%A5%BD%E5%87%86%E5%A4%87.），引用日期：2023 年 8 月 19 日。

② 见世界气象组织网站（https://public. wmo. int/zh-hans/%E9%A3%8E%E6%9A%B4%E6%BD%AE.），引用日期：2023 年 8 月 19 日。

③ 见韦氏词典网站（https://www. merriam-webster. com/dictionary/stake.），引用日期：2023 年 8 月 19 日。

是一个抽象名词短语，在翻译的时候建议补充动词"加强"或者"强调"，将短语变成一个句子，让译文更流畅。该句中还出现了大量的术语缩写，如果在口译过程中想不起来，可以直接以单词缩写的方式译出，确保信息完整、准确。

（二）汉译英

"智慧气象"
世界气象组织秘书长　佩特里·塔拉斯
2018 年世界气象日致辞

"智慧气象"——这是为 2018 年世界气象日所选的主题。如果我们再加入"水智慧"的口号，就完成了能源可持续发展的基本要素循环。

天气、气候和水对公众的福祉、健康和粮食安全至关重要。但是天气、气候和水也具有破坏性。（1）历来，像热带气旋、强降雨、热浪、干旱、冬季风暴和冻结低温等事件等高影响事件一直造成生命和生计损失。然而现在，气候变化正导致这些事件的强度和频率有所增加。

2018 年年初延续着 2017 年的状况：极端天气事件夺去了许多生命，也破坏了他们的生计。（2）2017 年，飓风季节给美国造成了前所未有的严重破坏——使得多米尼加等加勒比小岛屿发展中国家数十年的发展化为虚有。洪水使亚洲次大陆数百万人流离失所，同时，干旱也加剧了非洲之角的贫困和移民压力。

（3）毫无疑问，在世界经济论坛发布的《全球风险报告》中，环境已连续第二年成为全球领导人最关心的问题，其中包括极端天气、生物多样性丧失和生态系统崩溃、重大自然灾害、人为环境灾害，以及气候变化减缓和适应失败等。极端天气事件是其中最为突出的风险。

据记录，2017 年排在高温榜的前三名，是无厄尔尼诺事件的最热年份。由于温室气体排放造成了长期气候变化，未来地球会变暖，并伴有更多极端天气事件，水资源也将受到更多冲击。

（4）我希望所有的 WMO 成员最终都能做到"天气常备"和"气候智慧"，同时也实现"水智慧"。这对于支持可持续发展、减少灾害风险和适应气候变化的国际议程是非常必要的。

具体而言，我们需要完善多灾种早期预警系统，协调应对措施，为极端天气、气候和水事件做好准备。为了推进这一目标，WMO 将发布一个多灾种早期预警系统清单，这一重要实用工具旨在增强风险抵御能力。

（5）国家气象水文部门应以最浅显的表达为社会各界（从个人到社区再到工商各业以及决策者）准确、及时地提供针对各种事件的服务，包括从临近预报到次季节再到季节性天气和长期气候预测等。

建设极端天气和气候事件抵御能力的第一步是建立一个完善的观测网络。为了对极端天气和气候事件进行预报和预警，我们非常需要一个面向陆地、大气和海洋以及太空的广泛观测网络以获取资料。如有需要，WMO 致力于帮助各成员国升级观测基础设施，而气候服务的发展可为此提供一个很好的机会。

第二步，应基于预报科学和技术发展，建设社会对极端天气和气候事件的抵御能力。过去 30 年来，灾害性天气事件造成的人员死亡人数大幅降低，这主要归功于天气预报和预警的准确性显著提高，灾害管理部门间的协调也有所加强。随着数值天气预报的发展，今天的五天预报与 20 年前的两天预报一样好，而且数值预报还在继续发展，持续对早期预警提供支持。

实际上，早期预警是降低灾害风险的一个重要因素，可防止生命损失，还可减少灾害等危险事件造成的经济和实质性影响。

要有效发挥作用，需要让更多面临多种灾害风险的人和社区积极参与到早期预警系统中，需要促进公众对风险的认识并开展风险教育，需要有效传播信息和预警，并确保备灾成为常态。

为此，WMO 与各国国家气象水文部门合作，发起了建立全球标准化多灾种警报系统的倡议。

我们还积极与"气候风险和早期预警系统"倡议的合作伙伴以及全球气候服务框架开展合作，以便帮助最脆弱的群体。

水文服务也是抵御能力的重要组成部分。为此，主办方之一 WMO 拟于 5 月举办全球水大会，此次大会的主题是"通过水文服务实现繁荣"。

总而言之，WMO 旨在填补观测网络的空白，并打破障碍，以便所有的成员国家和地区可提供准确及时的预报和基于影响的多灾种预警服务，从而促进建设一个对天气、气候和水事件有抵御能力的社会。通过这样的行动，本组织将促进全面落实《联合国 2030 年可持续发展议程》和《仙台减灾框架》：我们将建设一个理想的世界。

我希望所有的 WMO 成员和参与 WMO 活动的人们度过愉快的世界水日（3 月 22 日）和世界气象日（3 月 23 日），也希望所有的国家都能很快实现

"天气常备""气候智慧"和"水智慧"。

[资料来源：见中国气象局网站（https：//www.cma.gov.cn/2011xwzx/2011xqxxw/2011xqxyw/201803/t20180322_464821.html），引用日期：2023 年 8 月 19 日。]

1. 词汇准备

"智慧气象"	"weather-ready, climate-smart"
"水智慧"	"water-wise"
热带气旋	tropical cyclones
《全球风险报告》	*Global Risks Report*
"天气常备"	"weather-ready"
"气候智慧"	"climate-smart"

2. 长难句点拨

（1）该句主语之前出现了一连串并列的天气事件可能会让口译学习者应接不暇，这是对口译学习者做笔记和气候专题词汇积累的考验，如果熟悉这些术语表达，则可以借助符号或者英文缩写进行记录。在听辨过程要善于提取句子主干，即"事件造成了损失"，因此，该句主语应为事件。值得注意的是，参考译文补充了 high-impact 这个修饰词，从语篇衔接上来看，效果更佳。

（2）在翻译"严重破坏"时，一般容易翻译为 severe damage，参考译文中的"the costliest"值得借鉴，将"使发展化为乌有"译为"eradicated decades of developments gains"也非常值得学习。该句中出现了一些相对陌生的地名如多米尼加（Dominica）、非洲之角（the Horn of Africa）。口译学习者应该有广博的百科知识，平时应加强百科知识的积累。该句列举了 2017 年发生的三次极端天气事件：美国飓风、亚洲洪水、非洲干旱。由于描述美国飓风那一句的信息相对其他两次事件多，翻译时可以将描述美国飓风的内容独立成一个句子，然后用 whilst 连接描述亚洲洪水和非洲干旱的两个句子，这样翻译的句子层次更加分明，逻辑更清楚。

（3）该句中包含气象主题术语极端天气（extreme weather）、生物多样性丧失（biodiversity loss）、生态系统崩溃（ecosystem collapse）、重大自然灾害（major natural disasters）、人为环境灾害（man-made environmental disasters），以及气候变化减缓（failure of climate-change mitigation）和气候变化适应失败（failure of climate-change mitigation and adaptation）。有些术语在之前的练习中

出现过，有些是第一次出现。翻译时要重视术语积累。该句由于有长列举，因此句子比较长，在翻译成英语时，可以考虑分成两句，然后用代词回指来实现语篇连贯（这也是参考译文的处理方法）。也可以用 which 引导非限制性从句，如参考译文译成："It is no surprise that, for the second consecutive year, the environment was by far the greatest concern raised by global leaders in *the World Economic Forum's Global Risks Report*, which includes extreme weather, biodiversity loss and ecosystem collapse, major natural disasters, man-made environmental disasters, and failure of climate-change mitigation and adaptation."

（4）该句中的"天气常备""气候智慧"和"水智慧"会对口译造成困难，但其实遇到这样的词不用慌，可以灵活运用英语的构词法。比如这三个词都处理为名词＋形容词，如 weather-ready、climate-smart、water-wise。

（5）该句是一个典型的长句，首先要找出主干（国家气象水文部门为社会各界提供服务），搭建译文的基本框架，再区分主要信息和次要信息。该段讲话中括号中的成分实际是在解释社会各界具体涉及哪些部门，在阅读时括号可以提示相关作用，但是在口译过程中，口译学习者无法直接看到文稿，必须在听力理解过程中根据上下文判断信息点之间的关系，并意识到这些列举是在进行补充说明。在口译时遇到多个列举的情况不妨使用 from … to … 句型。该句参考译文为："National Meteorological and Hydrological Services should be able to provide accurate and timely services for all events from nowcasting to sub-seasonal and seasonal weather and longer-term climate predictions to all—from the individual, to the community, to various business sectors and policy makers—in the most easily understandable language."

➡ 四、参考译文

● （一）口译实践

1. 英译汉

早期预警必须让人人受益
水文气象信息，助力防灾减灾

世界气象组织秘书长　佩特里·塔拉斯 2022 年世界气象日致辞
（2022 年 3 月 22 日）

请接受来自日内瓦世界气象组织秘书处的问候。

世界气象组织（WMO）的首要任务是每时每刻保护生命和生产生活免受天气、气候和水极端事件的影响。

因此，2022 年世界气象日的主题"早预警、早行动"令我非常欣慰。

这一主题赞扬了各国气象、水文部门在改进早期预警系统方面取得的巨大成就，同时也凸显了减少灾害风险的相关各方为确保早预警触发早行动所做的重要工作。

但我们不能沾沾自喜。我们面临着诸多挑战，特别是要确保早期预警到达"最后一公里"，帮助最需要它们的最脆弱人群。

世界各地极端天气频发，气候变化已经非常明显。我们正见证着更甚以往的热浪、干旱和森林火灾。大气中水汽增多，导致极端降雨和致命洪水；海洋变暖使热带风暴更为猛烈，海平面上升更加剧了其影响。

我们预计，这种负面趋势将持续下去。当前，温室气体浓度达到创纪录水平，气候变化将在未来几十年内持续，冰川融化和海平面上升将持续几个世纪。

除了减缓气候变化以外，适应气候变化也相当重要。早期预警系统正是适应气候变化的强有力手段。

去年，WMO 发表了一份关于过去 50 年间灾害的统计报告。报告显示，在过去 50 年间，1.1 万多起灾害与天气、气候和水带来的危害相关，几乎相当于每天发生一起；死亡人数达 200 万人，相当于每天死亡 115 人。在过去 50

年中，灾害数量增加了 5 倍，经济损失直线上升。

但好消息是，伤亡人数已大幅下降。在拯救生命方面，我们比以往任何时候都更出色。

超级计算机、卫星和科学进步极大提高了我们的预测准确性。手机预警和天气应用程序甚至能够覆盖偏远地区。

WMO 正在推动基于影响的天气预测。这对于高度依赖天气行事的广大用户和客户群体加强灾害防御、开展早期行动是必要的。

但我们仍任重而道远。

在 WMO 的 193 个会员中，只有一半建立了多灾种预警系统。

还有一个当务之急，就是提高多数会员基于影响的预报技能。

非洲、拉美部分地区以及太平洋和加勒比岛屿的气象水文观测网络存在重大空白，这影响了当地和全球预报能力。因此，WMO 创建了系统观测融资机制（SOFF），以推动对基本观测系统的投资、填补数据空白。

WMO 是气候风险与预警系统倡议（CREWS）的执行伙伴，该倡议旨在为气候变化下相对脆弱的国家和社区增强应变和恢复能力。

WMO 正在领导一个聚焦水与气候的新联盟，以更加关注与水有关的灾害和水资源短缺。在热带气旋、海岸洪涝、洪水和干旱等方面，我们已有成熟的计划和项目。

在日内瓦，我们与联合国减少灾害风险办公室携手成立了一个气候变化与灾害问题英才中心。

WMO 一直致力于建立一个机制，以向联合国人道主义机构提供可靠、权威的信息，从而能够在与天气有关的灾害前后优化人道主义援助。

我们正在与世界银行、欧盟、联合国开发计划署（UNDP）、绿色气候基金等融资机构合作，为早期预警服务划拨更多资金，并确保投资的可持续性。

当然，WMO 也一直致力于推动 2030 年在气候行动、可持续发展和减少灾害风险等方面的国际议程。

WMO 的愿景是：“到 2030 年，我们希望看到一个这样的世界：所有的国家，特别是最脆弱的国家，更有能力抵御极端天气、气候、水及其他环境事件的经济社会影响。”

早期预警是有效的。它们必须让人人受益，必须触发早期行动。

我恭祝大家世界气象日快乐。

［资料来源：见中国气象局网站（https://www.cma.gov.cn/2011xwzx/2011xqxxw/2011xqxyw/202203/t20220322_593688.html？from＝singlemessage），引用日期：2023 年 8 月 19 日。］

2. 汉译英

The Third High-Level Session of the Open Consultative Platform (OCP-HL-3)

YU Yong, Deputy Administrator of China Meteorological
Administration (CMA)
(June 20, 2022)

Thank you, Mr. Moderator.

This new white paper better explains the future roles played by analysts and also our responsibilities. The CMA is the national met service authority and is responsible for assisting the policy-making for the government and met forecast and hazard warning services for the general public as well as tailor-made and dedicated service for various sectors to promote socio-economic development. Therefore we formulate China meteorological development policies and regulate them in service sector.

In the past April, the State Council of China published the 2022 *to* 2035 *Guideline on Fostering High-Quality Meteorological Development*, which specified the pathway and objectives of this development. CMA strives to achieve sophisticated monitoring, precise forecasting, and a tailored service to promote the digital and smart transformation of met service with focus in four areas in particular.

First, safeguarding lives. Efforts will be made to improve the met hazard monitoring and early warning system to target specific hazards and key sectors, and to conduct reviews of hazard risks to develop impact-based forecast and risk warnings, so as to have in place a warning-led chain mechanism.

Second, enabling robust production. The "Met Plus" empowering action plan will be implemented to provide enhanced, precise and professional services to met sensitive sectors including agriculture, ocean and transportation.

Third, creating a better life for all. Service supply will be improved to have a service system that covers both the urban and the rural areas and provides personalized and tailor-made service available while ensuring the universal accessibility of a public met service.

Fourth, promoting a sound ecosystem. Climate change, monitoring evaluation will be strengthened to better protect the ecosystem and restore met barriers while promoting the reasonable utilization of climate resources.

In June this year, we published a new policy document to better nurture the met service market and to engage various players to provide guided met service, which includes, first of all, optimize the policy environment to promote the gradual opening of met data resources of different classes. Second, to improve the regulations so as to have a better monitoring and evaluation system in place, ensuring a market environment that encourages fair competition. Third, to better engage the private sector and to establish and improve government purchasing mechanism of met service and encourage the private sector to be a service provider in this sector. We therefore recommend that WMO in promoting public private partnership to uphold the utmost principle of safeguarding global public interest while seeking the common development of capacity of its members. Setting the international rules to be observed by both and NMSs and private sector. And therefore Guiding the engagement of the private sector in an appropriate manner and ultimately elevating the met service capabilities around the world.

Thank you.

[资料来源：本文是视频致辞，见 VIMEO 视频网站（https://vimeo.com/726713916），引用日期：2023 年 8 月 19 日。]

（二）口译练习

1. 英译汉

海洋，我们的气候和天气
世界气象组织秘书长　佩特里·塔拉斯2021 年世界气象日致辞
（2021 年 3 月 22 日）

2021 年世界气象日的主题是"海洋、我们的气候和天气"，以纪念世界气象组织（WMO）将地球系统内的海洋、气候和天气列为工作重点。

不断变化的气候正使海洋变暖，对天气产生了极大影响。WMO 全球气候状况年度报告显示，尽管拉尼娜现象使得太平洋降温，但 2020 年仍是有记录以来最暖的三个年份之一。2011 年到 2020 年是有记录以来最暖的十年。

这一年，海洋热量达到创纪录水平，海洋酸化仍在持续。海冰在融化，冰川、格陵兰岛和南极冰盖也在融化，海平面继续加速上升。

2020年，全球各地经历了长时间干旱，火灾季节相应延长。澳大利亚发生的毁灭性野火，与海洋温度异常带来的更干燥的季节性气候有关。

温暖的海洋助推大西洋飓风季创下纪录，并导致印度洋和南太平洋上的热带气旋异常强烈。这些区域风暴潮肆虐，显示了海洋的威力，对沿海地区造成破坏性影响。在非热带地区，海洋风暴继续威胁着海上船舶，并造成了更多生命和货物的损失。

北极2020年年度海冰最小覆盖范围，是有记录以来的最低值之一。极地社区遭遇了异常的沿海洪水和融冰带来的海冰危害。

有鉴于此，WMO全系统在支持海洋、大气、陆地和冰冻圈的研究、观测、预测和服务方面肩负着重大责任。

海上观测数据匮乏，阻碍我们在更长时间尺度上准确预测天气，特别是开展次季节到季节预测。2020年11月召开的WMO数据会议认识到，海洋数据存在重大缺口。地球系统数据的免费开放获取变得更为必要——最大化利用这些数据，能够大幅降低经济损失。

WMO拥有众多伙伴关系，包括联合国教科文组织政府间海洋学委员会，可以帮助我们更好地将海洋作为地球系统的一部分进行理解、观测和预测。

全球40%以上人口居住地距离海岸不到100公里，我们迫切需要保护这些社区的安全。WMO及其会员致力于加强多灾种早期预警系统建设，支持沿海地区管理和复原力建设。

全球近90%的贸易通过海运进行，面临着海上极端天气的威胁。WMO与国际海事组织和国际水道测量组织合作，提供标准化信息、预报和警报，确保海上生命和财产安全。

未来十年是适应和减缓气候变化关键的十年。作为"为地球奋斗奖"（2021至2030年）提名者，WMO正在寻求应对海洋和气候紧急挑战的解决方案。

今年对WMO也是重要的一年。联合国"海洋科学促进可持续发展十年（2021—2030）"从今年开启，WMO致力于推动多项工作参与到实现"安全海洋""预测海洋"和"透明海洋"的目标中来。

WMO正在与合作伙伴携手，努力使"地球系统科学"从一门科学走向一项服务。

要理解天气和气候，我们必须了解海洋。我们将不断为此努力，保护弱势社区，支持《仙台减少灾害风险框架》《联合国可持续发展目标》《巴黎气候变化协定》和《萨摩亚途径》。

在未来一年，WMO 将领导几项重要的全球倡议：

第一，进一步强化全球基本观测网络，建立创新性融资机制 SOFF（系统性观测融资机构），以确保天气和气候观测的系统性，特别是针对最不发达国家和小岛屿发展中国家。

第二，建立水与气候联盟，加快实现联合国"清洁饮水和卫生设施"的可持续发展目标。

第三，加强多灾种早期预警系统和相关服务。

祝大家世界气象日快乐。

［资料来源：见中国气象局网站（https://www.cma.gov.cn/2011xwzx/2011xqxxw/2011xqxyw/202203/t20220322_593688.html? from = singlemessage），引用日期：2023 年 8 月 19 日。］

2. 汉译英

Weather-Ready, Climate-Smart

Statement by Petteri Taalas WMO Secretary-General

for World Meteorological Day 2018

（March 18, 2018）

"Weather-ready, climate-smart"—this is the theme chosen for World Meteorological Day 2018. If we add the slogan water-wise, we complete the circle of fundamental elements that power sustainable development.

Weather, climate and water are vital to public well-being, health and food security. But they can also be destructive. High-impact events like tropical cyclones, heavy rainfall, heatwaves, droughts, winter storms and freezing temperatures have taken lives and livelihoods throughout the ages. But today, climate change is leading to an increase in the intensity and frequency of some of these events.

The start of 2018 has continued where 2017 left off—with extreme weather, which has claimed lives and destroyed livelihoods. The 2017 hurricane season was the costliest ever for the United States—and eradicated decades of developments gains in small islands in the Caribbean such as Dominica. Floods uprooted millions of people on the Asian subcontinent, whilst drought is exacerbating poverty and increasing migration pressures in the Horn of Africa.

It is no surprise that, for the second consecutive year, the environment was by far the greatest concern raised by global leaders in the World Economic Forum's *Global Risks Report*. These included extreme weather; biodiversity loss and ecosystem collapse; major natural disasters; man-made environmental disasters; and failure of climate-change mitigation and adaptation. Extreme weather events were seen as the single most prominent risk.

2017 was one of the three warmest years on record, and was the warmest year without an El Niño. Long-term climate change as a result of greenhouse gas emissions commit our planet to a warmer future, with more extreme weather and water shocks.

My wish is that all WMO Members will finally become "weather-ready" and "climate-smart" —and also water-wise. This is necessary to support the international agenda on sustainable development, disaster risk reduction and climate change adaptation.

Specifically, we need to prepare for extreme weather, climate and water through better multi-hazard early warning systems and more coordinated responses. In order to facilitate this, WMO is publishing a multi-hazard early warning systems checklist as an important, practical tool to boost resilience.

National Meteorological and Hydrological Services should be able to provide accurate and timely services for all events from nowcasting to sub-seasonal and seasonal weather and longer-term climate predictions to all—from the individual, to the community, to various business sectors and policy makers—in the most easily understandable language.

The first step in building resilience to extreme weather and climate events is the establishment of a robust network of observation. An extensive observation network— over land, air and sea as well as out of space—is imperative to provide the data to support forecasting and early warnings for extreme weather and climate events. WMO as a community is engaged to help Members who need to upgrade their observation infrastructure, and the development of climate services offers a good opportunity to do so.

Second, society's resilience to extreme weather and climate events should be developed based on advances in science and technologies for forecasting. The dramatic reduction in the lives lost due to severe weather events in the last thirty years has been largely attributed to the significant increase in accuracy of weather forecasting and warnings and improved coordination with disaster management authorities. Thanks to developments in numerical weather prediction, a 5-day forecast today is as good as a 2-day forecast twenty years ago. And that development is continuing and is supporting early warning.

Indeed early warning is a major element of disaster risk reduction. It can prevent loss of life and reduces the economic and material impacts of hazardous events including disasters.

To be effective, early warning systems need to actively involve the people and communities at risk from a range of hazards, facilitate public education on and awareness of risks, effectively disseminate messages and warnings and ensure there is a constant state of preparedness.

For this reason, WMO has launched an initiative to establish a global and standardized multi-hazard alert system in collaboration with National Meteorological and Hydrological Services worldwide.

We are also actively working with partners in the Climate Risk and Early Warning Systems initiative, as well as the Global Framework for Climate Services, to help the most vulnerable.

Hydrological services are also an important part of the resilience equation. For this reason, WMO is one of the sponsors of a major global water conference in May: Prosperity Through Hydrological Services.

In conclusion, WMO aims to fill the gaps in the observational networks and to break the barriers to the delivery of accurate and timely forecasts and impact-based multi-hazard warning services in all of its Members States and Territories in order to contribute to building a society resilient to weather, climate and water. By doing so, the Organization will contribute to fully implement *the United Nations* 2030 *Agenda for Sustainable Development* and *the Sendai Framework for Disaster Risk Reduction*: We will be building the world we want.

I wish a good World Water Day (22 March) and World Meteorological Day (23 March) to all Members and individuals engaged with WMO, with the hope that all nations will soon become weather-ready, climate-smart and water-wise.

[资料来源：见中国气象局网站（https://www. cma. gov. cn/en2014/20150311/20180323/ 2018031405/201803/t20180320_464627. html），引用日期：2023 年 8 月 19 日。]

第五章　世界旅游组织

➡️ 一、背景阅读

🔘 （一）汉语简介

【成立时间】1975年1月2日成立，2003年成为联合国专门机构，简称"世界旅游组织"。

【宗　旨】促进和发展旅游事业，使之有利于经济发展，国际相互了解，和平与繁荣以及不分种族、性别、语言或宗教信仰、尊重人权和人的基本自由，并强调在贯彻这一宗旨时要特别注意发展中国家在旅游事业方面的利益。

【成　员】159个正式成员国，6个准成员，500多个附属成员。

【组织机构】主要为全体大会、执行委员会、秘书处和地区委员会。

【总　部】西班牙马德里。

【主要负责人】现任秘书长祖拉布·波洛利卡什维利（Zurab Pololikashvili，格鲁吉亚籍）。2017年9月当选，2021年12月连任，任期至2025年。

［资料来源：中国外交部（https://www.mfa.gov.cn/web/gjhdq_676201/gjhdqzz_681964/lhg_681966/jbqk_681968/200704/t20070413_9380004.shtml），引用日期：2023年8月20日。］

🔘 （二）United Nations World Tourism Organization 英语介绍

1. What is UNWTO?

The United Nations World Tourism Organization（UNWTO，also known as WTO）is the United Nations agency responsible for the promotion of responsible, sustainable and universally accessible tourism.

As the leading international organization in the field of tourism, UNWTO promotes tourism as a driver of economic growth, inclusive development and environmental sustainability and offers leadership and support to the sector in advancing knowledge and tourism policies worldwide.

Priorities:

(1) Mainstreaming tourism in the global agenda

(2) Improving tourism competitiveness

(3) Promoting sustainable tourism development

(4) Advancing tourism's contribution to poverty reduction and development

(5) Fostering knowledge, education and capacity building

(6) Building partnerships

Members:

As an intergovernmental organization, UNWTO has 160 Member States, 6 Associate Members, 2 Observers and over 500 Affiliate Members.

2. History

➢ 1946

The First International Congress of National Tourism Bodies, meeting in London, decides to create a new international non-governmental organization to replace the International Union of Official Tourist Propaganda Organizations (IUOTPO), established in 1934.

➢ 1948

IUOTO is granted United Nations consultative status.

➢ 1967

The United Nations, following an IUOTO initiative, declares 1967 International Tourist Year (ITY), with the slogan Tourism, Passport to Peace.

➢ 1970

On 27 September, the IUOTO Special General Assembly meeting in Mexico City adopts the Statutes of the World Tourism Organization (WTO). From 1980 onwards, this day will be celebrated as "World Tourism Day".

➢ 1975

First WTO General Assembly meets in May in Madrid at the invitation of the Spanish Government. Robert Lonati is voted in as the first WTO Secretary-General and the Assembly decides to establish its headquarters in Madrid.

➢ 1976

The WTO General Secretariat is set up in Madrid on 1ˢᵗ January. The agreement is signed for WTO to become an executing agency of the United Nations Development Programme (UNDP), carrying out technical co-operation with Governments.

➢ 2003

The Assembly approves the transformation of WTO into a United Nations specialized body by resolution. The transformation is ratified at the United Nations General Assembly by resolution.

3. Governing Bodies

(1) General Assembly

The General Assembly is the principal gathering of the World Tourism Organization. It is considered the most important global meeting of senior tourism officials and high-level representatives of the private sector.

It meets every two years to approve the budget and programme of work and to debate topics of vital importance to the tourism sector. Every four years it elects a Secretary-General. The General Assembly is composed of Full Members and Associate Members. Affiliate Members and representatives of other international organizations participate as observers.

The World Committee on Tourism Ethics is a subsidiary organ of the General Assembly.

(2) Regional Commissions

UNWTO has six regional commissions—Africa, the Americas, East Asia and the Pacific, Europe, the Middle East and South Asia. The commissions meet at least once a year and are composed of all the Full Members and Associate Members from that region. Affiliate Members from the region participate as observers.

(3) Executive Council

The Executive Council is UNWTO's governing board. Its task is to take all necessary measures, in consultation with the Secretary-General, for the implementation of its own decisions and recommendations of the Assembly and report thereon to the Assembly.

The Council meets at least twice a year and consists of Full Members elected by the Assembly in the proportion of one Member for every five Full Members, in accordance with the Rules of Procedure laid down by the Assembly with a view to achieving fair and equitable geographical distribution. The term of office of Members elected to the Council is four years and elections for one-half of the Council membership are held every two years. Spain is a Permanent Member of the Executive Council. The Council elects one Chair and two Vice-Chairs from among its Members.

(4) Committees

Specialized committees of UNWTO Members advise on management and program content. These include: the Program and Budget Committee, the Committee on Statistics and the Tourism Satellite Account, the Committee on Tourism and Competitiveness, the Committee on Tourism and Sustainability, the World Committee on Tourism Ethics and the Committee for the Review of Applications for Affiliate Membership.

(5) Secretariat

The Secretariat is led by Secretary-General Zurab Pololikashvili from Georgia, who supervises 152 personnel at UNWTO's Madrid Headquarters. These are responsible for implementing UNWTO's programme of work and serving the needs of Members. The Affiliate Members are supported by a full-time Director at the Madrid Headquarters. The Secretariat also includes a regional support office for Asia-Pacific in Nara, Japan, financed by the Japanese Government. The official languages of UNWTO are Arabic, English, French, Russian and Spanish.

4. Tourism in 2030 Agenda

The year 2015 has been a milestone for global development as governments have adopted the 2030 Agenda for Sustainable Development, along with the Sustainable Development Goals (SDGs). The bold agenda sets out a global framework to end extreme poverty, fight inequality and injustice, and fix climate change until 2030. Building on the historic Millennium Development Goals (MDGs), the ambitious set of 17 Sustainable Development Goals and 169 associated targets is people-centred, transformative, universal and integrated.

Tourism has the potential to contribute, directly or indirectly, to all of the goals. In particular, it has been included as targets in Goals 8, 12 and 14 on inclusive and sustainable economic growth, sustainable consumption and production (SCP) and the sustainable use of oceans and marine resources, respectively.

Sustainable tourism is firmly positioned in the 2030 Agenda. Achieving this agenda, however, requires a clear implementation framework, adequate financing and investment in technology, infrastructure and human resources.

［资料来源：见联合国世界旅游组网站（https://www. unwto. org/who-we-are），引用日期：2023 年 8 月 20 日。］

5. 词汇表 Vocabulary List

Associate Members	准成员
Affiliate Members	附属成员
Observer	观察员
General Assembly	全体大会
Regional Commissions	地区委员会
Executive Council	执行委员会
World Tourism Day	世界旅游日
International Tourist Year（ITY）	国际旅游年
Least Developed Countries（LDC）	最不发达国家
Sustainable consumption and production（SCP）	可持续消费和生产
International Union of Official Travel Organizations（IUOTO）	国际官方旅游组织联盟
International Union of Official Tourist Propaganda Organizations（IUOTPO）	国际官方旅游宣传组织联盟

➡ 二、口译实践

● （一）英译汉

Tourism Can Help Lead the World to Recovery

Zurab Pololikashvili

Secretary-General of the United Nations World Tourism Organization

（September 26，2020）

The COVID-19 pandemic has hit global tourism harder than any other major economic sector. In an effort to contain the spread of the virus and keep their citizens safe, countries around the world introduced restrictions on international travel, bringing tourism to a standstill almost overnight. Indeed, at the peak of this lockdown, the United Nations World Tourism Organization (UNWTO) found that 100 percent of global destinations had either closed their borders to tourists completely or introduced strict measures such as compulsory quarantine for new arrivals.

(1) The sudden and unexpected fall in tourist arrivals also placed on hold the many social and economic benefits that tourism delivers. Globally, tourism supports one in ten jobs, and 80 per cent of the sector is made up of small businesses, including family operation. At the start of the crisis, UNWTO set out three possible scenarios for tourism in 2020, depending on when and how widely travel restrictions would be lifted. While it looks like we will avoid the worst-case scenario, we nevertheless expect global tourist arrivals to be down by as much as 70 percent this year compared to 2019.

The knock-on effect will be significant. The United Nations Conference on Trade and Development (UNCTAD) estimates that tourism's woes will cause global GDP to decline by as much as 1.5 per cent to 2.8 per cent. Furthermore, the fall in tourist numbers will likely translate into as many as 120 million lost jobs. (2) And, as always, the most vulnerable will suffer the most, including women and youth, for whom tourism is a leading source of opportunity, as well as those working in the informal economy.

Developing countries at greatest risk

No country has been left unscathed by the pandemic, including with regard to tourism. The effects, however, will be most profoundly felt in those destinations that are most reliant on tourism for livelihoods and economic well-being. For the majority of the world's Small Island Developing States (SIDS), as well as the least developed countries, most notably within Africa, tourism is a lifeline. On average, tourism accounts for 30 per cent of export revenues for SIDS, and in some cases this is much higher. Indeed, in Palau—the newest UNWTO member State, having officially joined in 2019—tourism generates 90 per cent of all exports.

As the United Nations Secretary-General's *Policy Brief on "COVID-19 and Transforming Tourism"* makes clear, the true cost of the pandemic's impact on tourism cannot be measured in GDP or employment figures alone. (3) Due to its unique cross-cutting nature, touching upon nearly every part of modern society, tourism is an essential contributor to the wider mission of the United Nations, including achievement of the Sustainable Development Goals. Again, as a leading employer of women, tourism leads the way in the journey towards gender equality. At the same time, tourism is a leading contributor to the promotion and protection of cultural and natural heritage, which is in jeopardy, including the ecosystems and wildlife that draw visitors to developing countries.

Building cooperation and a united response

Before the World Health Organization (WHO) officially declared COVID-19 to be a pandemic, UNWTO recognized both the unique vulnerability of tourism and also the sector's unique potential to drive wider societal recovery once the health crisis had been tackled. The visit of a UNWTO delegation to WHO headquarters in Geneva laid the foundations for the international, multi-organizational cooperation that has defined tourism's response to an unprecedented challenge.

(4) This, in turn, came on the back of heightened advocacy for tourism at the very highest political level, most notably at the European Commission at the start of the year, to make sure the sector is at the centre of the planned *European New Green Deal*, as well as at the most recent meetings of the G20 nations. This has allowed UNWTO to become an increasingly prominent voice within the United Nation. When the crisis hit, we were able to make sure that tourism was part of the conversation at both the governmental and United Nations levels.

The Global Tourism Crisis Committee, convened virtually in March and then meeting five times as the crisis evolved, brought together leading voices from member States and from the private sector. Only UNWTO was in a position to unite such a diverse sector. (5) This Crisis Committee channeled these diverse voices and concerns into a clear plan of action, the UNWTO Recommendations for Recovery. These Recommendations have been embraced across the public and private sectors and now inform recovery plans in every global region.

Sustainability takes centre stage

Central to the Recommendations is the principle that sustainability and inclusivity are at the heart of both the recovery process and the tourism sector that emerges out of this crisis. The pause in global tourism presents the global community with a chance to reassess its priorities. (6) It also allows us to put the principles that are central to the work of UNWTO—namely that tourism works for people and planet, and should be open to all and benefit all—front and centre of everything we do.

The number one priority, however, is to build trust and confidence. Only by making people feel safe and encouraging them to travel again will the benefits that tourism offers start to return. UNWTO, as the specialized United Nations agency for tourism, must lead by example. To this end, as soon as it was safely possible, in-person visits to member States resumed: to the Canary Islands and Ibiza in Spain, to Italy, and to Saudi Arabia. The decision was also made to hold a hybrid Executive Council meeting, the first in-person meeting of the tourism sector and the United Nations to be held since the start of the pandemic. This brought together 170 delegates from 24 countries, sending a clear message that safe international travel is now possible in many parts of the world, thus providing a vital confidence boost for the sector.

As tourism restarts in many parts of the world, with growing numbers of countries easing travel restrictions, the sector's position within the work of the United Nations has never been more relevant. UNWTO leads the restart guided by the principles of *the Tbilisi Declaration*, signed by our Member States in Georgia at the close of the UNWTO Executive Council (15 to 17 September 2020). *The Declaration* recognizes the importance of tourism to livelihoods, to economic prosperity and opportunity, and to preserving our shared and unique culture. Signatories also committed to building back better, prioritizing sustainability and equality, and ensuring that, as tourism builds a brighter future, nobody is left behind.

资料来源：见联合国网站（https://www. un. org/en/un-chronicle/tourism-can-help-lead-world-recovery），引用日期：2023 年 8 月 20 日。

1. 实践解析

本材料来自联合国世界旅游组织秘书长 Zurab Pololikashvili（祖拉布·波洛利卡什维利）于 2020 年 9 月 27 日发表的讲话。讲话中他表示：新冠疫情对全球旅游业造成了前所未有的重创，最受影响的是依赖旅游业的发展中国家，特别是小岛发展中国家和非洲最不发达国家。旅游业不仅对经济和就业产生影响，也是实现联合国可持续发展目标的重要组成部分。世界旅游组织积极倡导合作以应对挑战，以可持续和包容为核心，重建信任和信心，实现更加繁荣和公平的未来。这篇材料涉及话题较为常规，整体逻辑清晰，难度适中。

Small Island Developing States（SIDS）即小岛屿发展中国家。1992 年 6 月，联合国环境和发展会议在巴西里约热内卢举行，会议认为，"小岛屿发展中国家是发展中国家中一个独特的群体，在社会、经济和环境方面有其独特的脆弱性。小岛屿发展中国家包括联合国 38 个会员国，另有 20 个非联合国会员国/区域委员会联系成员"①。

Global Tourism Crisis Committee（GTCC）即全球旅游危机委员会。2020 年 3 月，世界旅游组织成立了全球旅游危机委员会，以指导世界旅游业应对疫情，并为未来的复原力和可持续增长奠定基础。该委员会由世界旅游组织成员国和附属成员的代表以及世界卫生组织、国际民用航空组织和国际海事组织组成。私营部门包括国际机场理事会、国际邮轮公司协会、国际航空运输协会和世界旅行和旅游理事会代表，以确保作出协调和有效的反应。②

Tbilisi Declaration 即《第比利斯宣言》。1977 年，联合国教科文组织和联合国环境规划署在第比利斯召开了政府间环境教育会议，阐明了环境教育的作用、目标和特点，并提出了环境教育的若干目标和原则。《第比利斯宣言》指出"环境教育在保护和改善世界环境以及世界各社区取得健康、平衡发展方面的重要作用"③。

2. 长难句点拨

（1）该句的主语是抽象名词名词短语（the sudden and unexpected fall in tourist arrivals），而实际上这个名词短语表达的是动作概念，因此在口译中，可以考虑词性转换，将形容词＋名词的偏正结构转换为名词＋动词的主谓结构（游客人数骤然下跌令人出乎意料）。该句的另一个理解困难可能是谓语部分，由于宾语过长且含有一个后置定语从句，为了保持语流流畅，讲话者使用了 place on hold sth.，听力理解过程中要等待一下宾语的出现。

（2）the most vulnerable（最弱势群体）是在各类演讲中经常涉及的一个概念，在文章中要结合语境理解具体含义。该句中的最弱势群体指的是妇女、

---

① 见联合国网站（https://www.un.org/zh/conferences/small-islands），引用日期：2023 年 8 月 20 日。

② 见联合国世界旅游组织网站（https://www.unwto.org/unwto-convenes-global-tourism-crisis-committee），引用日期：2023 年 8 月 20 日。

③ 见联合国教科文组织网站（https://unesdoc.unesco.org/ark：/48223/pf0000382407），引用日期：2023 年 8 月 20 日。

青年。英语的定语位置比较灵活，除了前置定语，往往在主句结束后还有一些补充成分，或者修饰成分，而汉语的修饰语基本都在被修饰对象之前，因此在英译汉过程中要根据句意调整句序。

（3）该句中 cross-cutting 的用法并不是常用意义，但是讲话者在句子后半段提供了解释（touching upon nearly every part of modern society），因此在语境中不难推测出文中的 cross-cutting 是跨领域的意思。英语的句子往往是围绕主语开展的，而该句的主语前有一个较长的原因状语，在听力理解过程中要使用等待策略，将前后信息相互联系才能更好地理解原文。这对短时记忆有一定要求。

（4）该句是典型的英语长难句，句子成分较多，结构复杂。该句的核心是主谓结构（This came on the back of heightened advocacy for tourism），而其他的成分通过各种语法手段聚集在主谓结构之后，on the back of 意思是在……的基础上，而 heightened advocacy for tourism 这个短语是用名词短语表示动词含义，在口译中如果将其翻译为动词则符合汉语习惯。其他的成分则应根据汉语语言习惯调整语序，参考译文为：与此同时，最高政治层面（尤其是今年年初的欧盟委员会会议）大力支持发展旅游业，以确保旅游业成为《欧洲绿色新政》计划以及二十国集团近期会议的核心。因此，世界旅游组织的声音在联合国内部越来越重要。此次危机袭来时，我们得以确保旅游业被纳入各国政府和联合国层面的对话中。

（5）该句结构并不复杂，channeled these diverse voices and concerns into a clear plan of action 可以理解成类似于 translate sth. into sth. 的用法，即汇总这些不同的声音和关切，将它们变成了明确的行动计划。the UNWTO Recommendations for Recovery 是 a clear plan of action 的同位语。

（6）该句最大困难是插入语很长，将谓语部分即 put the principles that are central to the work of UNWTO front and centre of everything we do 硬生生分成两个部分，这对于听力理解是一个挑战。鉴于插入语是 the principles that are central to the work of UNWTO 的详细解释，翻译时可以按照汉语的习惯，先译插入语，再翻译剩余的信息，让译文更加地道。

（二）汉译英

UNWTO 执行主任祝善忠在敦煌"一会一节"
开幕式暨高峰会议的致辞（上）

［第五届丝绸之路（敦煌）国际文化博览会，
第十届敦煌行·丝绸之路国际旅游节］
联合国世界旅游组织执行主任　祝善忠
（2021 年 9 月 24 日）

尊敬的各位领导，

女士们，先生们：

大家好！

（1）很高兴再次与各位相约"如意甘肃"，相聚"人类敦煌"，参加第五届丝绸之路（敦煌）国际文化博览会和第十届敦煌行·丝绸之路国际旅游节。在此，我谨代表联合国世界旅游组织向各位与会嘉宾表示诚挚的问候，并对活动的举办表示热烈的祝贺！

（2）作为全球规模最大的产业之一，旅游业贡献了全球 11% 的 GDP，每 10 个工作岗位就有 1 个与旅游业相关，是许多国家的支柱性产业。近年来，中国已成为名副其实的旅游大国。2019 年，中国的出境旅游市场规模持续增长，出境游客达到 1.55 亿人次，为世界旅游业做出了贡献。

众所周知，突如其来的新冠疫情重创了全球旅游业。（3）世界旅游组织的数据显示，2020 年全球国际游客较 2019 年减少 10 亿人次，下降 74%，旅游收入减少 1.3 万亿美元，直接影响工作岗位 1 亿至 1.2 亿个。这是自 1950 年以来，世界旅游业经历的最严重的一次危机。当前，危机仍在持续：2021 年 1 月至 5 月，国际游客较 2019 年同期减少 4.6 亿人次，下降了 85%。

世界旅游组织作为联合国的专门机构，承担了推动全球旅游发展、促进全球旅游合作的重要使命。（4）在疫情暴发的初期，世界旅游组织同世界卫生组织、国际民航组织等联合国机构及成员国共同成立了全球旅游危机管理委员会，密切关注全球疫情的形势变化，出台了一系列促进旅游业复苏的建设性意见，并积极指导各国旅游主管部门采取行动，减小疫情对旅游业的冲击。

自疫情以来，世界旅游组织多次发布《联合国世界旅游组织旅行限制报告》，系统梳理了全球 217 个国家和地区的国际旅行限制状况。（5）7 月份发布的最新报告显示，目前全球近 1/3 的国家边境处于完全关闭状态，34% 的国家边境处于半关闭状态，还有部分国家要求入境游客落地时必须提供核酸检测报告，并在指定地点进行隔离。

[资料来源：见丝绸之路（敦煌）国际文化博览会网站（https://www.gswbj.gov.cn/a/2021/11/05/11545.html），引用日期：2023 年 8 月 20 日。]

1. 实践解析

本材料选自联合国世界旅游组织执行主任祝善忠于 2021 年 9 月 24 日在"一会一节"开幕式暨高峰会议的致辞（节选）。第五届丝绸之路（敦煌）国际文化博览会和第十届敦煌行·丝绸之路国际旅游节在敦煌隆重举行。国内外嘉宾以线上线下相结合的方式，共商"一带一路"合作大计，共绘互利共赢美好蓝图。这在助推沿线国家文化交流与旅游合作，提升中华文化的国际影响力等方面取得了丰硕成果。祝善忠表示，新冠疫情对全球旅游业造成了严重冲击，而世界旅游组织作为联合国的专门机构，与其他组织合作应对危机，提出促进旅游业复苏的相关建议。材料是典型的致辞，用词风格偏正式，难度适中。

2. 长难句点拨

（1）该句中包含一些专业术语如"如意甘肃""人类敦煌""第五届丝绸之路（敦煌）国际文化博览会"和"第十届敦煌行·丝绸之路国际旅游节"。博览会和旅游节的名称直译即可，而"如意甘肃"和"人类敦煌"实际上是旅游节推广的口号，其中的文化含义对许多英语读者来说十分陌生，而此处的重点是突出博览会和旅游节的举办地点——甘肃省敦煌市，因此把地点信息传递出来即可，可以省略其他的成分。

（2）该句阐述了旅游业的作用，包含了不少数字，也包含涉及与旅游相关的表达，如"旅游大国""出境旅游市场""出境游客"等，在口译过程中应准确传达这些词汇。这里要注意"旅游大国"的含义，实际表达的意思是说中国是主要的旅游目的地，因此应译为 a major tourism destination。旅游专题也有许多高频词，需要熟悉，如"出境旅游"（outbound tourism）、出境游客（outbound tourists/tourists traveling overseas）、入境旅游（inbound tourism）、入境游客（inbound tourists）、边境游（border tourism）、自由行（independent travel）、跟团游（package tour）、自驾游（self-driving tour）。除了词汇方面，该句在翻译的时候应注意语篇衔接，可以通过代词等衔接手段让语篇更加流畅。

（3）该句中包含多个不同数位的数字以及关于数字变化趋势的表达，对数字口译技巧以及表达储备要求较高。在口译时，主语的选择尤为重要，如果使用 sth. witness/saw … 这个句型，信息的组织就会比较轻松。在翻译时要适当增补连词，让逻辑关系更加清楚。

（4）该句是汉语典型的流水句，包含了一系列动词（"成立""关注""出台""指导""减小"）。在口译中应从句意出发，进行合理断句，然后根据英语习惯和逻辑进行语言重组。该句包含两个层次的信息：全球旅游危机管理委员会的成立和委员会采取的措施。由于委员会采取的措施较多，拆成两个英语句子既减轻口译学习者组织译文的压力，也有助于听众理解。

（5）该句主要难点是词汇和句型选择，即如何准确、流畅地翻译"边境完全关闭""半关闭"，这对语言表达提出了一定的挑战。要充分理解原文，使用系表结构而省略"状态"这个词。除此之外，句式的选择也要注意，英文忌重复，因此，对于"1/3 的国家边境处于完全关闭状态，34% 的国家边境处于半关闭状态"，在口译中，后半句可以省略，让译文更简洁。

➡️ 三、口译练习

🔵 （一）英译汉

Making Tourism Stronger and Ready for the Future
（UNWTO's 2022 New Year Message excerpt）
Zurab Pololikashvili Secretary-General of the United Nations

World Tourism Tourism Organization

（December 27, 2022）

This has been another challenging year for our societies, our economies and tourism. （1）Many millions of jobs and businesses remain in peril, at the mercy of an evolving crisis and of the actions of governments.

However, we are by no means in the same place we were when the pandemic was declared in March 2020. In fact, we have succeeded in laying the foundations to restart tourism around the pillars of sustainability, innovation, people and investing for a resilient future.

Working together

Over the past year, much progress has been made in rolling out vaccinations and in both detecting and treating COVID-19. We have also seen significant progress made in finding the right balance between keeping people safe and keeping the vital lifeline of tourism intact, as illustrated by UNWTO's effective collaboration with the World Health Organization (WHO) since the very start of the pandemic.

A collaborative and multilateral approach is and must remain at the centre of capitalizing on the lessons we have learned in such a short space of time.

Ensuring harmonized travel protocols has been our message since day one. They are at the heart of tourism's restart in many parts of the world, most notably in the Northern Hemisphere destinations during the peak summer months.

We are also encouraged by the resilience and determination coming from the tourism sector itself, as well as from our Member States.

Like never before, the pandemic has made clear tourism's relevance to our economies and societies. Tourism is now part of the global conversation and at the heart of both national and international recovery action plan.

Expanding on our mandate

(2) Interest in UNWTO's innovation and start-up competitions keeps growing, showcasing the talent we have unleashed, and our shared readiness to hear new voices and embrace new ideas.

Our global innovation ecosystem is now made up of more than 12000 start-ups from 160 countries, with US $83 million mobilized and 300 corporate partners currently working on new tourism technologies.

And UNWTO's education Programs are reaching unprecedented numbers of people, welcoming more than 20000 students from 100 countries in just 18 months. We promote lifelong learning thanks to partnerships with the world's top five institutions in tourism and hospitality. Together, IE university, Les Roches, Glion Institute of Higher Education, École Ducasse and the Swiss Education Group offer 19 online courses in Spanish, English and Arabic—a true ' online university of universities'.

(3) Underpinning it all are data analytics on tourism investments powered by

our partnership with the *Financial Times*. Through this, we have produced the first UNWTO tourism investment guidelines, which we are now scaling up to create guidelines for doing tourism businesses by country.

Restarting tourism is unthinkable without green investments. We are collaborating with institutions such as the World Bank's International Finance Corporation and the Inter-American Development Bank. To date, more than 200 investors are part of UNWTO's global investment network advancing critical work such as supporting hotel chains from 50 countries to become more sustainable.

For people and planet

Tourism is ready to do the hard work and live up to its responsibilities to people and planet, as demonstrated by the huge interest we have received in *the Glasgow Declaration on Climate Action in Tourism*, launched at the UN Climate Summit COP26. (4) We are receiving a growing number of commitments to halve emissions by 2030 and to reach Net Zero by 2050 at the latest, with Member countries, individual destinations, global companies and local players as well as media outlets, hundreds are on board, and counting.

And for people, we are making sure the benefits tourism offers are enjoyed as widely and fairly as possible. That includes establishing the sector as a driver of rural development, as celebrated through the Best Tourism Villages by UNWTO initiative. (5) Launched to great enthusiasm this year, 44 villages from 32 countries were granted the recognition during our recent General Assembly, for showing a commitment to tourism development in line with the Sustainable Development Goals.

The 24th UNWTO General Assembly in Madrid brought our Members together to speak with one voice. Members commended UNWTO's work done during the pandemic and its vision for the future of both the Organization and the sector, endorsing key initiatives such as a first *International Code for the Protection of Tourists*. This landmark legal framework is designed to restore trust in travel, a vital ingredient for recovery.

I am very grateful for the wide support of our Members, who have put their trust in me to serve a second term as UNWTO Secretary-General.

......

The future begins now.

The way in which the pandemic has developed over the closing weeks of the year gives us all reason for concern and to again put public health above everything else.

But recent developments again validate our initial position: the only way forward is through collaboration and actions that are based on evidence rather than on speculation or political strategy.

(6) UNWTO is in a good place to use the achievements of 2021 as a springboard for building a better tourism in the years to come, with the sector ready to return once conditions are right. It is in this spirit that I wish everybody a safe and healthy 2022. UNWTO stands by your side, to keep on working together for our joint progress.

[资料来源：见世界旅游组织网站（https://www.unwto.org/news/making-tourism-stronger-and-ready-for-the-future），引用日期：2023 年 8 月 20 日。]

1. 词汇准备

to capitalize on …	充分利用；从……中获得更多的好处
Les Roches	瑞士理诺士国际酒店管理学院
Glion Institute of Higher Education	格里昂酒店管理学院
École Ducasse	法国杜卡斯学院
Swiss Education Group	瑞士教育集团
the Glasgow Declaration on Climate Action in Tourism	《格拉斯哥旅游气候行动宣言》
Inter-American Development Bank	美洲开发银行

2. 长难句点拨

（1）该句结构并不复杂，句子主干是 Many millions of jobs and businesses remain in peril。in peril 与 in danger 词组意思相同，即岌岌可危。at the mercy of 短语连接了两个并列的宾语，是对上文的补充说明。这个词组的意思是 "wholly in the power of: with no way to protect oneself against"①，此处可以译为 "受制于不断演变的危机和政府行动"。

（2）该句结构也不复杂，主干是 Interest in UNWTO's innovation and start-up competitions keeps growing。showcasing 这个动名词短语是一个伴随状语，而 our shared readiness to hear new voices and embrace new ideas 也是对主干的补充说

---

① 见韦氏词典网站（https://www.merriam-webster.com/dictionary/at%20the%20mercy%20of），引用日期：2023 年 8 月 20 日。

明。句子中含有多个抽象名词,口译中应进行词性转换。

(3) 第一句采用了倒装结构,避免句子主语过长产生头重脚轻的感觉。正确的语序应该是 Data analytics on tourism investments powered by our partnership with the *Financial Times* are underpinning it all。这可能会对听力理解造成困难。除此之外,第二句中含有一个非限制性定语从句,定语从句的结构也比较复杂,因此,在口译过程中可以采取顺序驱动的技巧,参考译文为:支撑这一切的是我们与《金融时报》合作提供的旅游投资数据分析。通过这些数据分析,我们制作了第一个联合国世界旅游组织的旅游投资指南,现在我们正在扩大其规模,以为各国的旅游业务提供指导。

(4) 该句是一个长句,结构并不复杂,"We are receiving a growing number of commitments" 是句子的主干,to halve 引导的短语和 to reach 引导的短语是对 commitments 的修饰说明,with 连接了一个独立主格结构。该句也建议采取顺句驱动的方式,参考译文为:我们收到了越来越多的承诺,到2030年将排放量减半,最迟在2050年达到净零排放,成员国、个别目的地、全球公司和当地参与者以及媒体机构,有数百人加入,而且还在不断增加。

(5) 在英语中,当行为的施事者在上下文中不言自明时,往往采用被动态来论述,让原文简洁干脆。但是在汉语中,施事者即使无须言明也不需要通过被动态来表达,可以通过一些语言结构实现意义被动。因此,对原文中的被动结构可以处理得更加灵活。参考译文为:今年,来自32个国家的44个村庄在我们最近的大会上获得了认可,因为它们展示了按照可持续发展目标发展旅游业的承诺,这引起了极大的热情。

(6) 该句是一个典型的长句,句子里信息比较密集,在口译过程中首先要厘清意群之间的关系,然后进行切分,并采用顺句驱动的技巧:"UNWTO is in a good place // to use the achievements of 2021 as a springboard // for building a better tourism in the years to come //, with the sector ready to return //once conditions are right."参考译文为:世界旅游组织可以很好地利用2021年的成就作为跳板,在未来几年建设更好的旅游业,一旦条件成熟,旅游业将恢复发展。

（二）汉译英

UNWTO 执行主任祝善忠在敦煌"一会一节"
开幕式暨高峰会议的致辞（下）

［第五届丝绸之路（敦煌）国际文化博览会，
第十届敦煌行·丝绸之路国际旅游节］

联合国世界旅游组织执行主任　祝善忠

（2021 年 9 月 24 日）

女士们，先生们，

（1）2013 年，中国国家主席习近平提出"一带一路"倡议，为世界提供了一个充满东方智慧的共同繁荣发展方案。八年来，"一带一路"朋友圈不断扩大，合作伙伴越来越多，合作质量也越来越高，发展前景越来越好。共建"一带一路"不仅为中国的开放发展开辟了新天地，同时也为世界各国提供了新机遇。

世界旅游组织充分认识到中国政府为促进"一带一路"国家间的双赢合作所做出的努力。（2）在中国政府强有力的领导下，中国的疫情防控取得了重大阶段性胜利，旅游业得以率先复苏。当前中国国内旅游市场已呈现出供需两旺的态势，为全球旅游业的复苏树立了典范。

（3）在前不久召开的金砖国家旅游部长会上，中方表示愿与各方共同探讨、建立健康码国际互认机制，为国际旅游复苏探索可行之路。中国用行动诠释了国际合作与交流的重要性，这是推进全球旅游业复苏的关键之举，体现了旅游大国的担当。

（4）甘肃省文化底蕴深厚，旅游资源独特且丰富。在省委省政府的正确领导下，甘肃省旅游产业发展迅猛，取得了可喜的成绩。此次丝绸之路国际文化博览会与国际旅游节的召开意义深远，它为全球文化与旅游业的复苏与发展提供了一个开放、包容的合作平台。世界旅游组织充分肯定甘肃省"一会一节"在全球文化与旅游发展中的积极作用，并将继续通过"丝绸之路项目"，加大对甘肃省"一带一路"文化与旅游产业发展的支持。（5）世界旅游组织还将携手世界银行，为甘肃省的文旅产业国际合作、文旅品牌国际推广、文化旅游机构能力建设等方面出谋划策，共同寻找产业发展的新机遇！

最后，我谨代表联合国世界旅游组织，感谢各级政府在这一特殊时期为"一会一节"筹备工作所付出的努力，预祝本次盛会取得圆满成功！

谢谢大家！

[资料来源：见丝绸之路（敦煌）国际文化博览会网站（https://www.gswbj.gov.cn/a/2021/11/05/11545.html），引用日期：2023 年 8 月 20 日。]

1. 词汇准备

丝绸之路（敦煌）国际文化博览会
The Silk Road (Dunhuang) International Cultural Expo
敦煌行·丝绸之路国际旅游节
Dunhuang Tour—Silk Road International Tourism Festival
金砖国家旅游部长会　　　　　BRICS Ministers of Tourism
健康码　　　　　　　　　　COVID health certificates
"丝绸之路项目"　　　　　　"Silk Road programs"
能力建设　　　　　　　　　　to build capacity

2. 长难句点拨

（1）该句中包含了一些中国特色表达，如"东方智慧""朋友圈"和"开辟新天地"，在口译中要思考是否保留其中的修辞效果，如何在准确传递原文含义的同时让英语听众理解。除此之外，句中包含了一些并列结构，如"合作伙伴越来越多，合作质量也越来越高，发展前景越来越好"，讲话者重复了三个相似结构，形成了排比，这是汉语的常用的修辞手法。但是英语忌重复，因此，口译中可以放弃排比结构，以传递意义为主。

（2）该句中包含了一些中国特色词汇，如"重大阶段性胜利""率先复苏""供需两旺"，在翻译这些词汇时，要充分考虑中西文化的差异。例如，"中国的疫情防控取得了重大阶段性胜利"在中国文化背景下非常好理解，但直译则显得奇怪，建议释义为"疫情防控取得重大进展""供需两旺"使用了四字格结构让语言更简练、有节奏，该词实际表达了"供应和需求都很旺盛"之意，在口译中清楚传递这一层意义即可。该句可以译为："Under the strong leadership of the Chinese government, significant progress had been made in the prevention and control of the COVID-19 pandemic, with tourism leading the way in recovery. At present, the strong rebound of tourism on the supply and demand sides in China provides a beacon of hope for the recovery of global tourism."

（3）该句中包含一个专业术语"健康码国际互认机制"，在翻译时应充分考虑文化差异。健康码是我国首创的、针对新冠肺炎疫情防控推出的个人健康信息、活动信息追踪研判系统。尽管其他国家也有类似的措施，但并不都以二维码形式存在，如法国是健康通行证，而澳大利亚是数字疫苗证书。因此，在口译中应该采取释义的策略，将"健康码"解释为 health certificates，方便具有不同文化背景的听众理解。

（4）该句没有生词，句子结构也简单，大部分口译学习者都可以准确翻译，可译为"Gansu Province has a profound cultural heritage and unique and abundant tourism resources."但是考虑到本发言是在旅游博览会和旅游文化节场景下，讲话者旨在突出甘肃丰富的旅游资源，该译文则显得较为平淡，无法达到交际效果。该译文中的 has 此处可以考虑用 excel in 这个表达，既能够让译文简洁、地道，还能够体现对"甘肃旅游资源很丰富"的传达。

（5）该句是汉语中典型的长状语结构，状语包含多个并列名词短语，即"文旅产业国际合作、文旅品牌国际推广、文化旅游机构能力建设"，需要在翻译时处理好这些并列内容的语序和表达方式。鉴于英语"前封闭、后开放"的特点，宜先翻译句子主干"世界旅游组织与世界银行合作为甘肃出谋划策"，再将其他部分以目的状语形式译出。

➡ 四、参考译文

● （一）口译实践

1. 英译汉

旅游业有助于引领世界实现复苏

联合国世界旅游组织秘书长　祖拉布·波洛利卡什维利

（2020 年 9 月 26 日）

全球旅游业是受 2019 年新型冠状病毒大流行冲击最严重的经济部门。为了遏制病毒传播，保护公民安全，世界各国对国际旅行采取了限制措施，导致旅游业几乎在一夜之间陷入停滞。事实上，联合国世界旅游组织（世旅组织）发现，在各国采取封锁措施的高峰时期，全球所有旅游目的地或完全向游客关闭了边境，或采取了严格的措施，例如对外来人员实行强制隔离。

　　游客人数的骤然下跌令人出乎意料，这也使旅游业无法继续产生社会及经济效益。旅游业为全球十分之一的人口提供就业机会，其中，家庭经营等小型企业占旅游业的80%。在这场危机爆发之初，世旅组织根据各国可能取消旅行限制的时间和程度，对2020年旅游业的情况提出了三种设想。我们似乎能避免最坏的情况出现，但今年的全球游客人数预计仍将比2019年减少70%。

　　这将引发一系列重大的连锁反应。联合国贸易和发展会议估计，旅游业所面临的困境将导致全球国内生产总值损失1.5%～2.8%。此外，游客人数的下降可能会导致多达1.2亿人失业。而且，妇女和青年等最弱势群体将依旧受到最大的影响。对于妇女、青年和非正规经济部门的从业人员来说，旅游业是他们最主要的就业机会来源。

发展中国家面临更大的风险

　　没有哪个国家未受此次大流行病的影响，各国的旅游业都未能幸免于难。但是，最依赖旅游业提供生计和经济福祉的旅游目的地受大流行病的影响将最大。旅游业是世界上大多数小岛屿发展中国家和最不发达国家的生命线，其中最不发达国家大多位于非洲。平均而言，旅游业创造的收入占小岛屿发展中国家出口总收入的30%，在某些国家，这一比例甚至更高。例如，帕劳于2019年正式加入了世旅组织，是加入时间最晚的成员国，该国的旅游业收入占出口总收入的90%。

　　联合国秘书长在《政策简报：2019年新型冠状病毒病和旅游业转型》中明确指出，大流行病给旅游业所造成的真实影响无法仅用国内生产总值或就业数据来衡量。旅游业具有独特的跨领域性质，几乎涵盖了现代社会的各个方面。因此，旅游业为履行联合国更广泛的使命（包括实现可持续发展目标）作出了巨大贡献。正如前文所说，旅游业为妇女提供了主要的就业机会，因此，旅游业在促进性别平等方面处于领先地位。同时，旅游业也为宣传和保护面临威胁的文化和自然遗产做出了重要的贡献，这些遗产包括吸引游客前往发展中国家的生态系统和野生动植物。

建立合作并做出团结一致的应对

　　在世界卫生组织（世卫组织）正式宣布2019年新型冠状病毒病为大流行病之前，世旅组织就已经认识到了旅游业特有的脆弱性，还认识到这场卫生危机一旦得到解决，旅游业在推动实现更广泛的社会复苏方面具有独特潜力。世旅组织代表团访问了世卫组织日内瓦总部，为实现国际化、跨组织的合作奠定了基础，而这一合作为旅游业应对此次前所未有的挑战指明了方向。

　　与此同时，最高政治层面（尤其是今年年初的欧盟委员会会议）大力支持发展旅游业，以确保旅游业成为《欧洲绿色新政》计划以及二十国集团近期会议的核心。因此，世旅组织的声音在联合国内部越来越重要。此次危机袭来时，我们得以确保旅游业被纳入各国政府和联合国层面的对话中。

今年3月，由世旅组织成立的全球旅游危机委员会在线上召开了首次会议。在此次疫情期间，委员会共在线上举行了五次会议，汇聚了来自成员国和私营部门的主要声音。只有世旅组织可以将如此多样的旅游业联合起来。全球旅游危机委员会将这些不同的声音和关切汇总起来，制订了一份明确的行动计划，即世旅组织关于旅游业复苏的建议。这些建议已被公共和私营部门采纳，并为全球各个地区的复苏计划提供了参考。

可持续性成为焦点

以上建议的中心原则是，需要将可持续性和包容性作为复苏和此次危机后旅游业的核心要素。全球旅游业的停滞为国际社会提供了重新评估优先事项的机会。世旅组织工作的重要原则是，旅游业应为人类和地球服务，应该向所有人开放并造福所有人。这次停滞也促使世旅组织把这些原则作为一切工作的中心。

但是，首要任务是建立信任和信心。只有让人们感到安全并鼓励他们再次旅行，旅游业的好处才能重新显现。作为联合国专门负责旅游业的机构，世旅组织必须以身作则。因此，在安全可行的情况下，世旅组织立即恢复了对成员国的访问，访问了西班牙的加那利群岛和伊维萨岛、意大利和沙特阿拉伯。世旅组织还决定举行一次执行委员会混合会议，这是自大流行病暴发以来旅游部门和联合国首次举办的线下会议。来自24个国家和地区的170名代表齐聚一堂，传达了一个明确的信息，即世界许多地方现在都可以安全开展国际旅行，这为旅游业的恢复增强了信心。

如今，世界许多地方已经重新开放旅游业，越来越多的国家放宽了旅行限制，旅游业在联合国工作中的地位比以往任何时候都更加重要。2020年9月15日至17日，世旅组织执行委员会会议在格鲁吉亚举行。世旅组织成员国在会议结束时签署了《第比利斯宣言》。在该宣言的指导下，世旅组织将领导旅游业重启。《第比利斯宣言》认识到旅游业的重要性：旅游业能够维持生计，促进经济繁荣，创造经济机会，并帮助维护我们共同的独特文化。签署国还承诺重建更美好的家园，优先考虑可持续性和平等，并确保在借助旅游业创造更光明的未来时，不让任何一个人掉队。

[资料来源：见联合国网站中文版（https://www.un.org/zh/106007），引用日期：2023年8月20日。]

2. 汉译英

UNWTO Executive Director ZHU Shanzhong's Speech at the Opening Ceremony and Summit of the Expo and Festival (I)

[The 5th Silk Road (Dunhuang) International Cultural Expo,
the 10th Dunhuang Tour-Silk Road International Tourism Festival]

ZHU Shanzhong, UNWTO Executive Director

(September 24, 2021)

Ladies and gentlemen,

Greetings!

It's a great privilege to be back with you at the Fifth Silk Road (Dunhuang) International Cultural Expo and the Tenth Dunhuang Tour Silk Road International Tourism Festival in Dunhuang, an ancient city in Gansu province. On behalf of the UNWTO, I send cordial greetings to all distinguished guests and congratulations to both great events!

As one of the largest industries worldwide, tourism contributes 11% to global GDP. That translates into one in ten jobs in the world related to tourism and the industry has been a pillar supporting economic development for many nation. Over the last several years, China has become a major tourism destination. China's outbound tourism in 2019 has seen continuous growth as tourists traveling overseas reached 155 million, a significant contribution to world tourism.

It became apparent to everyone that the COVID-19 outbreak hit the breaks hard on international tourism. 2020 saw a dramatic plunge in international tourists, down 74% from 2019, and a loss of USD 1.3 trillion in revenue, resulting in a risk to 100 million to 120 million related jobs, according to the data from the UNWTO. This has been the most severe crisis in the tourism industry since 1950. This year the ongoing pandemic continues to looms large over the industry globally; from January to May, international travelers dropped by an astonishing 460 million, down 85% compared to the same period in 2019.

The UNWTO is the United Nations agency responsible for the promotion of universally accessible tourism. In the early stage of the COVID-19 outbreak, UNWTO, together with other agencies of the UN such as the WHO and ICAO, jointly established the UNWTO Global Tourism Crisis Committee. The committee provides constructive input on how to recover tourism by closely following the evolving pandemic dynamics. It proactively provides guidance to countries on COVID-19 prevention and control to minimize the impact on their tourism industries.

Since the outbreak, the agency has frequently published its *Travel Restrictions Report*, providing an overall picture of travel restrictions in 217 nations and region. The latest-published issue on July indicates that 33% of the world's outbound traffic remains closed, 34% semi-closed and some other countries require new arrivals to present COVID-19 nucleic acid test results and to be quarantined.

（资料来源：参考译文来自"敦煌一会一节"直播号视频字幕转写。）

（二）口译练习

1. 英译汉

加强旅游业，为未来做好准备
（联合国世界旅游组织 2022 年新年致辞节选）
联合国世界旅游组织秘书长　祖拉布·波洛利卡什维利
（2022 年 12 月 27 日）

对我们的社会、经济和旅游业来说，这又是充满挑战的一年。数以百万计的工作岗位和企业仍然岌岌可危，受制于不断演变的危机和政府行动。

然而，我们绝不是处于 2020 年 3 月宣布大流行病时的状态。事实上，我们已经成功地围绕着可持续发展、创新、人民和投资一个有弹性的未来等支柱，奠定了重新启动旅游业的基础。

共同努力

在过去的一年里，推广疫苗接种以及检测和治疗 COVID-19 取得了很大进展。我们还看到，在保护人民安全和保持旅游业的重要生命线之间取得平衡的长足进步，世界旅游组织与世界卫生组织（WHO）自新冠大流行开始以来的有效合作就是一个例证。

要想利用好我们在如此短的时间内所学到的经验，我们必须并继续把合作和多边的方法置于核心地位。

从第一天起，我们就把确保统一的旅游协议作为我们的信条，它们是世界许多地区特别是北半球目的地在夏季高峰期间旅游业重新启动的核心。

我们也为旅游业本身以及我们的成员国所表现出的韧性和决心感到鼓舞。

这场大流行病比以往任何时候都清楚地表明了旅游业与我们的经济和社会的关系。旅游业现在是全球对话的一部分，是国家和国际恢复行动计划的核心。

扩大我们的任务范围

人们对世旅组织的创新和创业竞赛的兴趣不断增加，展示了我们所释放的天赋，以及我们对倾听新声音和接受新想法做好了准备。

我们的全球创新生态系统现由来自 160 个国家的 12,000 多家初创企业组成，筹集了 8,300 万美元，目前有 300 家企业合作伙伴正在研究新的旅游技术。

而世旅组织的教育项目正在影响着前所未有之多的人，在短短 18 个月内就接待了来自 100 个国家的 20,000 多名学生。得益于与世界排名前五的旅游业和酒店业院校的合作，我们促进了终身学习。IE 大学、瑞士理诺士国际酒店管理学院、格里昂酒店管理学院、法国杜卡斯学院和瑞士教育集团共同提供 19 门西班牙语、英语和阿拉伯语的在线课程——形成了一所真正的"大学中的在线大学"。

支撑这一切的是我们与《金融时报》合作提供的旅游投资数据分析。通过这些数据分析，我们制作了第一个联合国世界旅游组织的旅游投资指南，现在我们正在扩大其规模，以为各国的旅游业务提供指南。

如果没有绿色投资，重启旅游业是不可想象的。我们正在与世界银行的国际金融公司和美洲开发银行等机构合作。迄今为止，有 200 多个投资者加入了世旅组织的全球投资网络，推进关键工作，例如支持 50 个国家的连锁酒店的可持续发展。

为了人类和地球

旅游业已经准备好艰苦奋斗，履行其对人类和地球的责任，这也反映在联合国气候峰会 COP26 上，峰会发布的《格拉斯哥旅游气候行动宣言》对旅游业表现出巨大兴趣。越来越多人承诺，到 2030 年将排放量减半，并最迟在 2050 年实现净零排放，这包括我们的成员国、旅游目的地、跨国公司和本地公司以及媒体机构，成百上千人已经加入，并且数量还在增加。

对于人们来说，我们正在确保大家尽可能广泛和公平地享受旅游业带来的好处。这包括将旅游业确立为农村发展的驱动力，正如联合国世界旅游组织的"最佳旅游乡村"倡议所庆祝的那样。今年，来自 32 个国家的 44 个村庄在我们最近的大会上获得了认可，因为它们展示了按照可持续发展目标发展旅游业的承诺，这引起了极大的热情。

在马德里举行的第 24 届联合国世界旅游组织大会上，成员们齐聚一堂，呼声一致。成员们赞扬了世旅组织在新冠大流行期间所做的工作及其对世旅组织和旅游业未来的愿景，认可了诸如第一部《游客保护国际守则》等关键举措。这一具有里程碑意义的法律框架旨在恢复对旅游的信任，这是复苏的一个重要因素。

我非常感谢我们成员的广泛支持，他们对我担任世旅组织秘书长的第二个任期给予了信任。

……

未来始于现在

大流行病在今年最后几周的发展方式让我们有理由感到担忧，并再次将公共健康置于一切之上。

但最近的事态发展再次证实了我们最初的立场：前进的唯一途径是基于证据，而不是投机或政治策略的合作和行动。

世旅组织可以很好地利用 2021 年的成就作为跳板，在未来几年建设更好的旅游业，一旦条件成熟，旅游业将恢复发展。本着这一精神，我祝愿大家在 2022 年平安健康。联合国世界旅游组织与各位同行，继续携手合作，共同进步。

（资料来源：本篇译文为编者提供并整理。）

2. 汉译英

**UNWTO Executive Director Zhu Shanzhong's Speech at the
Opening Ceremony and Summit of the Expo and Festival（Ⅱ）**
［The 5th Silk Road（Dunhuang）International Cultural Expo, the
10th Dunhuang Tour-Silk Road International Tourism Festival］
ZHU Shanzhong, UNWTO Executive Director
（September 24，2021）

Ladies and gentlemen,

In 2013, President Xi Jinping announced "The Belt and Road Initiative", a plan for the world inspired by Oriental wisdom. Eight years on, "the Belt and Road" circle of friends has expanded beautifully, witnessing more friends and partners joining hands to build "the Belt and Road" together. Thus "the Belt and Road" cooperation has both created new horizons for China's development and opening-up, and generated new opportunities for all participating countries.

The UNWTO has fully recognized China's efforts to promote win-win corporation between the Initiative's participants. Under the strong leadership of the Chinese government, significant progress had been made in the prevention and control of the COVID-19 pandemic, with tourism leading the way in recovery. At present, the strong rebound of tourism on the supply and demand sides in China provides a beacon of hope for the recovery of global tourism.

At the recent meeting of BRICS Ministers of Tourism, China showed its willingness to work with all parties on a way to mutually recognize each other's COVID health certificates as a feasible means of recovering global travel. These concrete actions define the importance of international exchanges and cooperation and are fundamental for a recovery. They demonstrate China's commitment as a major tourism destination.

Gansu Province excels in its cultural riches and unique and abundant tourism offerings. Under the wise leadership of the Gansu provincial government, its tourism industry is booming. The expo and the festival have great importance in creating inclusive opportunities for the recovery of global tourism and culture. The UNWTO has given a full recognition of the active role played by both the expo and the festival hosted by the Gansu government. With the "Silk Road programs", we will therefore render greater support to Gansu for is tourism and cultural industries under "the Belt and Road". Moreover, our agency will work together with the World Bank to help develop ways for Gansu to promote international tourism and cultural cooperation, market their brands and build capacity for tourist organization.

In conclusion, on behalf of the UNWTO, I thank all levels of government for their efforts to make both events a reality amid these challenging times and wish both the expo and the festival a great success!

Thank you!

（资料来源：参考译文来自"敦煌一会一节"直播号视频字幕转写。）

第六章　联合国教育、科学及文化组织

➡️ 一、背景阅读

🔘 （一）汉语简介

【成立时间】1945 年，《联合国教育、科学及文化组织组织法》在伦敦通过，1946 年该组织成立，同年成为联合国专门机构，简称为"联合国教科文组织"。

【宗　旨】通过教育、科学及文化促进各国间合作，对和平与安全做出贡献，以增进对正义、法治及联合国宪章所确认之世界人民不分种族、性别、语言或宗教均享人权与基本自由之普遍尊重。

【成　员】194 个成员和 12 个准成员。

【组织机构】主要为大会、执行局和秘书处。

【主要负责人】总干事奥黛丽·阿祖莱（Audrey Azoulay，女，法国籍）。2017 年 11 月当选，2021 年 11 月连任，任期至 2025 年。

【总　部】法国巴黎。

［资料来源：见中国外交部（https://www.mfa.gov.cn/web/gjhdq_676201/gjhdqzz_681964/lhg_681966/jbqk_681968/200704/t20070413_9380010.shtml），引用日期：2023 年 8 月 20 日。]

🔘 （二）UNESCO 英语介绍

1. What is UNESCO?

UNESCO is the United Nations Educational, Scientific and Cultural Organization. It seeks to build peace through international cooperation in education, sciences and culture. UNESCO's programs contribute to the achievement of the Sustainable Development Goals defined in the 2030 Agenda, adopted by the UN General Assembly in 2015.

2. History

As early as 1942, in wartime, the governments of the European countries, which were confronting Nazi Germany and its allies, met in the United Kingdom for the Conference of Allied Ministers of Education (CAME). World War II was far from over, yet those countries were looking for ways and means to rebuild their education systems once peace was restored. The project quickly gained momentum and soon acquired a universal character. New governments, including that of the United States, decided to join in. Upon the proposal of CAME, a United Nations Conference for the establishment of an educational and cultural organization (ECO/CONF) was convened in London from 1 to 16 November 1945. Scarcely had the war ended when the conference opened. It gathered together representatives of forty-four countries who decided to create an organization that would embody a genuine culture of peace. In their eyes, the new organization was to establish the "intellectual and moral solidarity of mankind" and thereby prevent the outbreak of another world war. *UNESCO's Constitution* was adopted in London in 1945, it entered into force in 1946.

3. The Structure of UNESCO

(1) The General Conference

The General Conference consists of the representatives of UNESCO's Member States. It meets every two years, and is attended by Member States and Associate Members, together with observers for non-Member States, intergovernmental organizations and non-governmental organizations (NGOs). Each country has one vote, irrespective of its size or the extent of its contribution to the budget.

(2) The Executive Board

The Executive Board is one of the three constitutional organs of UNESCO (the others being the General Conference and the Secretariat) and it is elected by the General Conference. Acting under the authority of the General Conference the Board examines the programme of work for the Organization and corresponding budget estimates submitted to it by the Director-General. It consists of 58 Member States each with a four-year term of office.

(3) Secretariat

The Secretariat is the Executive Branch of the organization. It consists of the Director-General and the Staff appointed by him or her. The staff is divided into Professional and General Service categories. About 700 staff members work in UNESCO's 53 field offices around the world.

4. Vision

Political and economic arrangements of governments are not enough to secure the lasting and sincere support of the peoples. Peace must be founded upon dialogue and mutual understanding. Peace must be built upon the intellectual and moral solidarity of humanity.

5. Main Activities

(1) Two Priorities and Six Expertise：

UNESCO's global priorities are Africa and Gender Equality.

➢ Global Priority Africa

As such, UNESCO and development partners are attentive to 54 African countries with a stronger and better targeted strategy. The African Renaissance is underway, with the adoption of the African Union's Agenda 2063 and the 2030 Agenda for Sustainable Development paving the ground for the African Economic Community.

➢ Global Priority Gender Equality

UNESCO believes that all forms of gender-based discrimination are violations of human rights, as well as a significant obstacle to the achievement of the 2030 Agenda for Sustainable Development and its 17 Sustainable Development Goals.

(2) Six expertise：

➢ Education

➢ Natural Sciences

➢ Ocean Sciences

➢ Social and Human Sciences

➢ Culture

➢ Communication & Information

［资料来源：联合国教科文组织网站（https：//www. unesco. org/en），引用日期：2023

年 8 月 20 日。]

6. 词汇表 Vocabulary List

UNESCO Constitution	《联合国教育、科学及文化组织法》
Intergovernmental Organizations	政府间组织
Non-governmental Organizations	非政府组织
Professional and General Service categories	
	专业人员和一般事务人员职类
The intangible cultural heritage	非物质文化遗产
Coalition	联盟
GlobalPriority Africa	总体优先事项"非洲"
Global Priority Gender Equality	性别平等优先

➡ 二、口译实践

● （一）英译汉

Joint message from Ms Audrey Azoulay,
Director-General of UNESCO,
and Ms Phumzile Mlambo-Ngcuka,
Executive Director of UN Women,
on the occasion of the International Day of Women and Girls in Science
（February 11，2021）

The COVID-19 crisis has demonstrated, once again, the critical role of women and girls in science. Women researchers have led many crucial breakthroughs in the fight against the pandemic—from understanding the virus and controlling its spread, to developing diagnostic tests and vaccines.

（1）At the same time, there is growing evidence that the pandemic has hit women—and women scientists—harder than men, for example as a result of the unbalanced distribution of unpaid care and domestic tasks. All too often, women take charge of home schooling, elderly care, and other work created by stay-at-home orders, at the expense of their own employment.

(2) Gender stereotypes and gender-based inequalities continue to prevent many girls and women from taking up and remaining in careers in science across the world. UNESCO's forthcoming *Science Report* shows that only 33% of researchers are women, despite the fact that they represent 45 and 55% of students at the Bachelor's and Master's levels o study respectively, and 44% of those enrolled in PhD programs.

(3) We need to step up our efforts to close these gender gaps in science, and address the norms and stereotypes that create and preserve expectations of limited career paths for girls. (4) The task is all the more urgent given women's underrepresentation in areas critical to the future of work, such as renewable energy and digital fields, with only 3% of female students in higher education choosing information and communication technologies.

We need science, and science needs women. This is not only about making a commitment to equal rights; it is also about making science more open, diverse and efficient.

To be truly transformative, gender equality policies and programs need to eliminate gender stereotypes through education, change social norms, promote positive role models of women scientists and build awareness at the highest levels of decision-making. We need to ensure that women and girls are not only participating in STEM fields, but are empowered to lead and innovate, and that they are supported by workplace policies and organizational cultures that ensure their safety, consider their needs as parents, and incentivize them to advance and thrive in these careers. Recent survey findings across 17 countries underline that young women urgently want more government action, with 75% of female respondents aged 18-24 expecting their government to increase funding for gender equality.

(5) UNESCO and UN Women, together with all our partners, are committed to prioritizing gender equality in all aspects of our work: from promoting basic STEM education to acknowledging and supporting the work of female scientists around the world through initiatives such as the L'Oréal-UNESCO "For Women in Science" Program and the Organization for Women in Science in the Developing World, and by engaging companies in the STEM sector to make bold gender equality commitments

through the Women's Empowerment Principles. UNESCO, in line with its two global priorities, Africa and gender equality, is particularly active on the African continent, accompanying girls with online mentoring programs in Kenya, for instance, and providing school laboratories with micro science kits in the Democratic Republic of the Congo. (6) This year we are also seizing the unique opportunity offered by the Generation Equality Forum, convened by UN Women and co-chaired by France and Mexico, in partnership with civil society and youth, and its Action Coalition on Technology and Innovation for Gender Equality, to push forward transformative actions for a gender-diverse digital evolution.

Women scientists are a source of inspiration for young girls around the world eager to enter scientific fields. Today, as we celebrate the International Day of Women and Girls in Science, it is our duty to pave the way for them, to build a fairer and more equal future. In the words of Jennifer Doudna, laureate of the 2020 Nobel Prize in Chemistry, "I love the process of discovery." For all girls contemplating a career in science, it should be as simple as that.

［资料来源：见联合国教科文组织网站（https://unesdoc.unesco.org/ark：/48223/pf000 0375488。）］

1. 实践解析

本材料为联合国教科文组织总干事 Audery Azoulay（奥黛丽·阿祖莱）和联合国妇女署执行主任 Phamzile Mlambo-Ngcuka（普姆齐莱·姆兰博－恩格库卡）在妇女和女童参与科学国际日的联合致辞，发表于 2021 年 2 月 11 日。致辞中，她们表示，性别成见以及基于性别的不平等现象，一直阻碍着世界各地的许多女性在科学事业的发展。她们介绍了教科文组织和联合国妇女署促进性别平等的一系列行动举措，同时呼吁通过性别平等政策等方式缩小科学领域的性别差距，实现真正的变革。

材料逻辑清晰，总体生词不多，但文中频繁出现了组织名、地名和主题相关一些概念，较多复杂长句也可能给翻译带来一定难度。

STEM 即科学（Science）、技术（Technology）、工程（Engineering）、数学（Mathematics）4 个学科的英文单词首字母的缩写。STEM 这个教育概念源于美国，是科学、技术、工程、数学多学科融合的综合教育，不仅帮助学生更好地理解和应用学科知识，也有助于提高学生分析问题、解决问题的能力。①

UN Women 即联合国妇女署，于 2011 年 1 月 1 日开始运，是联合国促进两性平等和妇女赋权实体。它在两个方面开展工作：支持国际政治谈判，以制定全球认可的性别平等标准。它提供专门知识和资金支持，协助联合国会员国执行这些标准。联合国妇女署还协助其他联合国系统组织，在从人权到人类发展等广泛议题中推进两性平等②。

Women's Empowerment Principles 即赋权予妇女原则（WEPs），于 2009 年 3 月开始制订，于 2010 年 3 月正式发布，是一系列适用于企业的原则，指导企业如何在工作场所、市场及社区赋权女性③。

2. 长难句点拨

（1）该段的句子结构不复杂，但是由于语序不同，语流信息不连贯可能会给理解造成困难。在第一句中，讲话者增加了两个插入成分 "women scientists" 和 "for example" 对原文进行限定，让发言逻辑更加严密，这可能会影响对原文的理解。而第二句中宾语过长，条件状语置于句末，可能会给记忆造成负担。在口译过程中，口译学习者必须根据汉语习惯将原因状语和条件状语提前，让译文更加流畅。

（2）remain in careers in science 的意思并不难理解，但是在口译过程中要考虑和前面的短语 take up careers in science 的并列关系，为了让译文简练、地道，上述两个短语可以翻译为 "从事和继续从事科学事业"。为了突出性别成见和不平等，讲话者对比了女研究员和攻读本科、硕士、博士学位的女性人数。为了让表达多样化，讲话者用了不同的措辞来介绍数据，如果直译，译文会显得重复。但是在口译中，译者应考虑汉语的表达习惯，进行适当整合，可以译为："攻读学士、硕士和博士学位的学生中，女生分别占……"

（3）该句信息比较密集，其中 step up our efforts … 和 address the norms and stereotypes … 短语处于并列关系，stereotypes 后面有一个定语从句。厘清不同意群之间的逻辑关系有助于理解句子意思。除此之外，该句一些地道的表

---

① 见人民网（http://edu. people. com. cn/n1/2018/0613/c1053-30054668. html），引用日期：2023 年 8 月 20 日

② 见联合国网站中文版（https://www. un. org/zh/aboutun/structure/unwomen/index. shtml），引用日期：2023 年 8 月 20 日。

③ 见联合国妇女署亚太地区官网（https://asiapacific. unwomen. org/en/countries/china/chinese/weps），引用日期：2023 年 8 月 20 日。

达，例如：close gender gaps（缩小性别差距），address the norms and stereotypes（破除陈规俗见），create and preserve expectations of limited career paths for girls（形成并固化女性职业道路狭窄）。这可能会对口译造成困难。

（4）对于论述类文字，英语常常是结论在前，细节描述在后。以该句为例，讲话者先提出"The task is all the more urgent"（这项任务非常紧迫）这一论点，然后再详细解释为什么紧迫，并列举具体的行业、从业人数进行佐证。但是汉语的论述方式恰恰相反，语序和结构一般是由先到后、先因后果，先假设再推论，由事实到结论。因此在口译中，口译学习者要重组结构、改变语序。

（5）该句是一个结构比较复杂的英语长句，口译中有两个三个难点：首先，该段包含多个专有名词，如 UN Women（联合国妇女署）和 Organization for Women in Science in the Developing World（发展中国家女性科学家组织），L'Oréal-UNESCO "For Women in Science" Program（欧莱雅－教科文组织妇女与科学计划）和 Women's Empowerment Principles（赋权予妇女原则）。如果不熟悉这些表达，口译学习者在做口译笔记时可能会难以全部记下来。其次，虽然该句的主干非常清晰，但是为了补充说明主干信息，句子中包含了两个长介词短语（from promoting ... to acknowledging and supporting ... 和 by engaging ...），介词短语中又包含多个修饰成分，会对听力理解和记忆造成较大的负担。最后，由于汉英两种语言的语序存在较大差异，在口译过程中应调整方式状语的语序，（如 through initiatives such as ... 和 through the Women's Empowerment Principles 在口译中应该被提前到动词之前）。口译的即时性导致口译学习者没有太多思考的时间，翻译过程中可能会影响译文流利度。

（6）该句的主要难点是包含多个后置定语，如过去分词短语 offered by the Generation Equality Forum 短语修饰前面的名词 opportunity, convened by UN Women 和 co-chaired by France and Mexico 这两个过去分词短语修饰的对象是 Generation Equality Forum，而这一连串的修饰成分隔开了谓语 we are also seizing 和它的补充成分 in partnership with，而句末的动词不定式结构实际是谓语的目的状语。由于修饰关系比较复杂，会对原文理解造成困扰，在口译过程中也要根据汉语习惯，进行较大的语序调整。建议重点学习该句的参考译文，并仔细和原文进行对比，理解汉英的语序差异。

● （二）汉译英

联合国教科文组织第五届女童和妇女教育奖贺词
中国国家主席习近平夫人、联合国教科文组织促进女童和

妇女教育特使　彭丽媛

（2020 年 10 月 12 日）

尊敬的阿祖莱总干事，

女士们，

先生们，

朋友们。

大家好。（1）值此国际女童日之际，我谨向联合国教科文组织第五届女童和妇女教育奖的成功评选，向来自斯里兰卡、肯尼亚的获奖者表示衷心的祝贺。

在联合国教科文组织的引领和推动下，国际社会日益关注和重视女童和妇女教育事业，越来越多的机构和个人投入这项事业。（2）2015 年，中国同联合国教科文组织合作设立女童和妇女教育奖，旨在表彰为促进女童和妇女教育做出突出贡献的机构和个人，展示教育改变女童和妇女命运的重要作用，激励更多人投身教育性别平等事业。

五年来，在这一奖项的颁奖仪式和有关的会议中，我同获奖者们进行了深入的交流，了解到他们投身女童和妇女教育的感人事迹。他们以实际行动帮助女童和妇女获取知识和技能，点燃女童和妇女的人生梦想，为促进教育性别平等、推动社会发展贡献力量。这种奉献精神令我深受感动。

今年获奖的斯里兰卡、肯尼亚的项目为我们更好为女童和妇女提供知识技能、享有教育和发展权益作出了突出贡献。（3）在中国，也有千千万万的人为女童和妇女教育事业默默耕耘。其中有一位名叫张桂梅的女教师，她扎根云南贫困山区 40 多年，推动创建了中国第一所免费女子高中，自 2008 年建校以来已帮助 1600 多位女孩子圆梦大学校园。张老师被女孩子们亲切地称为"张妈妈"。她像一束希望之光，照亮孩子们的追梦人生。

今年是一个特殊的年份。（4）受新冠肺炎疫情影响，全球 15 亿学生被迫停课，对女童的影响尤其明显，我对此十分忧心。在这样一个特殊时刻，我们更要充分发挥女童和妇女教育奖的影响力，增强世界各国对女童和妇女教育事

业的关注，想方设法帮助女童复课复学，不让女童因疫情掉队。

女士们，先生们，朋友们，

全球成年文盲中63%是女性，让我们深感心情沉重。（5）**妇女得不到良好教育，就不会有人类社会发展进步。**女童和妇女教育功在当代，利在千秋。作为联合国教科文组织促进女童和妇女教育特使，我在此呼吁更多国家和各界人士积极支持和参与这一伟大事业。中国将继续同教科文组织合作，办好2021年至2025年第二期女童和妇女教育奖，推动国际教育交流合作，为促进女童和妇女教育实现联合国2030年可持续发展目标做出更大贡献。让我们携手努力，帮助女童和妇女享有平等、优质的教育，让女性拥有美好的未来。

［资料来源：见央广网（http://news.cnr.cn/native/gd/20201016/t20201016_525297831.shtml），引用日期：2023年8月20日。］

1. 实践解析

本材料是国家主席习近平夫人、联合国教科文组织促进女童和妇女教育特使彭丽媛于2020年10月12日通过视频给联合国教科文组织第五届女童和妇女教育奖的贺词。彭丽媛向来自斯里兰卡、肯尼亚的获奖者表示衷心祝贺。在致辞中她表示，全球成年文盲中，63%是女性。妇女得不到良好教育，就不会有人类社会发展进步。女童和妇女教育功在当代，利在千秋。她呼吁更多国家和各界人士积极支持和参与这一伟大事业。

本材料是一篇典型的致辞，难度适中，提到的事例也是大家所耳熟能详的，要重点关注如何将汉语转为符合英文习惯的地道表达。

教科文组织女童和妇女教育奖（UNESCO Prize for Girls' and Women's Education）："教科文组织女童和妇女教育奖表彰个人、机构和组织为推动女童和妇女教育所作出的杰出贡献和创新。这是联合国教科文组织首个此类奖项，旨在展示成功项目中发挥独特作用，促进和改善女孩和妇女的教育机会，从而提高她们的生活质量。该奖项由中华人民共和国政府资助，用于帮助获奖者进一步在女童和妇女教育领域开展工作。首个奖项于2016年由教科文组织总干事颁发。"①

---

① 见联合国教科文组织网站（https://www.unesco.org/zh/prizes/girls-womens-education），引用日期：2023年8月20日。

2. 长难句点拨

（1）该句是典型的礼仪性致辞，值……之际（on the occasion of …）、向……表示衷心的祝贺（extend my hearty congratulations to …）是这类演讲中的常见表达。除此之外，代表（on behalf of）、以……的名义（in the name of …）、宣布……开幕（declare … open）、祝……圆满成功（wish … a complete success）也是礼仪性致辞中的高频词汇。获奖者可以用 prizewinner 或者 winner of a prize 或者 laureate 来表达，如 Oscar winner, a Nobel laureate。汉语原文中"祝贺"一词的对象既包括奖项成功评选，也包括获奖者，但是在翻译成英语时要考虑到搭配问题，建议将奖项成功评选和获奖者分开处理，即译成"On the occasion of the International Day of the Girl Child, I wish to celebrate with you the fifth edition of the UNESCO Prize for Girls' and Women's Education, and extend my hearty congratulations to this year's laureates from Sri Lanka and Kenya."

（2）汉语中动词并不区分谓语动词和非谓语动词，动词的使用相对灵活，可以充当各种成分，因此，汉语句子中经常出现动词连用。比如，该句中就包含多个动词：设立、表彰、做出、展示、改变、激励、投身。但是英语中动词的使用限制较多，句子中通常只有一个谓语，需要借助非谓语或者其他词类来实现一些功能，因此，该句中这一连串动词不能全部以动词形式译出，而主语和谓语的选择就显得尤为重要。该句围绕"女童和妇女教育奖"来展开，"表彰""展示""激励"这三个词语都是突出奖项的目的，如果放弃沿用汉语句中的主语，以"女童和妇女教育奖"为主语，那么口译就会更加简单。

（3）该段讲述了中国女童和妇女教育事业的情况，以及张桂梅老师的事迹，"默默耕耘""扎根山区""圆梦大学""张妈妈""希望之光""追梦人生"都是汉语的习惯表达，以英文为母语的听众可能不熟悉。因此在口译时既要确保语言的准确性，也要讲好相关的故事，并传递字里行间透露出来的情感。有一些意象如"张妈妈""希望之光""追梦人生"在经过直译之后也不难理解，还能够比较直观地反映张桂梅老师的突出贡献，建议保留，让译文更直白地传递原文的情感，实现类似的交际效果。而"默默耕耘""扎根""圆梦"之类的表达，如果对其进行直译，则比较啰唆，翻译时应以传递意义为主，不必逐字翻译。

（4）该段有两个难点，首先是原文中包含汉语习惯表达，在口译过程中要充分考虑文化和语言差异，确保译文准确、地道。例如"想方设法"是对偶复意动词词组，"复课复学"是 ABAC 的动词重复结构，这些词不仅让原文更有节奏，也传递了强烈的情感，在口译中却不宜保留这种重复结构，可以通过其他方式来达到同样的效果。其次，该段第一句是流水句，小句一个个铺排下来，可断可连，有些小句主谓难分，有些小句有明显的主谓结构，在口译中要选择合适的主语，并充分考虑句子之间的逻辑关系，利用各种衔接手段和形式，让译文结构形式规范。

（5）该句是对妇女（女童）教育意义的总结，通过简洁有力的语言结构表达了强烈的情感色彩。在口译中，这一类文本的翻译难度非常大，首先要准确理解"功在当代，利在千秋"的含义，一般采取释义策略（paraphrasing），结合上下文传递演讲者所要表达的意思，但是也要考虑语言组织，尽量让译文简练、规整，富有节奏感。

➡ 三、口译练习

● （一）英译汉

New horizons of Heritage Conservation

Shahbaz Khan

Director and Representative of UNESCO office Beijing

（May 20，2022）

Distinguished Professor Duan Peng, Vice President of Communication University of China,

Dear experts and participants across the Internet,

Ladies and gentlemen,

Very good morning, and thank you all for joining together for the opening of the webinar series on "New horizons of Heritage Conservation", a very timely series. On behalf of UNESCO, I wish to thank the Communication University of China for co-organizing this webinar series. (1) In this challenging time, the Internet allows us to keep the conversation and knowledge-sharing alive, and pushes us to think beyond existing paradigms for creative solutions in this "new normal".

As you know, the year 2022 marks the 50th anniversary of *UNESCO's Convention concerning the Protection of the World Cultural and Natural Heritage*, also known as *the World Heritage Convention*. (2) Over half a century, the legacy of this very important international instrument manifest itself in a coalition of 195 State Parties that have ratified the Convention and a network of 1154 World Heritage sites in 167 countries, which are the testament to the universal appreciation and achievement of this groundbreaking legal framework. This landmark year comes at a watershed moment for conservation. The effects of climate change have been tangibly felt by sites around the world, while the increasing volume of tourism has put new environmental and social pressure on the properties and surrounding communities alike. The COVID-19 pandemic has revealed the vulnerability of heritage ecosystem in the face of sudden onset crisis, as demonstrated by the closure of 89% of World Heritage sites. More than ever, we need to explore and communicate the new horizons of heritage conservation in the face of such new challenges.

I wish to take this opportunity to highlight two areas that we could reflect on and address during the course of this webinar series.

One is the issue of climate change, which has become one of the most pressing threats to the World Heritage properties, potentially impacting their Outstanding Universal Value and their potential for economic and social development at the local level. (3) World Heritage properties also harbor options for society to mitigate and adapt to climate change through ecosystem benefits that they can provide. Cultural heritage, on the other hand, can convey traditional knowledge that builds resilience for change to come and leads us to a more sustainable future. (4) As China progresses towards achieving the goal of carbon peaking by 2030 and carbon neutrality by 2060, we need to continue raising awareness on this important role of heritage, both tangible and intangible, both natural and cultural, in informing and supporting our response to climate change.

(5) Second is the issue of gender equality, which is the global priority of UNESCO in many aspects of heritage, whether it involves the role of women and men in care-taking of heritage site, or how gender is commonly expressed, performed and even constituted in and through living heritage. Over the past few years, UNESCO has already made considerable endeavors in this field. For example, at Shilin in the Yi autonomous region of Yunnan, which is part of South China Karst World Heritage

site, women are empowered to practice their traditional embroideries as a source of income and as a source of creative design. Qiaoqi, a remote Tibetan town in the core zone of Sichuan Giant Panda Sanctuaries World Heritage site, has been taking women beekeepers for engaging in local governance and marketing their produce—the honey. China's vast scope of heritage, represented by its 56 World Heritage sites and 42 elements on the Lists and Register for Intangible Heritage, are certainly a great example to explore how to better empower women in culture and heritage.

The theme of UNESCO's 50th anniversary celebrations of *the World Heritage Convention* is "The Next 50", which invites the international society to reflect on how to conserve heritage, not just for the sake of heritage itself, but to let it become a better source of resilience, humanity and innovation. In this process, we need to join forces together to build capacity for the next generation, harness new trends and transform our societies. I thank you all for joining together for this webinar, and look forward to fruitful discussions and outcomes in the months to come for "The Next 50". Thank you very much.

[资料来源：见哔哩哔哩视频网（https://www. bilibili. com/video/BV1nv4y1374s/? p = 2&vd_source = 44251f1a886d2152f9e4cc85f6bc27b9），引用日期：2023 年 8 月 20 日。]

1. 词汇准备

New Horizons of Heritage Conservation	《遗产保护的新视野》
the Communication University of China	中国传媒大学
the World Heritage Convention	《世界遗产公约》
South China Karst World Heritage site	中国南方喀斯特世界遗产地
Sichuan Giant Panda Sanctuaries World Heritage site	
	四川大熊猫栖息地世界遗产地
living heritage	活态遗产

2. 长难句点拨

（1）该句整体难度不大，理解原文时要联系 2022 年新冠肺炎疫情尚未结束，许多交流活动转到线上召开的背景来理解一些词汇的意思。例如 "keep the conversation and knowledge-sharing alive"，在该句中显然不是保持生机的意思，而是 "保持对话和知识共享的畅通" 的意思；"new normal" 即 "新常态"，联系上下文指的是疫情期间主要通过线上会议或者论坛开展交流的情况，显然与经常提到的中国经济进入新常态不是同一个概念。一些熟悉的概念在不同语境下可能被讲话者赋予不同含义，因此，口译学习者要结合语境和讲话者的目的来理解。

（2）该句结构复杂，含有大量的抽象名词（legacy、instrument、coalition、network、testament、appreciation、achievement、framework）和某些不太常见的表达（sth. manifest itself in sth.），可能会对听力理解造成困难。首先，要结合上下文来准确理解抽象名词的具体含义，比如 legacy 是"遗产、遗留植物"，放在文中语境显然不合适，讲话者列举的各项数据都表明《世界遗产公约》具有深远的影响力，因此不妨据此进行释义。instrument 这里是"法律文件"的意思，但结合具体语境译为"文书"更好。而 coalition 也不宜翻译为"联盟、联合体"，该词具体指代的就是后半句所指的 195 个缔约国签署了《保护世界文化和自然遗产公约》这个事实，并不需要专门译出这个词。在口译中，对于这种结构比较紧凑、句式相对复杂的句子建议采取拆分技巧，如句子主干"the legacy of ... manifest itself in a coalition of ... that have ratified ... "应该拆解为两个句子，参考译文为《世界遗产公约》是非常重要的国际文书，体现在有 195 个缔约国签署了公约和遍布世界 167 个国家的 1154 处世界遗产上。

（3）该句虽然句子不长，但是包含的成分较多，加上一些口译学习者可能不太熟悉 harbor options 这个搭配（harbor 表示提供、拥有、包含，参考译文为即世界遗产地提供了一些解决办法），可能理解句子时会遇到困难。首先，要合理划分意群结构："World Heritage properties also harbor options // for society to mitigate and adapt to climate change //through ecosystem benefits //that they can provide. "然后根据汉语表述习惯重组切分后的意群，参考译文为：世界遗产通过其生态系统为社会应对并适应气候变化也提供了多种解决方法。

（4）该句涉及两个专业术语的理解，carbon peaking 即"碳达峰"，是指某个地区或者行业年度温室气体排放量的最高值，是温室气体排量由增转降的历史拐点。carbon neutrality（碳中和）是某个地区在一定时间内（一般指一年）人类活动直接或间接产生的温室气体排放总量，与植树造林、节能减排等形式，抵消自身产生的二氧化碳排放量，实现碳净零排放[①]。《中华人民共和国国民经济和社会发展第十四个五年规划和 2035 年远景目标纲要》提出，

---

① 见中国生态环境部网站（https://www.mee.gov.cn/ywgz/xcjy/xccpzyk/wsp/202105/t20210520_833789.shtml），引用日期：2023 年 8 月 20 日。

落实 2030 年应对气候变化国家自主贡献目标，制定 2030 年前碳排放达峰行动方案，锚定努力争取 2060 年前实现碳中和，这也被称为"30·60 目标"。除此之外，该句中包含了两个 both ... and 短语连接的插入语，译文容易受到连词结构影响。为了让译文更加流畅，翻译时建议放弃连词结构，直接以状语形式译出。

（5）living heritage，即活态遗产，这是非物质文化遗产的另一个说法。英文原文是较长的复合句，涉及多个并列和从属关系，该句的主句非常短——Second is the issue of gender equality，用 which 引导的非限制性定语从句对"the issue of gender equality"进行补充说明，而 whether 和 how 引导的两个从句具体阐述 many aspects 包含的内容。这两个从句里，how 从句使用了被动态，谓语部分包含三个并列的过去分词"expressed, performed and even constituted"，如果亦步亦趋地将其翻译为"性别是如何被表达、执行、构成"，就会非常拗口。在口译过程中宜通过增译、词性转换等技巧，让译文更加自然，流畅。

（二）汉译英

在 2022 年亚太地区教育部长会议上的讲话

中国教育部部长　怀进鹏

（2022 年 6 月 24 日）

尊敬的联合国教科文组织教育助理总干事贾尼尼女士，

各位部长，

女士们，先生们，

大家好！教育变革是今年九月即将召开的"全球教育变革峰会"的主题，也是 2030 年教育高级别指导委员会确定的全球重点关注主题之一。当前世界进入新的动荡变革期：百年变局和世纪疫情交织，科技与产业革命迅速发展，人类正在面临多种复杂和严峻的挑战。教育只有主动变革、主动作为才能实现 2030 年教育目标，才能为促进人类可持续发展和世界和平做出应有贡献。

过去两年多，中国统筹疫情防控、脱贫攻坚和推进教育现代化，克服诸多困难与挑战，实施 2030 年教育目标，取得了重大进展。结合中国实践，下面我愿提出三点建议。

一是重做教育目标与教育内容。教育培养什么人决定未来的世界会是什么样的。（1）应聚焦"立德树人"的根本任务，坚持"德智体美劳"五育并举，围绕更好适应和融入未来社会构建新的课程与教育体系，为学生实现全面发展与可持续发展打下坚实基础；应强化国际理解教育，增强人类命运共同体意识，在青少年心中埋下和平的种子；强化生态文明教育和生命教育，帮助学生学会与自然和谐相处，科学应对疫情等重大公共卫生危机；强化数字素养与技能培养，帮助学生提升数字化适应力、胜任力和创造力。

二是建设更具韧性、更加包容、公平的高质量教育体系。（2）两年多来抗击疫情的实践告诉我们：要统筹疫情防控与教育发展，坚持"生命第一"，提升学校疫情防控能力，大力发展线上教学与混合教学，最大程度减少学生学业损失；（3）应以推进基本公共教育服务均等化为抓手，健全包括家庭经济困难学生和残疾学生在内的各类困难群体平等受教育的政策保障体系，不断缩小城乡、区域和群体间教育的差距，让每个人都有人生出彩的机会；要不断优化普通高校和职业学校学科专业结构，大力推进产教融合与科教融合，提升高等教育与职业教育的适应性，为青年体面工作生活赋能；（4）应充分运用现代技术，努力向社会提供多种形式的终身教育服务，实现人人皆学、处处能学，时时可学；应把学校和教师作为改革发展高质量教育的关键基础，改进学校治理，激发学校创新活力；做好教师培养培训，切实提升教师专业素养，特别是应用新技术教学的能力，保障并不断提高教师，特别是乡村教师的工资待遇，使教师成为推动教育变革的主力。

三是大力推进教育数字化变革。世界范围内实施 2030 年教育议程的经验教训告诉我们：走传统的教育之路难以实现预期目标，难以适应未来需要。以教育数字化带动教育转型升级是我们必须抓住的重大历史机遇。（5）中国正实施国家教育数字化战略行动，以"应用为王、服务至上、简洁高效、安全运行"为总要求，整合各类资源，推出了国家智慧教育平台，聚焦学生学习、教师教学、学校治理，赋能社会和教育创新，向全社会免费提供覆盖各级各类教育的优质资源。同时，我们还将通过信息技术更新教育理念，变革教育教学模式，推动教育数字化治理，构建网络化、数字化、个性化、终身化教育体系。我们愿意积极探索在线教育国际合作和交流机制，共同打造数字教育未来新空间、新图景。

女士们，先生们，

亚太各国山水相连，命运与共。当前，受疫情影响，教育复苏形势依然严峻。我们应当共同行动，共克时艰，共创未来。中国愿与联合国教科文组织和亚太地区各国携手应对挑战。通过务实交流与合作，特别是加强职业教育和高等教育合作，共同探索面向未来的人才培养规律，共同推进教育数字化变革。

加快疫后教育复苏和实施 2030 年教育目标，为亚太地区教育实现更好发展，共创亚太美好未来而努力奋斗。

谢谢大家！

[资料来源：见 youtube 联合国教科文组织频道（https://www.youtube.com/watch？v = O9ZmspSF-0Q），引用日期：2023 年 8 月 20 日。]

1. 词汇准备

"全球教育变革峰会"	The Transforming Education Summit
2030 年教育高级别指导委员会	
	SDG4-Education 2030 High-Level Steering Committee
"立德树人"	foster virtue through education
"生命第一""生命至上"	the principles of putting life first
数字素养	digital literacy
混合教学	hybrid teaching
职业学校	TVET (Technical and Vocational Education and Training) schools
2030 年教育议程	Education 2030 Agenda

2. 长难句点拨

（1）首先，平时应重视积累常见的中国特色表达的英文，如"科教兴国"（invigorating China through science and education）、"新时代人才强国战略"（developing a quality workforce in the new era）、"为党育人、为国育才"（cultivating talent for the Party and the State）。通过积累学习不难发现，中国特色表达的翻译主要采取了释义的策略，因此，如果平时积累中有疏漏，在口译翻译该句中，"立德树人""五育并举"也可以采用同样的技巧。该句的另一个特点是无主语，在翻译时应补充主语。

（2）该句翻译过程中应注意词语的选择，如原文中的"抗击疫情的实践告诉我们"，结合文章后提到的具体措施，此处的"告诉"译为"prove"更加妥当。该句口译的另一个难点是小句多，逻辑关系隐含在字里行间，因此在口译过程中要选择合适的语法手段，让小句之间的逻辑关系更加清晰。例如，"统筹疫情防控与教育发展"的首要任务就是坚持"生命第一"这个原则，因此在口译中应选择动名词短语作为伴随状语，并且补充 the principles of。"提升疫情防控能力"和"大力发展线上教学与混合教学"是学校应采取的行动，而"最大程度减少学生学业损失"则是目的，通过并列结构和动词不定式短语，就能够比较清楚地展现以上这些逻辑关系出来。

（3）该句涉及中国文化和政策背景下的教育服务均等化措施，在口译中要选择合适的表达方式，确保以英语为母语的听众能够理解其中的含义和背景信息。例如，对于"以……为抓手""健全……保障体系"，建议在口译中放弃这些结构，重点解释文字的具体含义。除此之外，由于原文涉及多个并列和从属关系，口译时需要注意句子间的逻辑连贯，如"不断缩小城乡、区域和群体间教育的差距"的最终目的是"让每个人都有人生出彩的机会"，可以通过增加逻辑连词，显化句子逻辑。

（4）原文中的 AABC 四字短语（"人人皆学，处处能学，时时可学"）可能会让口译学习者觉得无从下手。实际上讲话者采用三个并列的短语分别突出"人人""处处""时时"（即对象、时间和地点），这种词汇重复在汉语中除了增加语言的文采与结构，另一个作用就是强调。因此，口译学习者在口译中只要把握信息重点，理解修辞效果，可以通过重写（rewriting）技巧来确保英语译文准确、流畅。参考译文为"We should leverage modern technologies to provide lifelong education services in various forms so that everyone can learn everywhere at anytime."

（5）该句中的四字短语"应用为王、服务至上、简洁高效、安全运行"可能会让口译学习者望而生畏，但其实在翻译过程中不必拘泥于原文的形式，要超越语言结构并从中看到信息核心，即强调相关资源的应用性、服务性、简洁性、高效性和安全性。考虑到英文中抽象名词的使用比较普遍，因此可以译为"emphasis on application, service, simplicity, efficiency and safety"。该句还包含"国家智慧教育平台"和"国家教育数字化战略行动"，对于这类术语，一般结合英语表达习惯进行直译即可。该句的句子重组也有较大难度，首先应把握句子的逻辑，即先总说，提出国家教育数字化战略行动，再分说，后半句详细解释实施战略行动的具体内容。此处应合理断句，避免句子过长给听众造成负担。后半句主要围绕国家智慧教育平台来展开，因此不妨以此为主语，再利用各种语法结构，将其他小句整合在一起。

➡️ 四、参考译文

🔵 (一) 口译实践

1. 英译汉

联合国教科文组织总干事奥黛丽·阿祖莱

和联合国妇女署执行主任普姆齐莱·姆兰博－恩格库卡

在妇女和女童参与科学国际日的联合致辞

(2021 年 2 月 11 日)

新型冠状病毒病危机再次证明了妇女和女童在科学领域的关键作用。在这场抗疫斗争中取得的许多关键性进展都是由女性研究人员主导的，无论是在了解病毒和控制其传播方面，还是诊断测试和疫苗开发方面。

与此同时，越来越多的证据表明，由于过多承担无酬照护和家务工作，这场疫情对女性和女性科学家的冲击比男性更为严重。女性往往以牺牲自己的就业为代价，承担起家庭教育、老年人照护以及由于居家禁足措施带来的其他工作。

性别成见以及基于性别的不平等现象一直阻碍着世界各地的许多女性从事或继续从事科学事业。教科文组织即将发布的《科学报告》显示，在攻读学士、硕士和博士学位的学生中，女生分别占比 45%、55% 和 44%，但在研究人员中只有 33% 是女性。

我们需要加紧努力，缩小科学领域的这些性别差距，破除那些形成并固化"女性职业道路狭窄"这一观念的陈规俗见。鉴于女性在对未来工作至关重要的领域（如可再生能源和数字领域）的代表性不足，并且只有 3% 接受高等教育的女生选择信息和通信技术专业，这项任务就显得尤为紧迫。

世界需要科学，科学需要女性。这不仅涉及对平等权利的承诺，也是为了让科学更加开放、多样且具有成效。

为了实现真正的变革，性别平等政策和计划需要通过教育消除性别成见，改变社会规范，宣传女科学家的积极模范作用，并在最高决策层面提高认识。

我们不仅需要确保女性参与 STEM（科学、技术、工程、数学）领域的工作，还要增强其领导和创新权能，并确保她们得到工作场所的政策和组织文化的支持，这些政策和组织文化可以保障她们的安全，考虑她们作为家长的需求，并激励她们在职业道路上不断进取发展。最近在 17 个国家开展的一项调查结果表明，年轻女性迫切希望政府采取更多行动，75% 年龄在 18 岁至 24 岁之间的女性受访者希望政府增加对性别平等的资助。

联合国教科文组织和联合国妇女署与我们的所有合作伙伴一道，致力于将性别平等作为我们各方面工作的优先事项，包括促进 STEM 基础教育，通过欧莱雅 – 教科文组织妇女与科学计划和发展中世界妇女科学组织等举措认可并支持世界各地女科学家的工作，以及动员 STEM 领域的企业通过增强妇女权能原则在性别平等方面作出大胆的承诺。教科文组织根据其非洲和性别平等两个总体优先事项，在非洲大陆积极开展行动，例如在肯尼亚为女生提供在线辅导课程，并在刚果民主共和国向学校实验室提供微科学工具包。今年，我们还抓住由联合国妇女署召集、由法国和墨西哥联合主办的平等一代论坛所提供的独特机会，与民间社会和青年及其促进性别平等技术和创新行动联盟合作，推动促进性别多样化数字发展的变革行动。

女科学家在激励世界各地渴望投入科学事业的年轻女性方面发挥着榜样作用。今天，在庆祝妇女和女童参与科学国际日之际，我们有责任为她们铺平道路，建设一个更公平、更平等的未来。2020 年诺贝尔化学奖获得者詹妮弗·杜德纳（Jennifer Doudna）说过，"我喜欢发现的过程。"对于所有考虑日后投身科学事业的女孩而言，出发点就应该这么简单。

［资料来源：见联合国教科文组织网站（https://unesdoc. unesco. org/ark：/48223/pf0000375488_chi？ posInSet = 80&queryId = N-213f4a64-a253-4688-943c-0e92ae94960d），引用日期：2023 年 8 月 20 日。］

2. 汉译英

Congratulatory message to UNESCO Prize for Girls' and Women's Education

PENG Liyuan, Wife of Chinese President XI Jingping & UNESCO Special Envoy for the Advancement of Girls' and Women's Education

(October 12, 2020)

Madame Director-General Audrey Azoulay,

Ladies and gentlemen,

Dear friends,

Greetings to you all! On the occasion of the International Day of the Girl Child, I wish to celebrate with you the fifth edition of the UNESCO Prize for Girls' and Women's Education, and extend my hearty congratulations to this year's laureates from Sri Lanka and Kenya.

Thanks to the leadership and commitment of UNESCO, the international community is paying closer attention to girls' and women's education, and more institutions and individuals are joining this great cause. This Prize, set up by China and UNESCO in 2015, is designed to honor outstanding contributions made by institutions and individuals to advance girls' and women's education, to showcase how education can change the destiny of girls and women, and to inspire more people to work for this lofty cause of promoting gender equality in and through education.

Over the past five years, at award ceremonies and meetings related to this Prize, I have had in-depth exchanges with many laureates and heard moving stories of their devotion to girls' and women's education. Through concrete actions, the laureates have given numerous girls and women access to knowledge and skills and empowered them to dream for the better future. They have thus contributed to gender equality in and through education and promoted social progress. Their commitment and dedication have touched me deeply.

This year's Prize recognizes projects from Sri Lanka and Kenya, two outstanding programs that provide girls and women access to knowledge and skills, and help them benefit from education and development. Here in China, there are tens of thousands of unsung heroes working tirelessly for girls and women's education. Among them is Zhang Guimei, a female teacher who has spent more than 40 years in the impoverished mountainous areas of China's southwest Yunan Province. She is the founder of China's first tuition-free high school for girls. Since it was opened in 2008, the school has sent more than 1600 girls to universities. Fondly addressed as "Zhang Mama" by the girls, Ms. Zhang is like the beam of hope, lighting the way forward for the girls to pursue their life dreams.

We face a special situation this year. School closures forced by COVID-19 have affected 1.5 million students worldwide, girls in particular. This is most perturbing. Special circumstances call for stronger action. We should better leverage the influence of the Prize to draw more attention to girls' and women's education in all countries. We should do everything possible to bring girls back to school and keep girls in the picture.

Ladies and gentlemen, friends,

Of all the world's illiterate adults, 63% are women. This saddens our heart. Without good education for women, there is no human progress to speak of. Girls' and women's education is a lofty cause that will not only empower this generation but also benefit generations to come. As UNESCO Special Envoy for the Advancement of Girls' and Women's Education, I call on more countries and people of different backgrounds to support and join this great endeavor. On China's part, we will continue to work with UNESCO on the second cycle (2021-2025) of the UNESCO Prize for Girls' and Women's Education to promote international exchanges and cooperation on education and contribute more to girls' and women's education and to the achievement of the Sustainable Development Goals. Let us join hands to give girls and women equal access to quality education. Let us work together to bring all women a brighter future.

资料来源：见央广网（http://news. cnr. cn/native/gd/20201016/t20201016_525297831. shtml），引用日期：2023 年 8 月 20 日。

● （二）口译练习

1. 英译汉

可持续发展的遗产保护新视野

联合国教科文组织驻华代表处代表　夏泽翰

（2022 年 5 月 20 日）

尊敬的中国传媒大学段鹏副校长，

线上的各位专家和参会人员，

女士们，先生们，

早上好！感谢大家参加《遗产保护的新视野》系列线上讲座的开幕仪式。我谨代表联合国教科文组织，衷心感谢中国传媒大学与我们共同举办这一系列线上讲座。在这个充满挑战的时代，互联网让我们得以保持对话和知识共享的畅通，并推动我们在"新常态"中跳出既定范式，思考创造性的解决方案。

2022 年是联合国教科文组织《保护世界文化和自然遗产公约》，也就是《世界遗产公约》50 周年纪念。半个世纪以来，这一开创性的国际文书取得了深远的成就和影响，体现在其 195 个缔约国以及分布在全球 167 个国家的 1154 处世界遗产地中。这是对这一开创性国际文书框架的普遍认可和成就的证明。这具有里程碑意义的一年同样也是遗产保护的分水岭，世界各地的遗产地都愈发切实地感受到气候变化的影响，而日益增长的游客量也给当地和周边社区带来了新的环境和社会压力。新冠肺炎疫情揭示了遗产生态系统在突发危机面前的脆弱性，最严重时 89% 的世界遗产地被关闭就证明了这一点。面对这样的新挑战，我们比以往任何时候都更需要探索和交流遗产保护的新视野。

我希望借此机会分享我们可以在系列在线讲座期间思考的两个领域。

首先是气候变化，气候变化已成为对世界遗产最紧迫的威胁之一，对遗产地的突出普遍价值及其在地方经济和社会发展中的促进作用都带来了潜在的负面影响。而与此同时，世界遗产通过其生态系统为社会应对并适应气候变化也提供了多种解决方法。此外，文化遗产可以传递传统知识，为应对未来的变化增强韧性，并引领我们走向更可持续的未来。随着中国稳步向 2030 年碳达峰、2060 年碳中和的目标迈进，我们需要继续提高人们对物质和非物质遗产、自然遗产和文化遗产在帮助我们了解和应对气候变化的影响方面的重要作用的认识。

其次是遗产领域的性别平等问题，这也是联合国教科文组织的全球优先事项之一。遗产领域的性别平等涉及方方面面，包括女性和男性在遗产地保护中发挥的作用、性别在活态遗产中的表达和构成等。在过去的几年中，联合国教科文组织已经在这一领域做出了很多努力。例如，在中国南方喀斯特世界遗产地组成部分之一的云南石林，妇女被鼓励将传统刺绣作为收入和创意设计的来源。在四川大熊猫栖息地世界遗产地核心区的硗碛藏族乡，女性养蜂人在合作社治理和蜂蜜营销中扮演着越来越重要的角色。中国有 56 处世界遗产地和 42 项全球非物质文化遗产为代表的丰富遗产，这无疑能够为探索如何在文化和遗产方面为女性赋能提供借鉴。

联合国教科文组织《世界遗产公约》50 周年的主题是"下一个五十年"，邀请国际社会思考如何保护遗产，不仅仅是为了遗产本身，而是让它更好地成为人性、文明和创新的源泉。在这一过程中，我们需要齐心协力提升未来一代的能力，把握新趋势和变革并传承知识。感谢大家参加今天的在线讲座，期待在此次系列线上讲座的几个月中，我们能够为下一个 50 年开展富有成效的交流。谢谢！

［资料来源：见哔哩哔哩视频网（https://www.bilibili.com/video/BV1nv4y1374s/？p = 2&vd_source = 44251f1a886d2152f9e4cc85f6bc27b9），引用日期：2023 年 8 月 20 日。]

2. 汉译英

Statement at APREMC2022

Mr HUAI Jinpeng

Minister of Education of the People's Republic of China

（June 24，2022）

Distinguished Madame Stefania Giannini，Assistant Director-General for Education of UNESCO，

Ministers，

Ladies and gentlemen，

Good afternoon! The Transforming Education Summit to be held in September this year takes education transformation as the overarching priority，it is also one of the major themes of global concern identified by the SDG4-Education 2030 High-Level Steering Committee. The world is now entering a new period of turbulence and transformation，as major changes of times are compounded with a once-in-a-century pandemic and the rapid development of science, technology and industrial revolution. Faced with a variety of complex and severe challenges, we must take the initiative to transform education to accelerate progress toward the achievement of SDG4 and make a due contribution to sustainable human development and world peace.

Over the past two years, China has advanced poverty eradication and education modernization against the COVID-19 impact and other challenges, and made significant progress in implementing the Education 2030 Agenda. Based on China's practices, I would like to propose three suggestions:

First, redefine education objectives and contents. The objectives of education shape the future of the world. We should focus on fostering virtue through education, promote all-round development of students through moral, intellectual, physical, aesthetic and labor education, and innovate curriculum and education system to facilitate a better transition and integration into the future society, to lay a solid foundation for students to achieve comprehensive and sustainable development. Education for international understanding should be strengthened to enhance the awareness of a community of shared future for mankind and plant the seeds of peace in the hearts of young people. Education for ecological civilization and life should be strengthened to enhance the capacity to get along with the nature and respond to major public health crisis such as the pandemic. Digital literacy and skills should be strengthened to improve digital adaptability, competency and creativity.

Second, build a more resilient, inclusive and equitable quality education system. Over the past two years, the fight against the pandemic has proven to us that we should promote education alongside pandemic prevention and control, adhering to the principles of putting life first. Aside from improving the capacity of schools in pandemic prevention and control, we should promote online and hybrid teaching modes to minimize students' learning loss. We should advance balanced provision of basic public education services to strengthen the policy foundation for equal access to education for disadvantaged groups, including students from economically disadvantaged families and students with disabilities, so that education gap across urban and rural areas, different regions and groups can be narrowed and everyone can have the opportunity to succeed in life. We should optimize the structure of disciplines in both general higher education institutions and TVET schools, vigorously promote integration of industry and education, of technology and education, and enhance the relevance of higher education and TVET to better empower young people for decent work and life. We should leverage modern technologies to provide lifelong education services in various forms so that everyone can learn everywhere at anytime. We should also take schools and teachers as the key foundation for high-quality education. By improving school governance, simulating school-level innovation, promoting teacher training to facilitate teachers' professional development, especially their digital competencies in teaching, guaranteeing and increasing teachers' welfare and remuneration, especially that of rural teachers, we should make teachers the main change maker for transforming education.

Third, promote digital transformation of education. The lessons learned from the worldwide incrementation of the Education 2030 Agenda is that if we followed the traditional path of education, we would fail to achieve the goals and respond to future needs. We must seize the historical opportunity to transform education through digitalization. China has rolled out the national strategy for digital transformation of the education system. With emphasis on application, service, simplicity, efficiency and safety, we launched a national smart education platform, integrating various resources. Focusing on supporting for teachers and students in teaching and learning, school governance, social empowerment and education innovation, the platform provides free and quality education resources covering all levels and all types of education to the public. Meanwhile, we will leverage ICTs to update education concepts, transform teaching and learning modes, and promote digital governance of education, so that a connected, digital, personalized and lifelong education system can be built. We are willing to explore innovative mechanism for international cooperation in online education to jointly create new visions and scenarios for the future of digital education.

Ladies and gentlemen,

We Asian-Pacific countries form a community with a shared future linked by the same mountains and rivers. Currently affected by the pandemic, the prospect for education recovery is still uncertain. We should act together to tide over the crisis and create a better future. Faced with the complex challenges, China is willing to join hands with UNESCO and fellow Asian-Pacific countries to advance practical cooperation, especially that in TVET and higher education, to explore innovative models for cultivating talents of the future, to promote digital transformation of education, and to accelerate the post-pandemic education recovery and the implementation of the Education 2030 Agenda. Let's work together to promote education transformation and create a better future for the Asian-Pacific region!

Thank you all.

［资料来源：见 youtube 联合国教科文组织频道（https://www.youtube.com/watch? v = O9ZmspSF-0Q），引用日期：2023 年 8 月 20 日。］

第七章　联合国粮食与农业组织

➡ 一、背景阅读

● （一）汉语简介

【成　立】正式成立于 1945 年 10 月 16 日，简称"粮农组织"，属联合国专门机构。

【宗　旨】提高各国人民的营养水平和生活水准；提高所有粮农产品的生产和分配效率；改善农村人口的生活状况，促进世界经济的发展，并最终消除饥饿和贫困。

【成　员】共有 194 个成员国、1 个成员组织（欧洲联盟）和 2 个准成员（法罗群岛、托克劳群岛）。

【主要负责人】总干事屈冬玉（中国籍），2019 年就任，2023 年连任，任期至 2027 年。

【总　部】意大利罗马。

【组织机构】（1）大会：最高权力机构，负责审议世界粮农状况，研究重大国际粮农问题，选举、任命总干事，选举理事会成员国和理事会独立主席，批准接纳新成员，批准工作计划和预算，修改章程和规则等；每两年举行一次，全体成员国参加。

（2）理事会：隶属于大会，在大会休会期间在大会赋予的权利范围内处理和决定有关问题；由大会按地区分配原则选出的 49 个成员国组成，任期 3 年，可连任，每年改选 1/3；在大会两届例会期间举行 5 次会议。（3）秘书处：执行机构，负责执行大会和理事会有关决议，处理日常工作。负责人是总干事，由大会选出，任期 4 年，在大会和理事会的监督下领导秘书处工作。

【主要活动】作为世界粮农领域的信息中心，搜集和传播世界粮农生产、贸易和技术信息，促进成员国之间的信息交流；向成员国提供技术援助，以帮助提高农业技术水平；向成员国特别是发展中成员国家提供农业政策支持和咨询服务；商讨国际粮农领域的重大问题，制定有关国际行为准则和法规。

【驻华代表机构】联合国粮农组织于 1983 年在北京设立驻华代表处。现任驻华代表为文康农（Carlos Watson，洪都拉斯籍）。

[资料来源：中国外交部网站（https://www. mfa. gov. cn/web/gjhdq_676201/gjhdqzz_681964/lhg_681966/jbqk_681968/201308/t20130821_9380026. shtml），引用日期：2023 年 8 月 21 日。]

（二）FAO 英语介绍

1. What is Food and Agriculture Organization (FAO)?

The Food and Agriculture Organization of the United Nations (FAO) is a specialized agency of the United Nations that leads international efforts to defeat hunger and improve nutrition and food security. It was founded on 16th October 1945.

The FAO is composed of 195 members (including 194 countries and the European Union). It is headquartered in Rome, Italy, and maintains regional and field offices around the world, operating in over 130 countries.

FAO's goal is to achieve food security for all and make sure that people have regular access to enough high-quality food to lead active, healthy lives.

2. History

During the World War II, in 1943, United States President Franklin D. Roosevelt called a United Nations Conference on Food and Agriculture, which brought representatives from forty-four governments to the Omni Homestead Resort in Hot Springs, Virginia from 18 May to 3 June.

The Conference ended with a commitment to establish a permanent organization for food and agriculture, which was achieved on 16 October 1945 in Quebec City, Canada, following the Constitution of the Food and Agriculture Organization.

In December 1946, FAO became a specialized agency of the United Nation.

3. The Structure of FAO

(1) FAO Conference

The supreme body of FAO is the all-member FAO Conference, which holds its regular biennial sessions in Rome in odd-numbered years. The conference determines the policy of FAO and adopts its budget. It makes recommendations relating to food, agriculture, fisheries, forestry, and related matters to member nations and to other international organization. It approves conventions and agreements for submission to member governments. It may establish commissions, working parties, and consultative groups and may convene special conferences. It periodically elects the Director General, as well as the member nations to be represented on the FAO Council. Each FAO member has one vote in the conference.

(2) FAO Council

The FAO Council, consisting of 49 member nations elected by the FAO Conference for three-year terms on a rotating basis (one-third of the membership stands down each year), meets at least once a year, under an independent chairman, as an interim governing body between meetings of the conference.

Council Committees include Programme Committee, Finance Committee, Committee on Constitutional and Legal Matters. Technical Committees include Committee on Agriculture, Committee on Commodity Problems, Committee on Fisheries, Committee on Forestry.

(3) Director-General

Under the supervision of the conference and the Council, the Director-General has full power and authority to direct the work of FAO.

The current Director-General is Qu Dongyu, who is the first Chinese national to head FAO. Qu won the nomination on the first round of voting at the 41st FAO Conference on 23 June 2019.

4. FAO *Strategic Framework 2022-2031*

(1) What is FAO's Strategic Framework?

Since 2010 all of FAO's work is guided by a Strategic Framework prepared for a period of ten to fifteen years, reviewed every four years.

FAO *Strategic Framework 2022-2031* articulates FAO's vision of a sustainable and food secure world for all, in the context of *the Agenda 2030 for Sustainable Development.*

(2) The four betters and leaving no one behind

FAO *Strategic Framework 2022-2031* seeks to support *the 2030 Agenda* through the transformation to MORE efficient, inclusive, resilient and sustainable agri-food systems for better production, better nutrition, a better environment, and a better life, leaving no one behind.

➢ Better production

➢ Better nutrition

➢ Better environment

➢ Better life

(3) A reinvigorated business model fit for purpose

FAO *Strategic Framework 2022-2031* also highlights the importance of a shift in FAO's working paradigm. FAO's reinvigorated, fit-for-purpose business model aims to ensure an inclusive and agile Organization that is transparent, open, innovative, responsible, effective and impactful to ensure the transformational change that is called for.

［资料来源：见国际粮农组织网站（https://www. fao. org/about/about-fao/en/。]

5. 词汇表 Vocabulary List

Food and Agriculture Organization of the United Nations

联合国粮食与农业组织

FAO *Strategic Framework 2022-2031*　粮农组织《2022—2031 年战略框架》

the Agenda 2030 for Sustainable Development　　《2030 年可持续发展议程》

a sustainable and food secure world for all

人人享有可持续发展、粮食安全有保障的世界

the 42nd session of the FAO Conference

联合国粮农组织大会第四十二届会议

food security	粮食安全
FAO Conference	粮农组织大会
The four betters	"四个更好"
better production	更好生产
better nutrition	更好营养

better environment	更好环境
better life	更好生活
agri-food systems	农业粮食体系

➡ 二、口译实践

● （一）英译汉

Global Conference on Green Development of Seed Industries
Opening Remarks（Excerpt）

Dr. QU Dongyu，FAO Director-General of FAO

（November 4，2021）

Excellencies，

Ladies and Gentlemen，

The world is facing a global population rise—that is expected to reach about 10 billion by 2050! We need to produce 50% more food to adequately feed everyone. The only way to achieve this target is by increasing crop productivity， through science and innovation.

（1）With innovative technologies and new business models we can do so in a sustainable manner， to protect our planet， our limited natural resources and biodiversity， and ensure profitability and social equality. We need to adapt our agri-food systems to mitigate the impacts of the climate crisis， and to reduce our environmental footprint.

Food insecurity has been increasing over the past six years. In 2020， almost 2 billion people did not have regular access to safe， nutritious and sufficient food. And up to 811 million people are currently facing hunger.

We need to speed up action， be efficient and effective， and coherent.

（2）We must produce more—more quantity and more food diversity with higher quality， with less—less inputs of resources and less impacts on the environment.

All the SDGs can be achieved， including SDG1 no poverty and SDG2 zero hunger.

But we need to do things differently. Business as usual is no longer an option.

(3) FAO's new *Strategic Framework for 2022-2031* supports *the 2030 Agenda.*

"Through the transformation to MORE efficient, inclusive, resilient and sustainable agri-food systems. For Better Production, Better Nutrition, a Better Environment and a Better Life, leaving no one behind."

This Global Seed Conference will contribute to the Four Betters, especially Better Production, for which "better seeds" are fundamental.

There are no good crops without good seeds. Seeds are the foundation of agri-food systems. We rely on seeds to produce food, feed, fibre, fuel, and they contribute to a friendly environment. Seeds play a crucial role in promoting food security and healthy foods, including food quality and food safety, and in supporting farmers' livelihoods, economic growth and rural development.

An improved and resilient crop variety can deliver a good and nutritious yield.

......

Dear Colleagues,

(4) FAO is a technical organization that generates, facilitates and promotes professional knowledge, and provides a neutral global platform for scientific and evidence based knowledge-sharing, including on affordable quality seeds, and planting materials of well-adapted and nutritious crop varieties. To support this work, we have identified five key themes to be covered over the next two days:

One, advanced technologies: including modern bio-technologies, such as gene editing and genetic improvement, are important tools for generating superior crop varieties.

(5) Two, conservation of plant genetic resources for food and agriculture, both in nature and in gene banks, and relevant data must be made available for research and breeding programs.

Three, crop varietal development and adoption: plant breeding should be encouraged as it generates progressively superior crop varieties adapted to different stress environments and requiring less external inputs.

(6) Four, seed systems: fit-for-purpose seed systems for delivering context-specific cropping systems solutions to farmers should become the norm.

Five, policy and governance effective policies, legislation and regulations must be in place to enable all relevant stakeholders to engage beneficially in the seed value chain.

Governments are the key drivers to eradicate hunger.

They should launch national seed actions to strengthen the seed value chain, and FAO will continue to support governments to develop and implement national policies, regulations and laws to create predictability and foster confidence in seed systems.

Over the next couple of days, prominent speakers will present their insights on developing and delivering solutions to farmers, to set the scene for a robust exchange of ideas. Ministers from different regions will share their thoughts on initiatives and policies aimed at making quality seeds of priority productive, nutritious and resilient crop varieties available to farmers. Participants will discuss progress on the various aspects of the seed industry value chain, and make recommendations to guide global work to promote the green development of global seed industries, in support of the *2030 Agenda*.

We only have nine harvests ahead of us before we reach our *2030 Agenda*. Let us sow the new seeds for promising future now! FAO is committed to leverage the momentum generated by this conference to transform the evidence provided into action on the ground.

Thank you.

[资料来源：见联合国粮农组织网站（https://www.fao.org/director-general/speeches/detail/en/c/1450918/），引用日期：2023 年 8 月 21 日。]

1. 实践解析

本材料是联合国粮农组织总干事 QU Dongyu（屈冬玉）博士于 2021 年 11 月 4 日在全球种业绿色发展大会上的开幕致辞。致辞中，屈冬玉提到针对解决粮食安全和可持续农业发展的挑战的一系列重要议题和行动方案。他强调了种子在农业体系中的重要性，呼吁推动绿色创新，建设可持续农业粮食体系。他表示，粮农组织作为技术型组织，致力于提供专业知识和种植材料。为实现2030 年议程助力，组织将积极采取行动，将本次大会的成果转化为实际行动，为粮食安全和可持续农业做出贡献。

本材料难点在于出现了不少农业种业、粮食作物的相关概念，特别是谈及全球种业绿色发展大会的四大目标和五大专题时，包含了 breeding programs、 gene editing、gene banks 等术语。文中直接引用粮农组织相关政策议程，需要对相关背景有一定了解才能快速作出反应。

Seed industry 即种业，《"十四五"现代种业提升工程建设规划》指出种业处于农业整个产业链的源头，是建设现代农业的标志性、先导性工程，是国家战略性、基础性核心产业。种业也被认为是农业的"芯片"。

Agri-food systems 即农业粮食体系，包含食品类和非食品类产品（种植业、畜牧业、渔业、林业和水产养殖产品）初级农业生产、非农产品（例如人造肉）生产、粮食供应链从生产者到消费者各环节和粮食最终消费者。①

Green Agriculture 即绿色农业，是"以可持续发展为基本原则，充分运用先进科学技术、先进工业装备和先进管理理念，以促进农产品安全、生态安全、资源安全和提高农业综合效益的协调统一为目标，把标准化贯穿到农业的整个产业链中，推动人类社会和经济全面、协调、可持续发展的农业发展模式"②。

Strategic Framework for 2022-2031 即联合国粮农组织《2022—2031 年战略框架》，于 2021 年 6 月在粮农组织第 42 届大会上批准通过，是在粮农组织职责领域面临重大全球和区域挑战（如 2019 年新型冠状病毒疫情）的背景下制定的，阐述了粮农组织在《2030 年可持续发展议程》背景下对人人享有可持续和粮食安全世界的愿景，着力推动转型，建设更高效、更包容、更有韧性且更可持续的农业粮食体系，实现更好生产、更好营养、更好环境和更好生活，不让任何人掉队。③

2. 长难句点拨

（1）该句的难点之一是句子结构和逻辑关系，句子中包含多个并列结构，如"we can do so in a sustainable manner, to protect our planet …"，其中 to protect 和 ensure 是并列关系，而 our planet 和 our limited natural resources and biodiversity 是动词 protect 的并列宾语。在口译时，需要处理好这些并列成分，确保句子之间的逻辑连贯。同时，对一些抽象名词如 biodiversity, profitability,

---

① 联合国粮农组织：《2021 年粮食及农业状况：提高农业粮食体系韧性，应对冲击和压力》，2021 年版，第 9 页。

② 见知网百科（https://xuewen.cnki.net/read-R2016093510000294.html），引用日期：2023 年 8 月 21 日。

③ 见联合国粮农组织网站（https://www.fao.org/strategic-framework/zh），引用日期：2023 年 8 月 21 日。

social equality，在组织译文时，要进行词性转换，让译文流畅、简洁。例如，将"ensure profitability and social equality"译为"兼顾效益的同时，确保社会平等"更佳。

（2）该句结构相对简单，语言理解没有什么困难，难点在于语言组织。讲话者通过使用 more 和 less 短语，形成了对比的效果。译文不仅要保持对比的效果，还要考虑让译文地道、简洁，如"要提升产量，实现优产、丰产、多样化"比译成"要生产更多食物，种类更多，质量更高"更简洁。为了形成对仗，"less inputs of resources and less impacts on the environment"可译为"要减少消耗，少投入资源，少影响环境"。

（3）该段中包含两个专有名词 Strategic Framework for 2022-2031（《2022—2031 年战略框架》）和 the 2030 Agenda（《2030 年议程》即《2030 年可持续发展议程》）。其中，《2030 年议程》是联合国所有会员国于 2015 年一致通过的，是指导国际和国家发展行动的整体框架，频繁出现在各类联合国相关会议和文件中，必须熟记。段落中的引文引用自联合国文件，整体风格偏正式，通过使用名词（transformation）来表达动词（transform）的含义，让表达更简洁。同时由于多用名词，因而增加了介词使用（through、to 和 for），凸显了英语静态的特点。然而汉语呈现出动态特点，倾向于多用动词，因此，对该段在口译中应该通过增补和词性转换技巧，让译文符合汉语特点。

（4）该句介绍了联合国粮农组织的作用，是典型的英语长句，包含了主从复句和多个并列结构。要准确翻译该句，首先要准确切分意群，并厘清意群之间的逻辑关系："FAO is a technical organization // that generates, facilitates and promotes professional knowledge//，and provides a neutral global platform //for scientific and evidence based knowledge-sharing//，including on affordable quality seeds, and planting materials of well-adapted and nutritious crop varieties."其中，generates、facilitates、promotes 三个动词是并列谓语，主语是 that（即主句中的技术组织），共同的宾语是 professional knowledge，这三个动词又与 provides 并列，provides 的宾语 platform 后面有 for 介词短语修饰，表示这个平台的目的，而 including 后面并列的名词和动名词短语则是知识分享的具体内容。

（5）该句的难点之一是涉及一些农业和遗传学方面的专业术语，如 plant genetic resources（植物遗传资源）、gene banks（基因库）、breeding programs（植物育种计划）。除此之外，该句由于是讲话者提到的未来两天探讨的五大话题之一，因而采用了标题式短语的形式，对动词进行了名词化处理，并省去了不必要的虚词和次要词。但是在翻译成汉语时，要充分考虑汉语习惯，将短语补充成短句。

（6）该句也是标题式短语，把词语挤压在一起，通过词语连用构成的新词。这种短语结构简单，但是信息量大，因此翻译时要联系上下文，提供准确流畅的译文，如将 fit-for-purpose seed systems 译为"切合所需的种业体系"，context-specific cropping systems solutions "因地制宜的耕作制度解决方案"。第五点关于政策与治理部分，原文采用被动态来表达一种客观、正式的语气。在口译过程中，由于汉语表述形式更加灵活，可以使用无主句来实现同样的效果，译为：有效的政策和法律法规要落实到位，使有关各方推进种业价值链建设。

（二）汉译英

国际粮食减损大会视频致辞（节选）
联合国粮农组织总干事 屈冬玉博士
（2021 年 9 月 9 – 11 日）

尊敬的各位嘉宾，

我很高兴围绕粮食减损这一重要议题发表讲话。

（1）从农田到餐桌，供应链的每个环节都面临着粮食损失和浪费问题。据联合国粮农组织估计，从收获到零售各环节中，全球范围内的粮食损失率高达 14%。此外，零售、餐饮和消费环节的粮食浪费率高达 17%。

（2）粮食损失和浪费现象触目惊心，每年导致 4000 亿美元的损失，总量相当于 12.6 亿人一年的口粮。更何况，当前全球粮食不安全与营养不良形势十分严峻，这一现象愈发令人扼腕痛惜。全球共有 8.11 亿人食物不足，30 亿人无力负担健康膳食。

（3）在中国，大家都知道："谁知盘中餐，粒粒皆辛苦。"粮食损失和浪费耗费了宝贵资源，引发温室气体排放，加剧气候危机影响。

不仅如此，粮食损失和浪费也印证了当前的农业粮食体系运转不良，全球亿万民众在新冠疫情危机期间对此有着切身体会。

女士们，先生们，

联合国秘书长将于本月联合国大会期间召开联合国粮食体系峰会，加快推动农业粮食体系转型。为此，我们要因地制宜，广泛采纳新思路、新想法。业态创新和制度安排创新，以及人工智能等各类技术与数字化方案都能促进减少粮食损失和浪费。

（4）联合国粮农组织是可持续发展目标第12.3项具体目标指标"粮食损耗指数"的托管机构。我们携手各方伙伴，尽可能准确掌握粮食损失和浪费的规模、发生的环节以及原因。唯有准确掌握信息，才能有效行动。

我们必须团结各方、群策群力、协调行动，共同减少粮食损失和浪费。比如，动员公共与私营部门、学术界、国际组织、金融机构、生产者、消费者与民间社会一起开展行动。我们通过"衡量和减少粮食损失和浪费技术平台"，推广最佳方法。

（5）联合国粮农组织期待与包括中国在内的全体成员共同努力，通过南北合作、南南合作及三方合作，跨国、跨区域和跨洲传播知识，促进对话，分享专长。

……

女士们，先生们，

在讲话的最后，我想提出三大要点作为总结：

首先，我们若不能降低粮食损失和浪费水平，就无法消除饥饿和各种形式的营养不良。

其次，我们必须对粮食损失和浪费的根本原因形成可靠、科学且立足实证的认识。我们能做到在实现增产的同时减少资源消耗，不对环境造成负面影响。

最后，承诺、协作、伙伴关系和各利益相关方加大支持力度至关重要。

联合国粮农组织致力于团结各方力量，推动更富雄心的协作，共同应对粮食损失和浪费问题，支持实现《2030年议程》，为所有人实现更好生产、更好营养、更好环境和更好生活，不让任何一个人掉队。

谢谢。

［资料来源：见联合国粮农组织网站（https://www.fao.org/director-general/speeches/detail/zh/c/1438516/），引用日期：2023年8月21日。］

1. 实践解析

这篇材料是联合国粮农组织总干事屈冬玉博士于2021年9月在国际粮食减损大会上的视频致辞。大会上，来自50多个国家及国际组织、企业、非政府组织的300多名代表围绕"减少粮食损失浪费，促进世界粮食安全"主题展开深入交流。致辞中，屈冬玉指出全球范围内粮食损失和浪费问题的严重性，呼吁加快推动农业粮食体系转型，通过业态创新、制度安排创新和技术应用等手段应对问题。同时，他也强调了联合国粮农组织的角色和行动，期望各方共同努力减少粮食损失和浪费，推动实现可持续发展目标。

材料长短句交错，总体难度适中，但涉及粮食相关术语概念，故需要译者掌握一定的背景知识。

粮食损耗指数（Food Loss Index）：指的是"从生产到（不包括）零售水平的粮食损失状况。它所衡量的是一个由 10 种主要大宗商品组成的篮子与基准期相比的损失率变化。粮食损耗指数有助于衡量可持续发展目标具体目标12.3 方面的进展状况"[1]。

三方合作（Triangular cooperation）：指"北方国家或国际多边组织与南方国家合作，向其他发展中国家提供援助支持。其中南方国家作为援助合作方的加入是三方合作与以往合作方式相比的不同之处"[2]。

2. 长难句点拨

（1）该段是典型的总分关系，先总述目前存在的问题，再分别阐述"粮食损失率"和"粮食浪费率"。从语篇层面来讲，应在译文中体现句子间的逻辑与连贯。除此之外，还应关注汉英文在数字相关表达上的差异。原文中数字出现在句末，如果采取直译策略，以"粮食损失率"和"粮食浪费率"为英文主语，则译文比较生硬。不如换个说法参考译文为："14% of food produced globally undergoes food loss. Furthermore, 17% of total global food production may be wasted at the retail, food-service and consumer stages."

（2）该句既没有专业词汇，也没有复杂的结构，翻译成英文并不难。但如果想让译文简洁、地道，应该考虑上下文的衔接与连贯，如"每年导致4000 亿美元的损失"这个短语是对主语"粮食损失和浪费现象触目惊心"的补充，可以考虑用同位语结构。除此之外，"当前全球粮食不安全与营养不良形势十分严峻"这个大背景衬托出问题的严重性，因此用"against a backdrop of"可以更好地突出意群之间的逻辑关系。

（3）该句的难点是诗句翻译，如果长期记忆中没有储备"谁知盘中餐，粒粒皆辛苦"的英译版本，对口译学习者来说，在短时间内斟酌出译文是一个不小的挑战。可以考虑放弃"盘中餐"这样的意象，采取释义的方法来解

---

[1] 见联合国粮农组织网站（https://www.fao.org/sustainable-development-goals-data-portal/data/indicators/1231-global-food-losses/zh），引用日期：2023 年 8 月 21 日。

[2] 袁晓慧：《三方合作：国际发展合作的新兴方式》，载《国际经济合作》2020 年第 6 期，第 21 页。

释诗句的意思，如 "A single grain of rice comes with a thousand drops of sweat."第二句是一个连动句，连续使用了"耗费""引发""加剧"三个动词，切忌将其处理成并列关系，而应该根据汉语意思厘清逻辑，并通过连词和介词在英文中显化逻辑关系，让译文更有层次。

（4）该句中有两个专有名词："粮食损耗指数"（Food Loss Index）和"托管机构"（custodian agency）。除此之外，该句后半段可以巧用 how much、where 和 why 等疑问词，而非逐字翻译为 "the scale of the loss" 和 "where food loss takes place"。

（5）该句结构较为复杂，含有多个并列结构，其中"通过南北合作、南南合作及三方合作""跨国、跨区域和跨洲"这两个并列成分实际是句子的状语，是动词短语"传播知识、促进对话、分享专长"的修饰语。在听力理解阶段要能够厘清意群之间的关系，并选择合适的语法结构。除此之外，也要熟悉对于"南北合作、南南合作、三方合作"的英语表述。

➡ 三、口译练习

● （一）英译汉

Gender in Agriculture and Rural Development（Excerpt）

Why consider gender in the analysis of agriculture and rural development? Gender inequality is not solely a matter of human rights. It is also an important issue interconnected with agricultural performance and food security.

......

Women's contributions to rural economic activities are indispensable in all region. Women often manage complex households and pursue manifold livelihood strategies. (1) They often play multiple productive, reproductive and community roles, such as producing crops, tending animals, processing and preparing food, working as wage laborers, fetching water and fuel, trading and marketing, educating children, caring for the elderly and sick and maintaining their homes. Women's share of the agricultural labor force in Central Asia is just below the world average at 41 %. In Europe, the average is 32 %, ranging from 29% in Eastern Europe to 45% in Southern Europe. Despite the significant variations across regions and countries, agriculture still remains one of the major sectors of employment for women. (2) However, many activities performed by women are neither captured by statistics nor defined as economically active employment in national accounts, even though they are essential to the well being of rural households. Thus, the real share of women in the agricultural labor force may be significantly higher than what is officially reported. (3) Time Use Surveys and estimates from various countries tell us that women provide 85% to 90% of the time spent on household chores, which often leads to their time poverty.

At the same time, women's crop production roles are expanding in some rural areas, in part due to the out migration of men and youth. For instance, in the Republic of Moldova, the recently conducted Agricultural Senses shows that there is no significant difference between the type of crops grown by female and male agricultural holders.

What role do women play in livestock production? Women are also heavily engaged in the livestock sector. Globally, about 66% of poor livestock keepers, 400 million people, are women. They are predominantly involved in managing poultry and dairy animals. However, women in general, tend to own smaller numbers of animals, which might be due to labor constraints or to their lack of access to loan.

Data from FAO's Rural Income Generating Activities database suggests that livestock holdings of male holders in Albania, Bulgaria and Tajikistan range between 30% to 50% higher than those of female holders. Land is an important productive asset for ensuring food and nutrition security, as well as supporting income generation. Land ownership and control over land means wealth status and power in rural societies, especially for those engaged in agriculture. Stark gender disparities in landholdings are acknowledged in all region. (4) Available data show that men make up the majority of total agricultural holders around the world. Moreover, male headed households in developing countries tend to have two or three times larger landholdings and those of female headed households. Male household heads, or holders in Albania, hold on average about 20% larger sized lands than their female counterparts. While in Bulgaria, this gender disparity is as high as 30 %. In the Republic of Moldova, 64% of the agricultural holders are men, yet 81% of the total area of agricultural holdings belongs to male holders. The results of a recently conducted agricultural census in the Republic of Mondova are in line with global trends in relation to the gender gap in access to technology. For instance, despite the fact that women make up more than one 3rd of all agricultural holders, they own only 9% of all tractors in the country.

What gains could be made from closing the gender gap in access to agricultural assets, services and productive resources? Research suggests that closing these gender gaps in access to resources would help women to achieve better yields on their farms, thus contributing to greater overall food security. (5) <u>It has been suggested that higher production would have additional impacts, including, for example, increased demand by farmers for labor, locally produce goods and services, increased availability of food and reductions in food prices.</u> Higher production could also increase women's employment as well as the incomes of female farmers. Closing the gender gap requires an improved understanding of the roles and relations and the opportunities and constraints of women and men involved in agriculture and rural development. Doing so requires collecting and using meaningful gender indicators and sex disaggregated data to inform policies and programs. A module on gender statistics will provide simple technical guidance on the production and collection of sexist aggregated data via a core set of gender indicators.

〔资料来源：见 youtube 联合国粮农组织频道（https://www.youtube.com/watch? v = Et2gHFzKCNk），引用日期：2023 年 8 月 21 日。〕

1. 词汇准备

Republic of Moldova	摩尔多瓦共和国
Rural Income Generating Activities database	农村创收活动数据库
Albania	阿尔巴尼亚
Bulgaria	保加利亚
Tajikistan	塔吉克斯坦

2. 长难句点拨

（1）该句结构相对简单，也没有专业术语，唯一的难点是为了解释 "multiple productive, reproductive and community roles" 列举了一连串的动词短语，对口译学习者的听力理解和做笔记的能力有较高的要求。除此之外，考虑到演讲的具体语境和场合，译文的措辞要正式，结构基本统一，让译文更富有节奏。可以翻译为：她们在生产、生育和社区中承担多项工作，包括生产农作物、照料动物、加工和准备食物、充当雇佣劳动者、取水和燃料、交易和销售、教育儿童、照顾老人和病人以及维护家园。

（2）该句涉及一个专业词汇"national accounts"即国民账户，是测量 GDP 的基本方法和框架。从语篇层面来讲，该句涉及的一些论述相对比较陌生，如"not captured by statistics"（妇女从事的许多活动没有被统计）和"economically active employment"（有被定义为国民账户中的经济活动就业），可能会造成理解困难。

（3）time use survey（TUS，时间利用调查）就是"针对人们从事各种活动的时间情况的抽样调查，通过客观、量化的测量手段将人们的'社会时间'对象化，使其能够被全面概述和了解"①。time poverty，即时间贫困，"劳动经济学家把工作时间超过某一特定时间限度的情况"② 称为时间贫困。

（4）该句涉及三个专业概念，厘清三者之间的关系，句子理解就迎刃而解。agricultural holder，即农业持有者，指的是在农业领域中拥有土地或从事农业活动的个体或家庭。这包括农民、农场主或农业经营者等。理解了这个概念，landholdings（持有土地）就不难理解了，male headed households 指的是户主为男性的家庭，那么与之相对的 female headed households 则指的是户主为女性的家庭。

（5）该句结构相对松散，要准确理解句子意思就要理解不同短语之间的关系，如 increased demand by farmers、increased availability 和 reductions in food price 这三者处于并列关系，而 increased demand by farmers for 的宾语则包括 labor、locally produce goods、services 三个成分。除此之外，在翻译过程中，对一些英语的抽象名词如 availability 和 reductions 要进行词性转换，使译文更加流畅、地道。

---

① 马缨、李晨熹：《时间利用调查及其在社会科学研究中的应用》载《统计理论与实践》2022 年第 9 期，第 20 页。
② 畅红琴：《中国农村地区时间贫困的性别差异研究》载《山西财经大学学报》2010 年第 2 期，第 9 页。

● （二）汉译英

依托家庭经营推进农业现代化（节选）
——在联合国粮农组织的演讲
中华人民共和国国务院总理　李克强

（2014 年 10 月 15 日）

尊敬的格拉齐亚诺总干事，

女士们，先生们，朋友们：

很高兴在金秋时节来到联合国粮农组织总部，参加第 34 个世界粮食日系列活动。刚才，一进粮农组织大楼，我就看到一层大厅墙壁上多种语言镌刻的"Food for All"——人皆有食。这是粮农组织的神圣使命，也是世界各国的共同目标。（1）长期以来，联合国粮农组织与世界粮食计划署、国际农发基金，紧紧围绕这一目标，帮助成员国以多种形式发展农业，为供养世界几十亿人口作出了十分突出的贡献。在此，我谨代表中国政府和人民，对粮农组织等机构、在座的各位和你们的同事所作出的不懈努力表示高度赞赏，对所取得的卓越成就表示诚挚敬意！

今年世界粮食日的主题是"家庭农业：供养世界，关爱地球"。我认为这个主题既立足现实，又着眼长远，勾画出了全球农业发展的美好愿景。依靠家庭农业解决吃饭问题，也符合中国的实际。（2）2000 多年前中国的先哲说过，"民以食为天"，这也是长久以来中国人所奉行的理念。大家都知道，中国人口多、人均耕地少，让十几亿人民吃饱饭，是我们最大的事情，也曾经是最大的难题。我年轻时在中国农村生活多年，亲身经历过吃不饱饭的艰难岁月。吃一顿饱饭可能很快就会忘记，但饥饿留下的印象永生难忘。30 多年前中国实行改革开放，就是从农村改革开始的。我们通过改革实现了农业大发展，粮食产量由 3 亿多吨增加到 6 亿多吨，成功解决了人民的温饱问题。这里有一条最基本的经验，就是发展家庭农业。

（3）20 世纪 80 年代初的农村改革，最主要的就是推行家庭承包经营制度。这项改革把农户确立为农业经营的主体，赋予农民长期而有保障的土地使用权和经营自主权，几亿农民的生产积极性迅速调动起来，每个人的力量都得到充分发挥，短短几年农业生产就迈上一个大台阶。在此基础上，几亿人摆脱了贫困，并提前达到联合国千年发展目标。近 10 年，中国粮食连续增产，今年又丰收在望。这些成绩的取得，家庭农业功不可没。

30多年来，中国家庭农业能够不断焕发出新的活力，也与科技、政策等创新密不可分。(4) 我们建立了一整套农业科技推广体系，大面积推广优良品种、农业机械，推广设施农业。仅杂交水稻一项，每年就带来数千万吨的增产。我们大力鼓励农民合作社、专业农户、企业公司以及政府服务组织等，为农民提供农业机械作业、农产品加工流通等服务。每年都有数十万台农业机械像候鸟一样，在中国大地上往返迁徙。当小麦成熟的时候，大批联合收割机一路由南往北，追赶着季节，为农民提供小麦收割服务，既解决了农民家庭机械作业的难题，也提高了农业机械的使用效率。中国政府还不断增加农业投入，支持建设农业基础设施、改善生产条件，农田有效灌溉率已提高到50%以上，农业抗灾能力不断增强。

…………

中国政府高度重视农业，始终坚持立足国内实现粮食基本自给。同时，也高度重视农业可持续发展。我们用低于世界平均水平的耕地和淡水资源，解决了世界近20%人口的吃饭问题，这本身体现了一种集约。但我们不满足于此，还要进一步促进农业高效集约发展。（5）与此同时，加强生态保护与建设，实施好退耕还林、天然林保护、防沙治沙、水土保持、草原治理等工程，支持农民改良土壤、减少污染、大规模建设高标准农田。通过努力，促进农业资源的永续利用，既满足当代人需要，也为子孙后代留下良田沃土、碧水蓝天。保护中国生态，也是关爱地球、保护地球。

女士们，先生们！

（6）人人有饭吃，是人类最基本的生存权利，是一切人权的基础。全球农业发展取得了长足的进步，但饥饿和贫困依然是一种"无声的危机"，是深深困扰全人类的"阿喀琉斯之踵"。目前世界上还有8亿多贫困人口面临着食物不足、营养不良的威胁。促进农业发展，消除饥饿和贫困，依然是世界面临的重大挑战，也是全人类肩负的共同责任。国际社会应当携起手来，加强农业合作，更多关注发展中国家，尤其是一些最不发达国家的诉求。应减少贸易保护，加强为最不发达国家提供农业技术、资金等支持，提高全球农业生产水平和粮食安全保障水平。

中国与世界各国特别是发展中国家的农业合作发展很快。近些年，我们在亚洲、非洲、拉美、太平洋等地区近100个国家，建立了农业技术示范中心、农业技术实验站和推广站，先后派遣农业专家和技术人员3万余人次，同时帮助这些国家培养了一大批农业技术人员。我们这一代中国人经历过饥饿的痛苦，我们与仍处在饥饿状态的人们感同身受，我们希望看到饥饿和贫困在全球被消灭，我们愿意与各国分享农业技术、经验和农业发展模式。中国的杂交水稻良种已经使很多国家受益。这里我宣布，未来5年，中国政府将向联合国粮农组织捐赠5000万美元用于开展"农业南南合作"，并加大对世界粮食计划署和国际农发基金的支持。

女士们，先生们！

中国作为世界上最大的发展中国家，任何时候都是维护世界粮食安全的积极力量。尽管中国农业进一步发展面临不少困难，但我们仍将不懈努力，用行动来兑现诺言，主要依靠自己的力量解决好吃饭问题。我们愿与世界各国携手奋进，共同创造一个无饥饿、无贫困、可持续发展的世界。

刚才总干事先生赠送我一本书，介绍他的国家提高粮食产量、减少饥饿的经验。我赠送给他一本反映大自然美好风光的画册。人们只有吃饱了饭，才有欣赏自然风光的心境，才有更高的精神追求。打牢粮食这个人类发展最重要的基础，人们的物质和精神生活才会更加美好，世界才会更加美好。谢谢各位！

［资料来源：见联合国粮农组织网站（https://www.fao.org/fileadmin/user_upload/newsroom/docs/Li%20Keqiang%20s%20Speech.pdf），引用日期：2023年8月21日。］

1. 词汇准备

"家庭农业：供养世界，关爱地球"

"Feeding the world, caring for the earth"

家庭承包经营制度	the household contract system
土地使用权和经营自主权	land use right and operational independence
联合收割机	combined harvester
退耕还林	returning farmland to forests
农业技术示范中心	agricultural technology demonstration centers
农业技术实验站和推广站	agricultural technology experimental stations and promotion station

2. 长难句点拨

（1）该句中除了联合国粮农组织（FAO），还出现了世界粮食计划署（the World Food Program，WFP）、国际农发基金（the International Fund for Agricultural Development，IFAD）这两个相对陌生的机构。该句另一个难点是句子中含有多个动词，谓语的选择至关重要。尽管该句的主干是"联合国粮农组织与世界粮食计划署、国际农发基金为供养世界几十亿人口作出了十分突出的贡献"，由于谓语之前有多个状语成分，且状语成分比较复杂，为了减轻记忆负担和语言组织的难度，建议采取顺句驱动的方式而非先译出句子主干，通过增补逻辑连词让句意更加清楚、明了。参考译文为："Over the years, the FAO, the World Food Program（WFP）and the International Fund for Agricultural Development（IFAD）, with a strong commitment to this goal, have helped the member states to develop agriculture in multiple forms, thus making outstanding contribution to feeding the billions of people in our world."

（2）该句的难点是"先哲""民以食为天"，在口译过程中要深刻理解原文，理解"先贤""先哲"指代的具体对象，如果只是笼统指代先人，一般译为"forefathers"或者"ancestors"；如果强调"哲"，即强调某个思想非常重要，一般译为"philosophers"。"民以食为天"是一句俗语，多次出现在政府领导人讲话中，一般采取意译的方式，参考译文为："Food is a paramount necessity for the people."或者"Food is the first necessity of the people."

（3）该句难度较大，首先是背景知识，涉及农村改革和家庭承包经营制度等术语，如"家庭承包经营制度"（household contract system）、"土地使用权"（land use right）和"经营自主权"（operational independence）。其次，原文句子较长，包含多个动词短语和修饰成分，在口译中，需要充分理解短语之间的逻辑关系，如第一句和第二句之间的衔接与过渡。"把农户确立为农业经营的主体"和"赋予农民长期而有保障的土地使用权和经营自主权"实际是改革的内容，而"几亿农民的生产积极性迅速调动起来，每个人的力量都得到充分发挥"是改革对农民的刺激作用，这里有两组并列关系，应体现在语法结构上。同时，还要增加连词，将因果关系显化。"短短几年农业生产就迈上一个大台阶"是这个制度带来的变化，此处也需要适当增补逻辑，通过灵活运用显化技巧，可以确保英语译文结构清楚，语言流畅。

（4）该句句式结构不难，主要难点是农业农民相关的术语和缩写，如优良品种（quality varieties）、农业机械（agricultural machinery）、设施农业（controlled-environment agriculture）、杂交水稻（hybrid rice）、农民合作社（farmers' cooperatives）和专业农户（specialized farming households）。在积累相关术语的时候，要理解术语意义，掌握其内涵，要知其然更要知其所以然。

（5）该句中包含一些与农田保护的术语，如退耕还林（returning farmland to forests）、天然林保护（protecting natural forests）、防沙治沙（desertification prevention and control）、水土保持（water and land conservation）、草原治理

（grassland management）和高标准农田（high-standard farmland）。首先必须记住和理解这些术语。同时，由于这些术语是以并列形式出现在谓语"实施"和宾语"工程"之间的，因此，该句宜先翻译主干部分，再用 such … as … 引出多个列举，参考译文为"We will further enhance ecological protection and improvement and effectively implement such projects as returning farmland to forests，protecting natural forests，desertification prevention and control，water and land conservation and grassland management."

（6）该句的难点之一就是文化差异和典故的运用，如"人人有饭吃"是中国文化特有的表达方式，口译学习者应选择合适的英文表达方式，使译文传达相同的意思和情感；而"无声的危机"（silent crisis）和"阿喀琉斯之踵"（Achilles' heel）则考察译者对于英语语言和文化的积累。除此之外，句子的整合也对译者提出了一定的挑战。"人人有饭吃"是这个句子的主语，如果将其处理成主语从句，整个句子就会显得累赘和复杂。宜处理为名词短语，"人类最基本的生存权利"和"一切人权的基础"看似处于并列关系，但是从意思上看有重叠的部分，因此不宜处理为并列关系。除此之外，在该句译文中，口译学习者需要妥善运用代词，让译文简洁明了。

➡ 四、参考译文

● （一）口译实践

1. 英译汉

全球种业绿色发展大会开幕致辞（节选）
联合国粮农组织总干事　屈冬玉博士
（2021 年 11 月 4 日）

各位阁下，
女士们、先生们，
世界人口保持增长态势，预计在 2050 年前将达 100 亿左右！粮食需要增产 50%，才能充分满足所有人的需求。唯有依靠科学与创新，提高作物生产水平，方能达成这一目标。

凭借创新技术和全新业务模式，我们能以可持续的方式落实这项工作，从而保护地球、有限的自然资源和生物多样性，并在兼顾效益的同时，确保社会平等。要调整农业粮食体系，减轻气候危机的影响，减少人类的环境足迹。

在过去六年中，粮食不安全形势日益严峻。2020 年，近 20 亿人不能按常获得安全、营养和充足的食物。目前，饥饿人口多达 8.11 亿。

要加快行动步伐，加强效率成效，保持步调一致。

要提升产量，实现优产、丰产、多样化，要减少消耗，少投入资源，少影响环境。

各项可持续发展目标有望一一实现，包括 SDG1（无贫困）和 SDG2（零饥饿）。

不过，要另寻他法。绝不能再对现状听之任之。

联合国粮农组织新版《2022—2031 年战略框架》助力落实《2030 年议程》，着力推动转型，建设更高效、更包容、更有韧性且更可持续的农业粮食体系，实现更好生产、更好营养、更好环境和更好生活，不让任何人掉队。

本次全球种业大会将推动实现"四个更好"，尤其是少不得"更好种子"的"更好生产"。

好收成离不开好种子。种子是农业粮食体系的立足之本，是我们赖以生产粮食、饲料、纤维、燃料的基础，有助于建设良好环境。种子的作用不可估量，既能增强粮食安全、提供健康食品，包括食品质量和安全，也能改善农民生计，促进经济增长，推动农村发展。

经过改良的韧性作物品种，能够长出有营养的好粮食。

…………

各位同事，

粮农组织是技术型组织，致力于创造、促进和推广专业知识，为分享基于实证的科学知识提供全球性中立论坛，包括分享实惠的优质种子，以及具有良好适应能力和营养价值的作物品种种植材料。为推进这方面工作，我们确定了五大专题，供接下来两天探讨：

一、先进技术：包括现代生物技术，例如基因编辑和遗传改良，都是开发优质作物品种的重要工具。

二、保护粮食和农业植物遗传资源：包括自然界和基因库中遗传资源，相关数据必须对科研和育种计划开放。

三、开发和应用作物品种：应鼓励植物育种，不断改良优质作物品种，使其适应各种不利环境，同时只需较少外部投入。

四、种业体系：打造切合所需的种业体系，为农民设计因地制宜的耕作制度解决方案，应成为常态；

五、政策与治理：有效的政策和法律法规要落实到位，使有关各方推进种业价值链建设。

政府对于消除饥饿发挥着关键作用，应出台国家种业行动，加强种业价值链，粮农组织则将继续支持政府制定并实施国家政策和法律法规，推进有章可循、可信可靠的种业体系建设。

在接下来的两天时间里，发言贵宾将发表真知灼见，畅谈如何为农民量身打造解决方案，从而为踊跃交流想法奠定基调。各区域国家部长将各抒己见，研讨向农民提供优选的高产、营养和抗逆作物优质种子的举措和政策。与会者将探讨种业价值链方方面面取得的进展，并出谋献策，指引国际社会着力推动全球种业绿色发展，助力落实《2030 年议程》。

距离实现《2030 年议程》最后期限仅剩 9 个年头。粮农组织力争把握大会形成的势头，力促将会上征集的实证转化为实地行动。

谢谢。

［资料来源：见联合国粮农组织网站（https://www.fao.org/director-general/speeches/detail/zh/c/1454774/，引用日期：2023 年 8 月 21 日。］

2. 汉译英

International Conference on Food Loss and Waste
Video Statement（Excerpt）

Dr QU Dongyu, FAO Director-General

（September 9-11, 2021）

Distinguished participants,

I am pleased to address you on this important topic.

Food loss and waste occur across the supply chain from tillage to table. FAO estimates that between the post-harvest and retail stages of the supply chain, up to 14% of food produced globally undergoes food loss. Furthermore, 17% of total global food production may be wasted at the retail, food-service and consumer stages.

These high levels of food loss and waste, valued at 400 billion US dollars annually, could feed around 1.26 billion more people per year. They are happening against a backdrop of severe global challenges in terms of food insecurity and malnutrition. Up to 811 million people in the world are undernourished, while 3 billion people cannot afford a healthy diet.

As a Chinese proverb says, "A single grain of rice comes with a thousand drops of sweat". Food loss and waste make up a waste of our scarce resources, while also contributing to the climate crisis impacts through Greenhouse Gas emission.

In addition, it also confirms poorly functioning agri-food systems, as millions of people around the world have experienced first-hand during the COVID-19 crisis.

Ladies and Gentlemen,

The UN Secretary-General will convene the UN Food Systems Summit during the UN General Assembly later this month, which will catalyze agri-food systems transformation. In finding solutions, we need to be open to new ideas, each one tailored to the specific context. Innovations in business models, institutional arrangements, technologies and digital solutions such as Artificial Intelligence can ALL contribute to reducing food loss and waste.

FAO is the custodian agency for the Food Loss Index, which is one of the indicators of SDG target 12.3. We are working, together with our partners, to know as accurately as possible how much food is lost and wasted, as well as where and why. This really matters and can make a difference.

We must get all the players on board to work collaboratively and in a coordinated manner towards reducing food loss and waste. This includes the public and private sectors together with academia, international organizations, financial institutions, producers, consumers and civil society. Through the Technical Platform on Measurement and Reduction of Food Loss and Waste, we can facilitate the adoption of good practices.

FAO is looking forward to working with our Members, including China, in disseminating knowledge, enhancing dialogue and exchanging expertise across countries, regions and continents through North-South, South-South and Triangular cooperation.

......

Distinguished Guests,

Ladies and Gentlemen,

In conclusion, I wish to summarize with three key messages:

First, we cannot end hunger and all forms of malnutrition if we do not address the high levels of food loss and waste.

Second, we must be informed by a solid, scientific and evidence-based understanding of the root causes of food loss and waste. We can produce more with less, without a negative impact on the environment.

And third, commitment, collaboration, partnerships and increased support from all stakeholders are crucial.

FAO is committed to working together to promote more ambitious collective actions to address the problem of food loss and waste in support of achieving *the 2030 Agenda* and ensure better production, better nutrition, a better environment and a better life for all, leaving no one behind.

Thank you.

［资料来源：见联合国粮农组织网站（https://www.fao.org/director-general/speeches/detail/en/c/1438511/，引用日期：2023 年 8 月 21 日。］

● （二）口译练习

1. 英译汉

农业农村发展中的性别问题（节选）

为什么在分析农业和农村发展时要考虑性别问题？性别不平等不仅仅是一个人权问题。它也是一个与农业绩效和粮食安全相互关联的重要问题。

············

在所有地区，妇女对农村经济活动的贡献是不可缺少的。妇女往往管理着复杂的家庭，并追求多方面的生计战略。她们往往在生产、生育/生殖和社区中承担多项工作，如生产农作物、照料动物、加工和准备食物、充当雇佣劳动者、取水和燃料、交易和销售、教育儿童、照顾老人和病人以及维护家园。中亚妇女在农业劳动力中的比例略低于世界平均水平，为 41%。在欧洲，平均为 32%，从东欧的 29% 到南欧的 45% 不等。尽管各地区和国家之间存在很大差异，但农业仍然是妇女就业的主要部门之一。然而，妇女从事的许多活动既没有被统计，也没有被定义为国民账户中的经济活动就业，尽管它们对农村家庭的福祉至关重要。因此，妇女在农业劳动力中的实际份额可能大大高于官方报告的数字。来自不同国家的时间使用调查和估计告诉我们，妇女提供了85%至90%的家务劳动时间，这往往导致她们的时间贫困。

同时，在一些农村地区，妇女的作物生产作用正在扩大，部分原因是男子和青年的外迁。例如，在摩尔多瓦共和国，最近进行的农业普查显示，女性和男性农业持有者种植的作物类型没有明显区别。

妇女在畜牧业生产中发挥什么作用？妇女也大量参与了畜牧业部门。在全球范围内，约有66%的贫困牲畜饲养者，即4亿人，是妇女。她们主要参与家禽和产乳类动物的管理。然而，一般来说，女性饲养的牲畜不多，可能是因为受到劳动力限制或她们无法获得贷款。

粮农组织农村创收活动数据库的数据表明，在阿尔巴尼亚、保加利亚和塔吉克斯坦，男性持有的牲畜比女性持有的牲畜高30%～50%。土地是确保粮食和营养安全以及支持创收的重要生产性资产。土地所有权和对土地的控制意味着农村社会的财富地位和权力，特别是对从事农业的人来说。所有地区都承认在土地所有权方面存在着明显的性别差异。现有的数据显示，在全世界的农业持有者中，男性占了大多数。此外，在发展中国家，男性户主家庭的土地持有量往往是女性户主家庭的两到三倍。在阿尔巴尼亚，男性户主或持有者所持有的土地面积平均比女性户主大20%左右。而在保加利亚，这种性别差异高达30%。在蒙多瓦共和国，64%的农业持有者是男性，但81%的农业持有总面积属于男性。最近在蒙多瓦共和国进行的农业普查的结果与全球在获得技术方面的性别差距趋势相一致。例如，尽管妇女占所有农业持有者的三分之一以上，但她们只拥有该国所有9%的拖拉机。

缩小在获得农业资产、服务和生产资源方面的性别差距可以带来哪些收益？研究表明，缩小这些在获取资源方面的性别差距，将有助于妇女在其农场获得更好的产量，从而有助于提高整体粮食安全。有人认为，更高的产量将产生更多的影响，包括，例如，农民对劳动力、当地生产的商品和服务的需求增加，粮食供应增加，粮食价格下降。更高的产量也可以增加妇女的就业和女性农民的收入。缩小性别差距需要提高对参与农业和农村发展的妇女和男子的角色和关系以及机会和限制的理解。这样做需要收集和使用有意义的性别指标和按性别分类的数据，为政策和计划提供信息。一个关于性别统计的模块将通过一套核心的性别指标，为制作和收集性别分类的汇总数据提供简单的技术指导。

（资料来源：本篇参考译文为编者翻译整理。）

2. 汉译英

Promote Agricultural Modernization Through Family Farming

Remarks at the Food and Agriculture Organization of the United Nations

H. E. LI Keqiang

Premier of the State Council of the People's Republic of China

(October 15, 2014)

Director-General José Graziano da Silva,

Ladies and Gentlemen,

Dear Friends,

It gives me great pleasure to be here at the headquarters of the Food and Agriculture Organization of the United Nations (FAO) in this golden autumn season to attend the event for the 34th World Food Day. Upon arriving at the FAO building minutes ago, I saw the multi-lingual inscription—Food for All—in the hall of the first floor. Food for all represents the noble mission of the FAO as well as the common goal of all countries. Over the years, the FAO, the World Food Program (WFP) and the International Fund for Agricultural Development (IFAD), with a strong commitment to this goal, have helped the member states to develop agriculture in multiple forms, thus making outstanding contribution to feeding the billions of people in our world. Hereby, I wish to extend, on behalf of the Chinese government and people, great appreciation to the FAO and other institutions, and to all of you present and your colleagues for your unremitting efforts, and sincere respect for the remarkable achievements you have made.

The theme of this year's World Food Day is Family Farming: "Feeding the world, caring for the earth". I think this theme is based on realities and focuses on the future as well, and it charts a bright future of global agricultural development. Ensuring adequate food supply for the people through family farming also suits China's realities. Over 2000 years ago, China's philosophers said, food is the first necessity of the people, and this is also what the Chinese have always believed in. As is known to all, China has a huge population but low per-capita arable land availability. To feed the over one billion Chinese people is our top priority and was once the biggest challenge we had to face. When I was young, I lived in China's rural areas for some years, and personally experienced the hard time of not having enough food. A big meal that I had might be easily forgotten, but the feeling of hunger left me a lifelong impression. In fact, China's reform and opening-up that began over 30 years ago was launched from rural areas. Since then, we have been able to achieve great agricultural development through reform and China's grain output has increased from over 300 million tons to over 600 million tons, successfully resolving the subsistence issue of the people. And a piece of most fundamental experience we got was to develop family farming.

In rural reforms that started in the early 1980s, the most important part was to promote the household contract system. Through this reform, rural households became the mainstay of farming and farmers were given long-term and guaranteed land use right and operational independence, thus rapidly unleashing the enthusiasm of hundreds of millions of farmers for production and giving scope to the capabilities of individual farmers. As a result, agricultural production made huge headway in just a few years. Building on that, hundreds of millions of people have been lifted out of poverty and the UN Millennium Development Goals have been reached ahead of schedule. In the recent decade, China has enjoyed continuous increase in grain output, with yet another bumper harvest to be expected this year. Without family farming, these achievements would not have been possible.

We also owe the constant new vigor in China's family farming over the past 30-plus years to innovation in science, technology and relevant policies. We have established a whole system for disseminating agricultural science and technology and extensively promoted quality varieties, agricultural machinery as well as controlled-environment agriculture. Hybrid rice alone has increased annual output by tens of millions of tons in China. We greatly encourage farmers' cooperatives, specialized farming households, businesses and government service organizations to provide farmers with services in terms of agricultural machinery and the processing and distribution of agricultural produce. Every year, hundreds of thousands of agricultural machines are taken to different parts of China to serve agricultural seasons, like birds that migrate back and forth with the season. When wheat ripens, an army of combined harvesters would advance from the south to the north of China, helping farmers with wheat harvesting. This not only provides much-needed agricultural machinery to rural households, but also helps raise efficiency in the use of farming machines. The Chinese government is still increasing input in agriculture to support agricultural infrastructure and improve production condition. For instance, the effective irrigation rate of farmland in China has been raised to over 50% and China's agriculture is now more resilient to disasters.

......

The Chinese government attaches great importance to agriculture and has always managed to ensure basic self-supply of food by relying on domestic production. At the same time, the Chinese government also gives priority to sustainable agricultural development. We have managed to feed nearly 20% of the world's population with a share of arable land and fresh water resources lower than world average. That in itself is intensive operation. But that's not enough. We still need to further promote efficient and intensive agricultural development. At the same time, we will further enhance ecological protection and improvement and effectively implement such projects as returning farmland to forests, protecting natural forests, desertification prevention and control, water and land conservation and grassland management. We will support farmers in their efforts to improve the soil, reduce pollution and develop high-standard farmland on a large scale. Such efforts will promote the sustainable use of agricultural resources, thus not only serving the need of the people in our time but also passing on fertile land, green water and blue sky to our future generation. In that sense, protecting China's ecology is also one way of caring for the earth and protecting our planet.

Ladies and Gentlemen,

Food for all is, for mankind, the most fundamental right of survival, which serves as the basis for all other human rights. Great progress has been made in the global agricultural development. Yet hunger and poverty have remained a "silent crisis". They are like the "Achilles' heel", deeply troubling all human beings. Over 800 million poor people in the world still face the threat of food shortages and malnutrition. To promote agricultural development and eradicate hunger and poverty remains a major challenge of the world and a common responsibility of mankind. The international community may join hands to enhance agricultural cooperation and pay greater attention to the calls of developing countries, in particular certain least developed countries (LDCs). Efforts should be made to curb trade protectionism and increase the technical and financial assistance to the agricultural sector of the LDCs so as to raise the global agricultural productivity and increase food security.

China's agricultural cooperation with other countries, in particular developing countries, has been on the fast track. In recent years, we have set up agricultural technology demonstration centers, experimental stations and promotion stations in nearly 100 countries in Asia, Africa, Latin America, and the Pacific. We have sent over 30000 agricultural experts and technicians to these countries and helped them to train a large number of technicians of their own. The Chinese of my generation had suffered from hunger, so we share the feelings with people who are still suffering from hunger. We hope to see hunger and poverty eliminated in the whole world and we are willing to share with other countries agricultural technologies, experience and development models. In fact, China's improved hybrid rice strains have already benefited many countries. Here I wish to announce that the Chinese government will donate US \$ 50 million to the FAO in the next five years for carrying out South-South cooperation on agriculture and will increase support to the WFP and the IFAD.

Ladies and Gentlemen,

As the largest developing country, China will always be an active force for safeguarding world food security. Although China faces quite a few difficulties ahead in its agricultural development, we will continue to work tirelessly to deliver on our commitment through action. We will ensure adequate food supply mainly on our own. We are ready to work with countries around the world to create a world of sustainable development that is free from hunger and poverty.

The Director-General just now gave me a book about his country's experience in raising grain output and reducing hunger, and I returned him with an album of beautiful natural sceneries. I believe that only when people have had enough food in their stomach, will they be in the mood to enjoy the beauty of nature and pursue a life of higher cultural attainment. Only when we could ensure the production and supply of food as the most important foundation for human development, will the people enjoy better material and cultural life and the world become a better place for us to live in. Thank you.

[资料来源：见英文巴士网（https://www. en84. com/nonfiction/remarks/201410/00015489. html），引用日期：2023 年 8 月 21 日。]

第八章　联合国工业发展组织

➡ 一、背景阅读

● （一）汉语简介

【成立日期】1966 年成立。1985 年 6 月成为联合国专门机构，简称"联合国工发组织"。

【宗　旨】通过工业发展推进扶贫和环境友好型经济增长，提高全世界人民，尤其是最贫困国家人民的生活水平和生活质量。

【成　员】截至 2022 年 6 月，共有 170 个成员国。

【主要负责人】总干事格尔德·穆勒（Gerd Mueller，德国籍），2021 年 12 月上任，任期 4 年。

【总　部】奥地利维也纳。

【组织机构】（1）大会：最高权力机构，由全体成员参加，每两年举行一届大会。（2）理事会：由大会选出的 53 个成员国组成，任期 4 年，每年改选一半，可连任，每年举行一次例会。（3）秘书处：大会和理事会的执行机构。负责人是总干事，由大会根据理事会的推荐任命，任期 4 年，可连任。

【主要活动】工发组织是联合国系统促进可持续工业发展和国际工业合作的专门机构，通过发挥其全球论坛职能及与发展中国家技术合作等活动，主要开展三大核心业务：减贫、贸易能力建设、能源和环境。

工发组织每两年举行一次大会，每年举行一次工发理事会会议和一次方案预算委员会会议。

【驻华代表机构】1998 年 9 月以前，工业发展组织驻华代表机构设在联合国开发计划署内。1998 年 9 月，工发组织成立独立的驻华代表处。2006 年底升级为工发组织驻中国、蒙古、朝鲜和韩国的区域代表处。现任代表康博思

（Mr. Stephen Bainous Kargbo，塞拉利昂籍），2021 年上任。

［资料来源：见中国外交部网站（https://www.mfa.gov.cn/web/gjhdq_676201/gjhdqzz_681964/lhg_681966/jbqk_681968/201308/t20130821_9380028.shtml），引用日期：2023 年 8 月 23 日。］

（二）UNIDO 英语介绍

1. What is UNIDO?

The United Nations Industrial Development Organisation（UNIDO）is the specialized agency of the United Nations that promotes industrial development for poverty reduction, inclusive globalization and environmental sustainability. The mandate of UNIDO is to promote and accelerate sustainable industrial development in developing countries and economies in transition. The organization draws on four mutually reinforcing categories of services: technical cooperation, analytical and policy advisory services, standard setting and compliance, and a convening function for knowledge transfer and networking.

2. History

On 17 November, 1966, the United Nations General Assembly passed resolution 2152（XXI）establishing the United Nations Industrial Development Organization（UNIDO）as an autonomous body within the United Nations, with a mission to promote and accelerate the industrialization of developing countries.

In 1975, the General Assembly, in resolution 3362（S-V II）, endorsed the recommendation of the Conference that UNIDO be converted into a specialized agency. In 1979, the UN conference on the "Establishment of UNIDO as a specialized agency" adopted the new Constitution which entered into force in 1985.

In 1997, Member States adopted a Business Plan for the Future Role and Functions of UNIDO to enable it to better respond to the changing global economic environment. In 2001, UNIDO adjusts its programs in the light of the United Nations Millennium Development Goals.

3. Institutions

UNIDO has two policy making organs: the General Conference and the Industrial

Development Board. The Programme and Budget Committee is a subsidiary organ of the Industrial Development Board.

The General Conference determines the guiding principles and policies of the Organization and approves the budget and work programme. Every four years, the Conference appoints the Director-General. The GC also elects the members of the Industrial Development Board and the Programme and Budget Committee. The Conference meets every two years.

The Industrial Development Board reviews the implementation of the work programme, the regular and operational budgets and makes recommendations to the Conference on policy matters, including the appointment of the Director-General. The Board meets once a year. Programme and Budget Committee members are elected for a two-year term. It is a subsidiary organ of the Board which provides assistance in the preparation and examination of the work programme, the budget and other financial matters. The Committee meets once a year.

4. UNIDO's focus

➢ 2030 Agenda and the SDGs

The Sustainable Development Goals (SDGs) constitute the core of the 2030 Agenda for Sustainable Development and guide all global, regional and national development endeavor until the year 2030. Adopted in 2015, the SDGs seek to build on the Millennium Development Goals and complete what these did not achieve. They are universal, integrated and indivisible, and seek to balance the three dimensions of sustainable development: the economic, social and environmental dimension. The breadth and scope of the SDGs reflect the complexity and scale of challenges to be addressed in the modern era.

➢ Inclusive and Sustainable Industrial Development (ISID)

According to its Lima Declaration, UNIDO aims to eradicate poverty through inclusive and sustainable industrial development (ISID). UNIDO advocates that ISID is the key driver for the successful integration of the economic, social and environmental dimensions, required to fully realize sustainable development for the benefit of our future generations

➢ The Medium-term Programme Framework (MTPF) 2018-2021

The medium-term programme framework (MTPF) 2018-2021 provides strategic guidance for UNIDO to continue increasing the impact of its services. In doing so, the MTPF integrates all levels of the organizational performance and development results—from the management of UNIDO's internal operations to the progress towards the Sustainable Development Goals.

The four strategic priorities of the Medium-term Programme Framework (MTPF) 2018-2021 are: creating shared prosperity, advancing economic competitiveness, safeguarding the environment and strengthening knowledge and institution.

[资料来源：见联合国工业发展组织（https://www.unido.org/about-us/who-we-are），引用日期：2023 年 8 月 23 日。]

5. 词汇表 Vocabulary List

the United Nations Industrial Development Organisation

联合国工业发展组织

Industrial Development Board 工发理事会

Inclusive and Sustainable Industrial Development (ISID)

包容性和可持续性工业发展

The Medium-term Programme Framework (MTPF) 中期方案框架

SMEs (small and medium-size enterprise) 中小企业

➡️ 二、口译实践

🌑 （一）英译汉

Global Collaboration is Key to Economic Recovery
Remarks at World Industrial Design Conference 2020
LI Yong, Director General of UNIDO (2013-2021)
（November 25, 2020）

Excellencies,

Distinguished Guests,

Ladies and Gentlemen,

It is my pleasure to address you on the occasion of the World Industrial Design

Conference 2020. First of all, I would like to thank the Ministry of Industry and Information Technology, the People's Government of Shandong Province and the China Industrial Design Association for hosting and organizing this event.

It has been an extraordinary year for all of us with the COVID-19 pandemic. It has and continues to affect economies and societies globally. We also know that at the same time, the crisis unveils an opportunity for all to "build back better". We must seize this opportunity. To help us do this, we need to prioritize innovation and intelligent design, which will drive solutions to help us accelerate the achievements towards the Sustainable Development Goals as envisaged in the Decade of Action.

The World Industrial Design Conference is an important platform for international exchange and cooperation among stakeholders in industrial design. It can play a crucial role particularly under the current circumstances where global collaboration is key to economic recovery. The conference can help guide and accelerate the use of technologies of the Fourth Industrial Revolution for industrial design. (1) Advances in robotics, artificial intelligence, additive manufacturing and data analytics, offer huge potential to accelerate industrial innovations, increasing value-added content of production and promote sustainability. The theme of the conference "Intelligent Design · Road to the Future" is therefore very timely and well chosen.

Ladies and gentlemen, in the plans to "build back better", it is envisaged that the circular economy will play an important role. (2) Intelligent design is a linchpin of circular economy. The central tenets of the circular economy include the ambition to design out waste and pollution and to keep products and the materials in use. Today's manufacturing model primarily involve taking raw material from the environment, creating new products and disposing them after use. This we know, is not a sustainable model. The circular economy allows us to rethink our approach at every stage of a product's life cycle.

We at UNIDO are strong supporters of innovative circular design as a means to achieve inclusive and sustainable industrial development. UNIDO contributes to circular economy through three main types of intervention. (3) Our research helps us understand the market, institutional and policy conditions under which the circular economy works, and provides policy advice to support governments in the transition. Our technical cooperation projects and normative work support the adoption of sustainable industrial solutions for pollution reduction and resource efficiency. Lastly, through our convening function in the global fora, UNIDO brings together stakeholders at all levels to advocate for the circular economy agenda.

(4) In the spirit of providing a global forum for discussions, UNIDO, in response to the needs of its Member States, is organizing global consultations to facilitate exchanges on best practices, emerging innovations and how to adopt circular economy principles and practices in industries. The regional consultations for Asia and the Pacific were held two weeks ago. I am confident that industrial design and eco-design in particular will continue to play a critical role as we take these consultations forward.

The circular economy concept has been a part of UNIDO's work for a while now. (5) In 2009, UNIDO and the United Nations Environment Programme created the Joint Resource Efficient and Cleaner Production (RECP) programme to ensure the mainstreaming of resource-efficient and cleaner industrial production. The programme facilitates the implementation of RECP methods and tools. This includes retrofitting production sites, introducing new technologies, phasing out hazardous materials, reducing waste and increasing efficiency in the use of raw materials. Enterprises have benefited from increased resource productivity and realized savings opportunities. More than $30 million have been raised in funds from multiple donors, over 50 national cleaner production centers have been established, and around 70 RECP service providers globally have joined the Global Network for Resources Efficient and Cleaner Production.

Ladies and gentlemen, China has become a major international player for design and technology and will remain so in the future. The government has systematically pursued a vision of exploring the power of innovation for many years. Increased investments in R&D and the application of cutting-edge industries have been one of its goal. China is today leading in many areas such as new energy vehicles, new materials, aircraft engines among others. UNIDO has been collaborating with China in advancing its innovation agenda including in the promotion of intelligent manufacturing in SMEs. We have built strong connections with the China Industrial Design Association and with local universities, research institutes, design companies, manufacturing enterprises and industrial parks.

(6) Two years ago, we launched the "Design for Poverty Alleviation

Initiative" with CIDA and others at the WIDC. The aim of this initiative has been to support China in alleviating the remaining pockets of poverty in the country by 2020. Our collaboration shows how versatile industrial design can be to advance our common development agenda as envisaged by the 2030 Agenda.

I am confident that in the future WIDC will remain a major platform disseminating innovative experiences from China to the rest of the world. I hope it will remain as a forum that facilitates the exchange of viable knowledge and best practices on the integration of new industrial innovations, smart manufacturing and circularity.

I look forward to seeing the outcome of this year's edition of WIDC and wish WIDC2020 a great success. Thank you!

[资料来源：见哔哩哔哩视频网（https://www.bilibili.com/video/BV1BV411a7NP? spm_id_from=333.337.search-card.all.click&vd_source=3d3de4c7e40eef5c7d263107db51ce64），引用日期：2023 年 8 月 23 日。]

1. 实践解析

本材料选自 2020 年 11 月 25 日，联合国工业发展组织总干事 LI Yong（李勇）在烟台国际博览中心举行的 2020 年世界工业设计大会上的开幕致辞。李勇表示，世界工业设计大会是工业设计利益相关者之间进行国际交流与合作的重要平台，将为全球经济复苏发挥至关重要的作用。在致辞中，他强调了循环经济概念、联合国工业发展组织就循环经济做出的贡献，以及中国推动创新议程的相关进展。

本材料语体风格正式，难点之一在于出现了较多制造业、环境术语，同时还涉及相关组织和倡议概念，需要对背景知识具有一定了解。

Decade of Action 即行动十年。"2019 年 9 月，联合国秘书长呼吁社会各界在三个层面上开展'行动十年'：在全球层面，采取全球行动，为实现可持续发展目标提供更强的领导力、更多资源和更明智的解决方案；在地方层面，政府、城市和地方当局的政策、预算、制度和监管框架应进行必要的转型；在个人层面，青年、民间社会、媒体、私营部门、联盟、学术界和其他利益攸关方应发起一场不可阻挡的运动，推动必要的变革。"[①]

---

① 见联合国网站（https://www.un.org/sustainabledevelopment/zh/decade-of-action/），引用日期：2023 年 8 月 23 日。

Additive manufacturing 即增材制造，又名 3D 打印，是"以数字模型文件为基础，通过计算机软件与专门的控制系统将专用的材料等，通过多种制造方式逐层堆积，制造出实体物品的制造技术"①。

Intelligent design 即智能设计，"智能设计在传统科研设计模式的基础上，灵活融入了智能制造、虚拟建模、大数据、信息工程等现代化技术，能够依据不同行业的具体设计需求形成与之相匹配的智能化研发设计系统"②。

Resource Efficient and Cleaner Production 即资源高效和清洁生产，由联合国工业发展组织（UNIDO）和联合国环境规划署（UNEP）共同倡议。在实践中，RECP 要求在流程、产品和服务中持续应用预防性环境战略，以提高效率并降低对人类和环境的风险。③

Design for Poverty Alleviation Initiative 即设计扶贫倡议。2018 年 4 月，第二届世界工业设计大会大会组委会与联合国工业发展组织、中国工信息部以及有关国家和地区设计行业组织、专业人士共同发布了《设计扶贫宣言》，倡议开展更大范围、更深层次的设计扶贫工作，为实现联合国 2030 可持续发展议程目标做出贡献。④

2. 长难句点拨

（1）该句中包含许多技术相关的术语，如 robotics（机器人技术）、artificial intelligence（人工智能）、additive manufacturing（增材制造）和 data analytics（数据分析）。英语呈句首封闭、句尾开放的特点，修饰语多后置（例如该句中 potential 的修饰成分 to accelerate industrial innovations, increasing value-added content of production and promote sustainability）。然而汉语修饰语一般前置，因此，该句在翻译过程中要调整语序，让译文更符合汉语表述习惯。

（2）该句并不长，但是句中包含的一些词汇可能会对听力理解带来困难，如 linchpin（the most important member of a group or part of a system, that holds

---

① 刘洋、周建平、张晓天：《增材制造技术在载人航天工程中的应用与展望》，载《北京航空航天大学学报》2023 年第 1 期，第 83 页。

② 芮雪：《智能设计技术在机械研发制造中的应用》，载《南方农机》2022 年第 16 期，第 175 页。

③ 见联合国工业发展组织网站（https://www.unido.org/our-focus-safeguarding-environment-resource-efficient-and-low-carbon-industrial-production/resource-efficient-and-cleaner-production-recp），引用日期：2023 年 8 月 23 日。

④ 见中国工业设计协会网站（https://m.chinadesign.cn/20/201804/1103.html），引用日期：2023 年 8 月 23 日。

together the other members or parts or makes it possible for them to operate as intended）和 tenet（one of the principles on which a belief or theory is based），a linchpin of circular economy 就是循环经济的关键，central tenets of the circular economy 即循环经济的重要宗旨。除此之外，在口译过程中要考虑英语和汉语在搭配上的差异，如 include the ambition 不宜采取直译策略。

（3）该句结构比较复杂，涉及多个并列的名词短语和动词短语，如 helps us understand 和 provides policy advice 是并列谓语，非谓语动词 understand 的宾语包括 the market、institutional 和 policy conditions，而 policy conditions 后接了一个由 under which 引导的定语从句。在口译中应处理好语序和修饰关系，并根据汉语习惯调整语序。

（4）该句是一个典型的英语长句，由于英语重形合，句中多个介词短语、不定式短语和疑问词引导的从句作为状语成分或者插入语，句子结构相对复杂。在口译中要首先要厘清各个成分之间的关系，充分理解句意，在口译中可以采取顺句驱动技巧，将长句分解为若干个小句，从而使译文符合汉语句子较短、结构松散的特点。

（5）该句中包含两个专有名词，其中 the United Nations Environment Programme 是联合国环境规划署，Joint Resource Efficient and Cleaner Production（RECP）即"资源效率和清洁生产联合方案"，切记望文生义。该句的另一个理解难点是 mainstream 一般作名词使用，而该句中作动词，意思为"become part of the most typical, normal, or conventional ideas or activities"①。

（6）该句中包含了专有名词，"Design for Poverty Alleviation Initiative" 即"设计扶贫倡议"，CIDA 即 China Industrial Design Association（中国工业设计协会），pocket of poverty 是英语中比较地道的表达方式，表示贫困地区的意思。

① 见柯林斯英语字典网站（https://www.collinsdictionary.com/zh/dictionary/english/mainstream），引用日期：2023年8月23日。

● （二）汉译英

商务部部长助理李成钢在联合国工发组织第十八届大会上的发言（上）
（2019 年 11 月 18 日）

主席先生：

我作为中华人民共和国商务部钟山部长代表出席本届大会。

首先，我代表中国代表团，祝贺你当选本届大会主席，并感谢上届主席和主席团对本届大会工作的杰出贡献。我还要感谢阿拉伯联合酋长国政府承办本届大会，并给予中国代表团周到的礼遇安排。

（1）在全球制造业面临深刻变革，新一轮产业和科技革命方兴未艾，2030 年可持续发展议程进入深度落实阶段的背景下，各国在本届大会围绕"工业 2030——创新、联通、改变我们的未来"主题进行深入讨论，对包容与可持续工业发展具有十分重要的意义。（2）我们高兴地看到，工发组织第十七届大会以来，在李勇总干事率领下，工发组织自身机构治理不断规范改进，技术合作执行规模、接受自愿捐款数量都保持了良好势头。工发组织倡导的包容与可持续工业发展理念深入人心，国别伙伴关系方案（PCP）试点取得积极进展，得到广大成员国高度认可。中方对工发组织取得一系列工作成绩表示祝贺，支持工发组织继续致力于包容与可持续工业发展事业，为广大发展中国家提升工业化水平提供帮助。

主席先生，

（3）当今世界正面临前所未有的大发展、大变革、大调整，单边主义、保护主义不断蔓延，以联合国为代表的多边主义体系和以世界贸易组织为核心的多边贸易体制正面临严峻挑战，世界经济运行的风险和不确定性显著上升。当前，全球经济正处在新旧动能转换的关键时期，给广大发展中国家同时带来机遇和挑战。我们应当抓住新一轮科技革命和产业革命的契机，凝心聚力、同舟共济，共同推进包容与可持续工业发展事业。基于中国的工业化实践与经验，中方愿与各方分享一些看法和体会，可以归纳为"4 个 I"：创新（Innovation）、互联（Interconnectivity）、包容（Inclusion）和落实（Implementation）。

一、创新（Innovation）。创新是引领发展的第一动力。（4）当前，全球新一轮科技革命孕育兴起，大数据、人工智能（AI）、区块链等新兴技术与产业正在深刻影响世界发展格局，深刻改变人类的生产生活方式，深刻变革工业发展模式，为广大发展中国家走新型工业化道路提供了更多可能。近年来，中国秉持创新、协调、绿色、开放、共享的发展理念，加快发展先进制造业，利用新技术为实体经济打造新的"助推器"，实现了更高质量、更有效率、更可持续的工业发展。

二、互联（Interconnectivity）。（5）面对单边主义、保护主义不断抬头的"逆流"，各国应更加紧密团结在一起，构建全球互联互通伙伴关系，实现共同繁荣。近年来，中方一方面积极推进"一带一路"国际合作，与各方共同努力实现政策沟通、设施联通、贸易畅通、资金融通、民心相通的合作蓝图，另一方面不断提升对外开放水平，先后在 18 个省、市设立自由贸易试验区，探索建设自由贸易港，制定新的《外商投资法》，实施外商投资准入前国民待遇加负面清单管理模式，举办中国国际进口博览会，不断提升互联互通水平，为世界各国发展创造新机遇。

[资料来源：见中国商务部网站（http://vienna. mofcom. gov. cn/article/jmxw/201911/20191102914380. shtml），引用日期：2023 年 8 月 23 日。]

1. 实践解析

2019 年 11 月，联合国工业发展组织第十八届大会在阿拉伯联合酋长国首都阿布扎比召开，时任中国商务部部长助理李成钢代表商务部部长钟山出席会议，并发表演讲。本材料即选自时任中国商务部部长助理李成钢于 2019 年 11 月在阿拉伯联合酋长国首都阿布扎比联合国工业发展组织第十八届大会上的讲话。大会主题为"工业 2030——创新、联通、重塑未来"，讨论性别平等、循环经济、青年与企业家精神、工业 4.0、工业园区和可持续能源等议题。李成钢在发言中指出，当前新一轮产业和科技革命孕育兴起，全球制造业面临深刻变革，世界经济处于新旧动能转换的关键时期，给广大发展中国家同时带来机遇和挑战。中方呼吁各方以创新、互联、包容、落实为着力点，携手共建全球互联互通伙伴关系，共同推进包容与可持续工业发展，实现共同发展繁荣。

本材料是发言的上篇，包含中国工业化实践与经验的"创新""互联"两部分，内容较为常规，但长句居多，信息密集，材料涉及面较广，提到"一带一路"、对外开放等具体的中国政策措施，需要对相关背景有一定了解。

国民待遇分为准入后国民待遇和准入前国民待遇。外商投资准入前国民待遇（pre-establishment national treatment）是指"外国投资者和东道国本国国民在投资的部门和领域、股权形式等方面具有大致相同的待遇，外资企业和内资企业在企业的设立、扩大、破产等阶段有相同的法律地位"①。

负面清单（negative list）：即以清单的形式列出不符措施，是一种义务承诺模式，其背后的法理是"法无禁止即可为"②。我国《外商投资法》采用了准入前国民待遇与负面清单相结合的模式。

2. 长难句点拨

（1）方兴未艾是汉译英中的常见成语，一般译为"to be unfolding""to be on the rise"或者"to be thriving"，具体措辞要结合具体语境选择。该句中包含多个小句，前三句都是会议召开的背景，如果将三个短语以状语形式译为并列的短语或者句子，则翻译出的句子会特别长，且头重脚轻。汉语的逻辑意义往往隐藏在字里行间，因此，口译中要先分析短句的功能和句子之间的逻辑，进行适当的拆分和组合。对该段可以将前两个短语用 in the face of 进行连接，作为一个宏观背景，将第三个小句"2030 年可持续发展议程进入深度落实阶段的背景下"与主句进行整合，利用时间状语从句，让各个句子之间更有层次，逻辑更清楚。

（2）该句考察译文组织能力。汉语原文包含了主从复句，在译成英语时可以保留这个结构。主要难点是从句句子结构和句式选择，可以用介词短语来引出两个状语结构（"自……以来"和"在……率领下"），保留从句里两个并列的谓语，最后一个小句采取被动句结构，避免句子主语过长。参考译文为："We have witnessed with great pleasure that since the 17th session of the UNIDO General Conference and under the leadership of Director General Li Yong, UNIDO's own institutional governance has been continuously standardized and improved, and a good momentum has been maintained in terms of the delivery of technical cooperation and the amount of voluntary contribution."

---

① 沈敬容：《外商投资法"准入前国民待遇"的必然性研究》，载《重庆行政》2019 年第 5 期，第 63 页。

② 戴林莉、康婷：《论我国自贸试验区外商投资准入负面清单的价值与功能》，载《经济体制改革》2018 年第 2 期，第 57 页。

（3）该句关于国际环境的论述在我国领导人的发言中反复出现，口译学习者对其中的一些高频表述应该熟练记忆，如"大发展、大变革、大调整"（great development，great transformation and great adjustments）、"单边主义、保护主义不断蔓"（"Unilateralism and protectionism are on the rise."）、"以联合国为代表的多边主义体系"（the multilateral system as represented by the United Nations）以及"以世界贸易组织为核心的多边贸易体制"（the multilateral trading system with the World Trade Organization at its core）。三个短句看上去是并列关系，在口译过程中如果能够增补衔接词，语篇会更加连贯。

（4）该句中包含新技术的术语，如"大数据"（big data）、"人工智能"（artificial intelligence，AI）和"区块链"（block chain）。这些术语本身并不难，但是在积累相关术语的英语表达的同时要重视对其基本原理的理解。该句包含并列结构（深切影响……，深切改变……，深切变革……），三个短句结构整齐匀称，有节奏感。但是英语重视表达形式多样化，倾向避免重复，因此在口译过程中不宜采取亦步亦趋的直译方法，保留三个 profoundly，而应该从句意出发，理解意群之间的逻辑关系，即生产生活方式和工业发展模式都发生变革，从而为广大发展中国家走新型工业化道路提供了更多可能。应该补充两者之间的逻辑关系。

（5）该句中包含"逆流"（countercurrent）这个意象，如果词汇储备中有这个词，则翻译起来就会比较得心应手。如果不知道这个表达，也可以避虚就实，即表达出目前单边主义、保护主义不断抬头即可，即将其处理为"Since unilateralism and protectionism are on the rise，countries should……"。而该句后半段的三个动词短语（紧密团结在一起，构建全球互联互通伙伴关系，实现共同繁荣）不应被处理为并列关系，而应该理解三者之间的逻辑关系，将逻辑显化。

➡️ 三、口译练习

🌑 （一）英译汉

UNIDO Director General's Remarks atthe Ministerial Round Table of Future Minerals Forum

Gerd Müller, Director General of UNIDO

（January10, 2023）

Excellencies,

Ladies and Gentlemen,

Good morning,

Let me start first by congratulating the Kingdom of Saudi Arabia and thanking his Excellency, the Minister of Industry and Mineral Resources for convening this important meeting and thank you so much for inviting me as the Director General of UNIDO.

UNIDO is the UN Organization that focuses on global sustainable industrialization, with headquarters in Vienna and 170 Member States. Especially developing countries, including major mining countries.

The mining industry plays a very important role in worldwide industrial production. The ores and metals drawn from mines are the basis of all industrial production. Without them, there would be no airplane production, no auto industry, no solar panels, no windmills—no machines can be produced without these basic resources. Without mining, our world would stand still.

(1) Research by the World Bank reports that global industry will need more than three billion tons of minerals and metals to produce low-carbon technologies-cobalt, nickel, lithium. All this is necessary for the transition toward a sustainable world economy by 2050.

Ladies and Gentlemen,

Great developments mean also great challenges. Extraction and processing of minerals currently accounts for about 10% of global greenhouse gas emission. The environmental impact of mining practices can lead to deforestation, contamination of water of land.

The health and safety, the labour conditions of mine workers is a major factor. Globally, over fifteen thousand miners are killed every year. And these are only official numbers. So, development of standards in workplace safety, minimum wages, and establishing ecological standards are absolutely fundamental.

My thanks go to the Saudi government. They are recognizing these problems and challenges. There are solutions on the way to sustainable mining! Large mining companies are taking proper measures. In recent years, responsible mining became a major priority on the international agenda.

(2) Increasing regulatory requirements through mandatory due diligence has become a new trend among most-developed countries to address trading with "Conflict Minerals". The Organization of Economic Cooperation and Development—OECD— has introduced due diligence guidance on responsible supply chain. The International Organization for Standardization and the International Labour Organization have conventions and standards for protecting the health and safety of miners. But, the challenge is the implementation of these standards in least developed countries.

Ladies and Gentlemen,

We are faced with some central questions which we must all together find answers to:

First: how can the predicted doubling or even tripling of worldwide production be accomplished responsibly?

(3) Second: a huge share of mining takes place in the so-called Artisanal and Small-Scale Mining (ASM) sector.

The social and ecological conditions there, for eighty to one hundred million workers are, if I may say it generally, not acceptable and far too often outright exploitative: wages at the lowest level, barely any job security, no implementation of environmental standards—and even child labour.

Third: new due diligence regulations in industrialized countries will encourage world markets to withdraw from sourcing from unregulated ASM mining sectors. However, many will not be able to comply with due diligence standards, and will not stop ASM miners from continuing working.

Therefore the question is:

(4) How can we successfully have a transfer of innovation, of modern production standards, training of workers in the relevant countries: a new cooperation with the ASM sector?

A decisive factor is: how can we implement standards also in the ASM sector without millions of people losing their jobs? What kind of support can the least developed countries receive? And by this I mean support from the rich countries where the refining industries are situated, where the profit is made. We must together find an answer to these questions!

Ladies and Gentlemen,

(5) UNIDO as the UN specialized agency for sustainable industrialization stands ready to work with you at the Future Minerals Forum to advance not only dialogue but also actions towards a Global Alliance for Responsible Minerals. Innovation through technology, knowledge transfer, vocational training can be the vehicle for sustainable industrialization—responsible mining—in these countries.

We have to understand: mining is a global business with global effects on our planet, and a global responsibility! Mining has enormous economic growth potential for the economies of the future and a particular place especially in developing countries.

We have the knowledge and the technological solutions to overcome the challenges we face.

Thank you so much.

[资料来源:见联合国工发组织网站(https://www.unido.org/news/ministerial-round-table-future-minerals-forum-riyadh-saudi-arabia),引用日期:2023 年 8 月 23 日。]

1. 词汇准备

ore	铁矿石
cobalt	钴
nickel	镍
lithium	锂
mandatory due diligence	强制性尽职调查
Conflict Minerals	冲突矿产
Artisanal and Small-Scale Mining (ASM)	手工和小规模采矿

2. 长难句点拨

（1）该句的结构很简单，主要难点在于一些金属名称。这些词语平时并不常见，在口译过程中，如果因为缺乏相关储备而不知道如何翻译，不妨采取省略的策略，因为此处讲话者列举这些金属名称是对上文 minerals and metals to produce low-carbon technologies 的补充，属于次要信息，即使省略了也不影响整体理解。

（2）该句涉及了大量的专业术语和专门机构名称，如 mandatory due diligence（强制性尽职调查）、Conflict Minerals［冲突矿产，又称 3T1G，即钨（Tungsten）、锡（Tin）、钽（Tantalum）、金（Gold）和钴（Cobalt），是指在武装冲突和侵犯人权的情况下所开采的矿物，特别是指在刚果民主共和国东部省份，由刚果政府军和其他许多武装叛乱集团，诸如卢旺达民主解放力量、保卫人民国家议会所控制的矿场所开采的资源①］、Organization of Economic Cooperation and Development（OECD 经济合作与发展组织）、The International Organization for Standardization（国际标准化组织）和 the International Labour Organization（国际劳工组织）。如果对相关背景不够了解，可能会在翻译中遇到困难。除此之外，由于英语句子中包含插入成分，在翻译过程中需要进行语序调整。

（3）该句中包含采矿业的一个专业术语 Artisanal and Small-Scale Mining（ASM），即手工和小规模采矿。该句中信息较多，还有插入语等成分给原文理解带来困难，在口译中应联系上下文充分理解原文含义，再根据汉语表述习惯调整句序，让译文更加流畅

（4）该句中 a transfer of 短语连接了并列结构，因此在口译过程中应确保意思准确。除此之外，应准确理解 transfer 的含义，即 a transfer of innovation 和 a transfer of modern production standards 并不是"创新转换"和"现代生产标准的转换"，而是转换的目标是实现创新，实现现代生产标准，因为手工和小规模采矿并不具备这些内容。

（5）该段第一句是一个典型的英语长句，句子中包含插入成分和并列成分，在口译过程中可以采取顺句驱动的技巧，将短句依次译出，减轻记忆负担，同时通过重复和增补关联词，让译文更加顺畅。可以译为：联合国工发组

----

① 见东莞市科优达电子有限公司官网（https://www.dgkyd.com/news/42.html），引用日期：2023年8月23日。

织是联合国可持续工业化的专门机构，随时准备在未来矿产论坛上与各位合作，不仅推动对话，而且推动为建立负责任矿产全球联盟而采取的行动。第二句中包含系表结构，然而主语（innovation）和表语（vehicle）都是抽象名词，可能会造成理解困难。可以利用顺句驱动来进行翻译，参考译文为：通过技术、知识转让和职业培训进行创新，可以成为这些国家实现可持续工业化——负责任的采矿业——的手段。

（二）汉译英

商务部部长助理李成钢在联合国工业发展组织第十八届大会上的发言（下）
（2019 年 11 月 18 日）

三、包容（inclusion）。（1）对美好生活的向往是各国人民的共同愿望，经济全球化是不可阻挡的历史潮流。各方应秉持"共商、共建、共享"原则，共同为包容与可持续工业发展目标不懈努力。作为负责任的大国，中方正在通过国际产能合作、建设境外经贸合作区等方式，切实帮助有关国家提高产业发展水平、积极融入全球价值链与产业链，使发展成果真正惠及世界。（2）截至2018 年 9 月，中国企业在 46 个国家建设合作区，累计投资 426.9 亿美元，上缴东道国税费 40.9 亿美元，为当地创造就业岗位 36.7 万个，对促进东道国经济社会发展、社会民生改善发挥了积极作用。

四、落实（implementation）。联合国 2030 年可持续发展议程已经进入深度落实阶段。发达国家应当继续切实履行向发展中国家特别是最不发达国家的援助承诺，在工业发展资金和技术方面给予支持。发展中国家应当继续深化南南合作，在工业发展领域实现优势互补、共同进步。（3）作为南南合作的坚定支持者、积极参与者和重要贡献者，中方积极承担与自身能力相匹配的国际义务，特别是落实中非合作论坛重要成果，从基础设施、能力建设、扩大投资等领域入手，帮助非洲国家走上包容与可持续工业发展道路。

主席先生，

今年是中华人民共和国成立 70 周年。70 年来，特别是改革开放以来，在中国共产党的领导下，中国开展了大规模工业化建设，完成了发达国家用几百年走过的工业化进程。（4）近年来，中国坚持创新驱动等新发展理念，构建制造业创新体系，不断调整优化产业结构；中国企业不断加大技术改造力度，积极发展绿色制造、智能制造，全面融入全球产业分工体系。根据联合国统计，中国2018年制造业增加值规模占全球比重超过28%，深刻改变了全球经济与工业发展格局。

中国政府一贯高度重视与联合国工发组织的合作关系。自20世纪70年代以来，双方在工业发展、贸易能力建设、环保等领域开展了大量卓有成效的合作。中方愿继续通过工发组织平台，与其他成员国共商包容与可持续工业发展大计，共建"一带一路"合作倡议，共享新一轮科技和产业革命机遇。同时，中方将继续通过提供自愿捐款、鼓励企业参与等方式，支持工发组织国别伙伴关系方案试点，充分发挥工发组织在技术专长、政策咨询、资源筹集等方面的优势，帮助发展中国家实现可持续工业发展。（5）面向未来，工发组织也应继续强化工业发展专门机构的职能优势，推动和引领各方加强伙伴关系，各施所长、各尽所能，形成发展合力，特别是落实"第三个非洲工业化十年"倡议，稳步推进国别伙伴关系方案试点，帮助成员国应对工业化挑战。

谢谢主席先生。

（资料来源：见中国商务部网站（http://vienna. mofcom. gov. cn/article/jmxw/201911/20191102914380. shtml.），引用日期：2023年8月23日。）

1. 词汇准备

"共商、共建、共享"原则

"Joint consultation, joint construction, and joint sharing"

境外经贸合作区　　　　　　overseas economic and trade cooperation zones

中非合作论坛　　　　　　　China-Africa Cooperation Forum

"第三个非洲工业化十年"倡议

the Third Industrial Development Decade for Africa initiative

工发组织国别伙伴关系方案试点

UNIDO's pilot Programme for Country Partnership

2. 长难句点拨

（1）本材料是中国商务部部长助理李成钢在联合国工业发展组织第十八届大会上的发言的后半部分，涉及中国工业化实践与经验的"包容""落实"两部分。该句中包含一些汉语习惯表达，如"对美好生活的向往""各国人民的共同愿望""不可阻挡的历史潮流"。在口译过程中要充分考虑文化和语言差异，在传递原文信息的同时，确保译文符合英语的表述习惯，而"共商、共建、共享"原则是一带一路相关话题中的高频表述，应该熟记参考译文。

（2）该句信息密集，含有多组数字，口译难度较大。首先，口译学习者应熟悉汉英数字转换的技巧，特别要熟悉关键数位的表达，如万亿（trillion）、十亿（billion）、百万（million）、千（thousand）。演讲稿中提到的数字一般不会太复杂，可以通过移动小数点来快速转换，如将 426.9 亿译为 46.69 billion，36.7 万可以译为 0.367million，也可以处理为 367 thousand。该句的另一个难点是句子中包含多个信息，信息之间并不全是并列关系，在口译过程中还要适当增加衔接手段，让逻辑关系更加清楚。

（3）该句中的很多表达，如坚定支持者（a staunch supporter）、积极参与者（an active participant）、重要贡献者（an important contributor）、与自身能力相匹配的国际义务（international obligations that match its own capabilities），以及能力建设（capacity building）都是中国政府官员在许多演讲中反复使用的常见表达，应牢记汉英版本。汉语原文包含的小句较多，在口译中应首先找到句子主干，即"中国承担国际义务，帮助非洲国家走上工业发展道路"。然后，将其他成分用介词短语连接，再根据英语表述习惯调整语序、组织语言。

（4）该句中包含一些专有名词，如创新驱动（innovation-driven）、制造业创新体系（an innovative manufacturing system）、绿色制造（green manufacturing）、智能制造（intelligent manufacturing）等。在翻译成英语时，应使用准确的专业术语。同时，也应该学习这些专业术语的翻译方法，观察规律，从而举一反三。该句主要包含两层：第一层是中国近几年的措施，第二层是中国企业的做法。因此在口译中，建议分别以 China 和 Chinese companies 做主语，译成两个英语句子。在口译过程中，要充分理解小句之间的关系，如"创新驱动等新发展理念"是指导性原则，而"构建制造业创新体系，不断调整优化产业结构"是具体措施。因此，第一个小句可以用 guided by … 来引出，后面两个短句做并列谓语。

（5）"第三个非洲工业化十年"倡议是一个相对陌生的专有名词，英语为 the Third Industrial Development Decade for Africa initiative。如果缺乏相关词汇储备，口译中可以采取直译的方法，也可以采用概述策略（generalization），如译为 an initiative for African Industrial Development。原文中的另一个难点是四字格的使用，如"各施所长""各尽所能""发展合力"。四字格是汉语中运用广泛的语言形式，言简意赅，富有节奏感。在口译中应考虑英语重形合、忌重复的特点，对重复的意义进行合并，并通过增加衔接手段，显化句子逻辑。比如，"各施所长"和"各尽所能"其实是重复的，而"形成发展合力"则是目标，可以用介词 for 或不定式 so as to 来体现这种逻辑关系。具体的措辞可以根据实际情况选择。

➡ 四、参考译文

● （一）口译实践

1. 英译汉

全球通力合作是世界经济复苏的关键
2020 世界工业设计大会致辞
联合国工业发展组织总干事　李勇
（2020 年 11 月 25 日）

各位阁下，
尊贵的客人，
女士们，先生们，

　　我为能在 2020 年世界工业设计大会上向您致辞感到非常荣幸。首先，我要感谢工业和信息化部、山东省人民政府和中国工业设计协会主办并组织了这次活动。

　　因为新冠疫情，今年对于我们所有人来说都是一个不平凡的一年，疫情已经对全球的经济和社会造成了持续性的影响，不过我们也知道，这场危机同时也为所有人提供了"重建美好"的机会，我们必须把握住这次机会。为此，我们需要优先考虑创新和智能设计，这是加快实现"行动十年"计划所设想的可持续发展目标的答案。

　　世界工业设计大会是工业设计利益相关者之间进行国际交流与合作的重要平台，它可以发挥至关重要的作用，尤其是在当下，因为全球合作是经济复苏的关键。此次大会可以帮助指导和加快第四次工业革命的技术在工业设计中的应用，机器人技术、人工智能、增材制造和数据分析方面的进步为加速工业创新、增加生产的附加值和促进可持续性提供了巨大潜力，因此，会议主题"设计·智向未来"真是恰合时宜。

女士们、先生们，循环经济将在"重建美好"的计划设想中发挥重要作用，智能设计是循环经济的关键。循环经济的核心原则是在保持产品和材料使用的同时，预先在设计中消除废物和污染。目前的制造模式基本是从环境中获取原材料、创造新产品并在使用后对其进行处理。众所周知，这不是一个具有可持续性的模式。循环经济使我们能够在产品生命周期的每个阶段重新思考我们现有的方法。

我们联合国工业发展组织是创新循环设计的有力支持者，此设计是实现包容和可持续工业发展的方法，联合国工业发展组织通过三种主要干预措施为循环经济做出了贡献。我们的研究有助于我们理解适用于循环经济的市场制度和政策条件，并提供政策建议来帮助政府过渡。我们的技术合作项目和规范性工作会对以减少污染和提高资源效率为目的而采用的可持续工业方案给予支持。最后，通过我们在全球论坛的召集职能，联合国工业发展组织将各级利益相关方聚集在一起，倡导循环经济议程。

本着提供一个全球讨论论坛的精神，联合国工业发展组织应其成员国的需求，正在组织全球磋商，以促进就最佳实践、新兴创新以及如何在工业中采用循环经济原则和实践进行交流。两周前举行了亚洲及太平洋区域协商会议，我相信随着这些磋商的推进，工业设计尤其是生态设计将继续发挥关键作用。

循环经济的概念成为联合国工业发展组织工作的一部分已经有段时间了。2009 年，联合国工业发展组织和联合国环境规划署共同创建了"资源效率和清洁生产联合方案"，以确保将资源有效性和清洁工业生产纳入主流。该联合方案促成了资源效率和清洁生产（RECP）方法和工具的实施，这包括改造生产场地、引进新技术、淘汰有害材料，减少浪费并提高原材料使用效率。企业也从提高的资源生产率和实现节约机会中获益，多个捐助者捐助的资金已超过 3000 万美元，建立了 50 多个国家清洁生产中心。全球约有 70 个资源效率和清洁生产（RECP）服务供应商加入了全球资源高效和清洁生产网络。

女士们，先生们，中国已经成为设计和技术的主要国际参与者，并且在将来依然会如此。多年来，政府一直系统地追寻着探索创新力量的理想，增加研发投入和尖端产业的应用一直是其中的一个目标。今天，中国在许多领域都处于领先地位，例如新能源汽车、新材料、飞机发动机等。联合国工业发展组织一直与中国合作推进创新议程，包括在中小企业中促进智能制造。我们已经与中国工业设计协会以及本地大学、研究机构、设计公司、制造企业和工业园区建立了牢固的联系。

两年前，我们与中国工业设计协会（CIDA）及其他机构在世界工业设计大会（WIDC）上发起了"设计扶贫倡议"，倡议的目标是到 2020 年为中国剩余贫困地区提供脱贫支持。我们的合作展示了多姿多彩的工业设计是如何促进共同发展议程的，而这些成果正是 2030 年议程的愿景。

我相信，世界工业设计大会在未来仍将是一个把创新经验从中国传播到世界其他地区的主要平台。我希望它将继续作为这样的一个论坛来融合新工业创新、智能制造以及可持续发展，并交流知识、分享实践经验。

我期待看到今年世界工业设计大会的成果，并祝愿 2020 年世界工业设计大会取得圆满成功，谢谢大家！

［资料来源：见哔哩哔哩视频网（https://www.bilibili.com/video/BV1BV411a7NP? spm_id_ from＝333. 337. search-card. all. click&vd_source＝3d3de4c7e40eef5c7d263107db51ce64），引用日期：2023 年 8 月 23 日。］

2. 汉译英

Speech by Assistant Minister LI Chenggang at the 18th Session of UNIDO General Conference（Ⅰ）
（November 18, 2019）

Mr. President,

I am attending this session of the UNIDO General Conference as the representative of Mr. Zhong Shan, the Minister of Commerce of the People's Republic of China.

First of all, on behalf of the Chinese delegation, I would like to congratulate you on your election as the President of this session and pay tribute to the President and the Bureau of the last session for their outstanding contributions to the work of this session. I would also like to express my gratitude to the government of the United Arab Emirates for hosting this conference and for the thoughtful and courteous arrangements it has made for the Chinese delegation.

In the face of profound changes in the global manufacturing industry, a new round of industrial and technological revolution is unfolding at a rapid pace. At a time when the 2030 sustainable development agenda has entered an intensive implementation stage, an in-depth discussion by all the countries during this conference focusing on the theme "Industry 2030—Innovate, Connect, Transform Our Future" will be of great significance to the inclusive and sustainable industrial development. We have witnessed with great pleasure that since the 17th session of the UNIDO General Conference and under the leadership of Director General Li Yong, UNIDO's own institutional governance has been continuously standardized and improved, and a good momentum has been maintained in terms of the delivery of technical cooperation and the amount of voluntary contribution. The concept of inclusive and sustainable industrial development advocated by UNIDO has become increasingly popular. The pilot Program for Country Partnership (PCP) has made positive progress and has been highly acknowledged by the member states. China congratulates UNIDO on its various achievements in its work and supports UNIDO in its continued commitment to inclusive and sustainable industrial development and in its efforts to assist the developing countries in improving their industrialization.

Mr. President,

The world today is facing an unprecedented great development, great transformation and great adjustments. At the same time, unilateralism and protectionism are on the rise. The multilateral system as represented by the United Nations and the multilateral trading system with the World Trade Organization at its core are faced with severe challenges. The risks and uncertainties in the operation of the world economy have risen remarkably. At present, the global economy is in a critical period of conversion of old and new kinetic energy, bringing opportunities and challenges to many developing countries at the same time. We should seize the opportunity of a new round of technological revolution and the industrial revolution and jointly push forward the inclusive and sustainable industrial development in a united and collective manner. Based on China's industrialization practices and experience, China would like to share some views and experiences here focusing on 4 words: innovation, interconnectivity, inclusion and implementation.

First, Innovation. Innovation is the No. 1 driving force to promote development. At present, a new round of global technological revolution is happening, and emerging technologies and industries such as big data, artificial intelligence (AI) and block chain are profoundly affecting the patterns of world's development, profoundly changing the ways of human production and the models of industrial development, which have offered more possibilities for developing countries to embark on the new paths to industrialization. In recent years, China has adhered to the concept of innovation, coordination, green, openness and sharing, accelerated the development of advanced manufacturing, and used new technologies to create new "boosters" for the real economy, thus achieving higher quality, more efficient and more sustainable industrial development.

Second, Interconnectivity. Faced with the "countercurrent" of unilateralism and protectionism, countries should be more closely united to build a global interconnected partnership and achieve common development and prosperity. In recent years, on the one hand, China has actively promoted the international cooperation in line with the Belt and Road Initiatives and worked together with all the relevant countries to realize the blueprint for cooperation in terms of linkages and connectivities of policies, facilities, trade, financing, and people. On the other hand, China has continuously improved the level of its opening up to the outside world, with 18 provinces and municipalities having set up free trade pilot zones, explored the construction of free trade ports, formulated new laws for foreign investment, implemented the management model of the pre-establishment national treatment with a negative list, convened the China International Import Expo, and continuously improved the level of interconnectivity, which has provided new opportunities for development of many countries in the world.

[资料来源: 见中国商务部网站 (http://vienna. mofcom. gov. cn/article/chinanews/201911/20191102915077. shtml), 引用日期: 2023 年 8 月 23 日。]

● (二) 口译练习

1. 英译汉

联合国工发组织总干事在未来矿业峰会部长级圆桌会议上的讲话
联合国工业发展组织总干事　格尔德·穆勒
(2023 年 1 月 10 日)

各位部长阁下,
女士们、先生们:

　　早上好, 首先, 请允许我祝贺沙特阿拉伯王国, 并感谢国王陛下和工业和矿产资源部召开本次重要会议, 感谢您邀请我作为联合国工发组织总干事参加会议。

联合工发组织是联合国的下属机构，专注于全球可持续工业化，总部设在维也纳，拥有 170 个成员国，特别是发展中国家，包括一些主要矿业国。

采矿业在世界工业生产中起着非常重要的作用。从矿山中提取的矿石和金属是所有工业生产的基础。没有它们，就没有飞机生产，没有汽车工业，没有太阳能电池板，没有风车——没有这些基本资源就无法生产机器。如果没有采矿业，我们的世界将停滞不前。

世界银行的研究报告称，全球工业将需要超过 30 亿吨的矿物和金属来生产低碳技术，这些金属包括钴、镍、锂。所有这些都是到 2050 年实现可持续世界经济转型的必要条件。

女士们、先生们：

巨大的发展也带来了巨大的挑战。目前，矿物开采和加工约占全球温室气体排放量的 10%。采矿活动对环境的影响可能导致森林砍伐、水污染和土地退化。

煤矿工人的健康和安全、劳动条件是一个主要因素。在全球范围内，每年有超过一万五千名矿工丧生。这些只是官方数字。因此，制定工作场所安全标准、最低工资标准和建立生态标准绝对是十分重要的。

我要感谢沙特政府，他们认识到了这些问题和挑战。可持续采矿的道路上有各种解决方案！大型矿业公司正在采取适当措施。近年来，负责任地采矿已成为国际议程上的一个主要优先事项。

为了应对"冲突矿物"贸易的新趋势，大多数发展中国家的一个新趋势是通过强制性尽职调查提高监管要求。经济合作与发展组织（经合组织）出台了关于负责任供应链的尽职调查指南。国际标准化组织和国际劳工组织也有保护矿工健康和安全的公约和标准。但是，挑战在于如何在最不发达国家执行这些标准。

女士们、先生们：

我们面临着一些我们必须共同寻找答案的核心问题：

第一：如何以负责任的方式实现全球产量翻一番甚至三倍的预计目标？

第二：大部分采矿活动发生在所谓的手工和小规模采矿。我可以笼统地说对于 800 万到 1 亿工人来说，这些手工和小规模采矿的社会和生态条件，是不可接受的，而且经常是绝对的剥削：工资处于最低水平，几乎没有任何工作保障，没有实施环境标准——甚至还有童工。

第三：工业化国家新的尽职调查条例将鼓励世界市场不再从不受管制的手工和小规模矿产开采部门采购。然而，许多人将无法遵守尽职调查标准，也无法阻止手工和小规模采矿者继续工作。

因此问题是：

我们如何能够在相关国家实现创新改革，实行现代生产标准和开展工人培训？如何与手工与小规模采矿部门开展新型合作？

一个决定性因素是：我们如何在不使数百万人失业的情况下，在手工与小规模采矿部门实施相关标准？我们可以从最不发达国家可以得到什么样的支持？我指的是来自富裕国家的支持，这些国家有产生利润炼油工业。我们必须一起找到这些问题的答案！

女士们、先生们：

作为联合国可持续工业化的专门机构，联合国工发组织随时准备在未来矿产论坛上与各位合作，不仅推动对话，而且推动为建立负责任矿产全球联盟而采取的行动。通过技术、知识转让和职业培训进行创新，可以成为这些国家实现可持续工业化——负责任的采矿业——的手段。

我们必须明白：采矿是一项全球性的事业，对我们的星球有着全球性的影响，也是一项全球性的责任！采矿业对未来的经济、具有巨大的经济增长潜力，在发展中国家也有非常重要的一席之地。

我们拥有知识和技术解决方案来克服我们面临的挑战。

谢谢大家！

（资料来源：本参考译文为编者提供并整理。）

2. 汉译英

Speech by Assistant Minister LI Chenggang at the 18th Session of UNIDO General Conference（Ⅱ）

（November 18，2019）

Third, Inclusion. The pursuit for a better life is the common aspiration of the people of all countries. Economic globalization is an irresistible historical trend. All parties should uphold the principle of "Joint consultation, joint construction, and joint sharing" and work together for the goal of inclusive and sustainable industrial development. As a responsible big country, China is helping the relevant countries through various means such as international cooperation in production capacity and establishing overseas economic and trade cooperation zones, with a view to effectively helping these countries improve the level of their industrial development and actively integrate into the global value chain and industrial chain, so that the development results truly benefit the world. As of September 2018, Chinese enterprises have invested in cooperation zones in 46 countries, with a total investment of 42.69 billion US dollars, paid 4.09 billion US dollars of taxes and fees to the host countries, and created 367000 jobs for the local communities, thus playing an active role in promoting the economic and social development of the host countries and improving the people's livelihood.

Fourth, Implementation. The UN 2030 Agenda for Sustainable Development has entered an in-depth implementation phase. Developed countries should continue to earnestly fulfill their aid commitments to developing countries, especially the least developed countries by providing them with industrial development funds and technology. Developing countries should continue to deepen South-South cooperation and achieve complementary advantages and common progress in the field of industrial development. As a staunch supporter, an active participant and an important contributor of South-South cooperation, China actively undertakes international obligations that match its own capabilities, especially in terms of implementing the important achievements of the China-Africa Cooperation Forum and helped African countries embark on the path of inclusive and sustainable industrial development in areas such as infrastructure, capacity building, and investment expansion.

Mr. President,

This year marks the 70th anniversary of the founding of the People's Republic of China. In the past 70 years, especially since the reform and opening up, under the leadership of the Communist Party of China, China has carried out large-scale industrial development and has completed the industrialization process that took developed countries hundreds of years to accomplish. In recent years, guided by the new development concepts such as innovation-driven development, China has built an innovative manufacturing system and has constantly adjusted and optimized the industrial structures. Chinese companies have continued to strengthen technological transformation, actively developed green manufacturing and intelligent manufacturing and have fully integrated into the global industrial division of labor. According to UN statistics, China's manufacturing value-added accounted for more than 28% of the global value added in 2018, profoundly changing the global economic and industrial development pattern.

The Chinese government has always attached great importance to its cooperative relationship with the United Nations Industrial Development Organization. Since the 1970s, the two sides have carried out a lot of fruitful cooperation in the fields of industrial development, trade capacity building and environmental protection. China is willing to continue to work with other member states to discuss inclusive and sustainable industrial development through the UNIDO platform, jointly develop the Belt and Road Cooperation Initiatives, and share the opportunities offered by a new round of technological and industrial revolution. At the same time, China will continue to support the UNIDO's pilot Programme for Country Partnership by providing voluntary contributions and encouraging its enterprises to participate in these programs. China will also give full play to UNIDO's advantages in technical expertise, policy advice, resource mobilization, etc., to help developing countries achieve sustainable industrial development. Looking to the future, UNIDO should also continue to strengthen its functional advantages as a specialized agency for industrial development, promote and lead all parties to strengthen partnerships, and give full play to their respective strengths to form a joint force for development. Special efforts should be made to implement the Third Industrial Development Decade for Africa initiative and steadily promote the pilot Programme for Country Partnership in order to help member states meet the challenges of industrialization.

Thank you, Mr. President.

[资料来源：见中国商务部网站（http://vienna.mofcom.gov.cn/article/chinanews/201911/20191102915077.shtml），引用日期：2023 年 8 月 23 日。]